THE
EXPERT IMPROVER

DANNY ROTH is a writer, player and coach who specializes in teaching bridge to beginners and intermediates. An experienced and successful player at club, county and tournament level, he represented Great Britain in the European Pairs' Championships in 1987. He has written several other books on bridge, aimed at the more advanced player, and is author of *The Expert Beginner*, also published by HarperCollins.

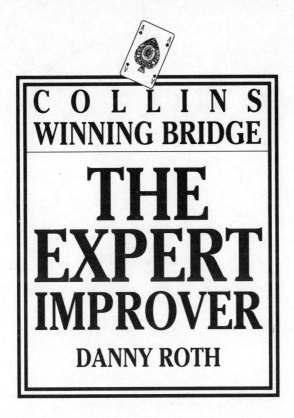

COLLINS
WINNING BRIDGE

THE EXPERT IMPROVER

DANNY ROTH

CollinsWillow
An Imprint of HarperCollins*Publishers*

First published in 1992 by
Collins Willow
an imprint of HarperCollins*Publishers*, London

Distributed in the United States by
HarperCollins *Publishers*
10 East 53rd Street
New York
NY 10022

**A CIP catalogue record for this book
is available from the British Library**

ISBN 0 00 258201 5

Set in Palatino by Wearset, Boldon, Tyne and Wear
Printed and bound in Great Britain
by Cox & Wyman Ltd

Contents

Introduction

Welcome back! I am assuming that you have read the introductory book, *The Expert Beginner*, and are now itching to get to the table to start a long and successful career as a bridge player.

First of all, a gentle word of warning. As S J Simon so aptly put it in his classic *Why you Lose at Bridge* (published by Nicholson and Watson, 1945): 'A little knowledge is at least twice as dangerous.' That will rank as one of mankind's greatest understatements. I have played a great deal over nearly four decades now and despite intensive study, notably over the last few years, still have much to learn. Even the world's top players, many even more trained and experienced than I am, are still light years away from perfection as tournament after tournament illustrates. Such is the variety and complexity of the game that one can never stop learning and even if you know that beginners' book backwards, and I hope you do, you have scarcely scratched the surface of bridge knowledge.

Let us briefly review what we learnt in the first book. I tried to explain that the 'Let's start playing and we'll learn as we go along' approach was a recipe for disaster and that, in order to have some idea of what was going on, it was necessary to develop a 'platform' of basic knowledge. That basically consists of three elements:

1 Familiarizing yourself with the deck of cards;
2 Learning and understanding the basic rules and procedure of the game;
3 Knowing the scoresheet backwards.

We then worked through the concept of winning tricks and studied plays in common card combinations in a single suit. We followed by learning to appreciate the differences arising if there was a trump suit outside. We emphasized that not only did it matter which side won the tricks, but also which partner of a pair and in what order. At the end of the play section, we played some simple examples to illustrate the application of the various principles.

We then turned to bidding and learnt how to value a hand on a first view and then appreciated the adjustments necessary as the auction progressed. It was emphasized (and will constantly be repeated without apology) that the uppermost consideration in our mind was the likely final contract. With that heavily imprinted on our minds, we studied the first two complete rounds of bidding and learnt one or two basic conventional calls. Emphasis was placed on the meaning of every call, in particular whether it was forcing, invitational (i.e. optional) or sign-off. We then allowed the opponents to join in the fun and learnt the two main uses of the double. Finally, we had a short chapter on defence, bearing in mind that the defenders' point of view had already been considered during the play problems.

Having taken great pains to equip you with a good pair of trunks and a little knowledge of what the pool has in store for you, we are now going to jump into the shallow end and are only now going to adopt the 'Let's start playing . . .' approach. However, once again, you will find that my method is rather different from those of other teachers. In the beginners' book, I set out a number of 'parrot-type' rules which teachers tend to give their pupils and which are consequently blindly followed for life. Sadly, as I explained at the time, there are so many exceptions that it is almost better not to know them in the first place.

When we study play and defence, heavy emphasis will be placed on the use of the one-closed-hand exercise which we learnt in the beginners' book, and it will now be extended to two hands. We shall learn to reconstruct the unseen hands with a view to playing with 'all four hands exposed', rather than trying to play in the dark. This obviously will involve extra mental effort but the rewards will be incalculable and you will not regret it – anyway, I certainly didn't!

I should emphasize that it is crucial not only to know what to do in a given situation, but why! Only then will you develop an understanding of when to break the rules.

Once again, all you will need are the same tools that you had for the first book – a large table in front of you, a deck of cards, pen and paper and a stop-watch. You will then be ready to start.

SECTION 1:

Basic Plays at No-trump Contracts

In *The Expert Beginner*, we learnt that no-trump contracts usually involve some sort of race between the declarer and defenders to see who can set up their long suit first, bearing in mind that established long cards will always score as they cannot be ruffed. Once the dummy goes down, you should go through each suit and decide:

1 How many rounds you expect to be played;
2 How many you expect to win;
3 How many you expect to lose,
   bearing in mind that your answers in 2 and 3 must add up to that in 1 and that the total rounds in the four suits must total thirteen;
4 If you have to give up tricks to establish a long suit, i.e. knocking out opponents' high cards, how many times will you have to lose the lead and
   a Have you any control over which defender will win those tricks?
   b Is that important? We learnt in the beginners' book that, if we can lose a trick to a defender who has no cards in his partner's long suit, the partner cannot cash long cards in that suit unless he has an entry in another suit;
5 Whether the total number of tricks you expect to win total those needed for your contract?

In the beginners' book, we looked at a number of examples illustrating these points and some of them were quite difficult.

However, you were allowed to see all four hands and we went through them, trick by trick.

Now we are going to repeat the exercise but, this time, under match conditions, seeing only your hand as declarer (South) and dummy's (North). In each case, we shall discuss the bidding in detail. Let us start with a simple example:

Hand No. 1
Dealer South
Neither vulnerable

♠ 9 8 6
♡ 8 5
♢ K Q J 10 9
♣ 6 4 3

W	N	E	S
			1♣
Pass	1♢	Pass	2♡
Pass	3♢	Pass	3NT
end			

```
      N
  W       E
      S
```

♠ A K 4
♡ A 7 6 2
♢ A 2
♣ A 8 5 2

South opens 1♣ with his 19 points, his goal contracts at this stage being 3NT, 4♡ or possibly 5♣. North replies with 1♢; again 3NT is favorite but 5♣ and 5♢ are also possible. Now South has enough to insist on game with 25 points guaranteed between the two hands, but notice he does not rush into 3NT. His partner can still have four hearts, in which case 4♡ is likely to be a better contract. This particularly applies here as the South hand is full of top controls, or *quick tricks*. These are more conducive to trump contracts, whereas a large number of queens, jacks and tens, *slow tricks*, are more suited to no-trump, one less trick being required for game.

After 2♡, it is debatable whether North should give preference to 3♣ or repeat his diamonds. In view of the strength of the diamond suit and poor quality clubs, it is probably better to emphasize the main trick-taking source of the hand in preference to showing three poor clubs which will probably offer no more than one heart ruff in a club contract. (Of course, South does not have to have more than three clubs anyway.) South now, with the spades well stopped (as the unbid suit, they are most likely to be led), goes for the no-trump game, his ♢A being sure to help establish some long diamond tricks.

Let us pause there for a moment. Notice the way the auction was conducted. That is the way you should always consider bidding sequences – as a cooperative conversation between the two partners.

West, as expected, leads the ♠Q. Now when the dummy goes down, there are a number of questions I shall want you to answer against the stop-watch:

1   a   How many round of spades do you expect will be played during the course of play?
     b   How many do you expect to win?
     c   How many do you expect to lose?

2–4   Same three questions for hearts, diamonds and clubs.

5   Do you know anything about the likely lie of the enemy cards, considering both length and strength? So far, the auction and opening lead are the only clues, but you will be amazed how much you can find out from those alone.

6   Do your total winners add to the number needed for your contract?

7   Do your total losers add up to the number the opponents need to set you?

8   Do you foresee any problems in the play, not only for you, but also for the opponents, and how do you think they will be tackled?

9   Having considered all the above, how do you propose to play the hand?

10   How do you think the defenders will try to stop you achieving your contract?

What a mouthful for a minute or two – and we haven't played a single card yet! But these are the questions you have to ask yourself on every hand and, of course, they apply, if anything with greater force, to the defenders.

When I wrote my early books for tournament players, I spent one introduction after another laying heavy emphasis on working out everything at trick one. This is very often critical because the vast majority of contracts which hang in the balance are decided by the play at the early tricks when least is known about the lie of the outstanding cards.

Afterwards it occurred to me that, if an expert can count up to thirteen, albeit in several disciplines (viz. suits and tricks) and to forty (in points), then why not a beginner? It just takes some training and that is what all the 'familiarizing yourself with a deck of cards' exercises were about. We are now going to put them into practice. In the above hand:

1   We can insist on three rounds of spades, of which we will obviously be winning two and losing one. Note, however, that, if the defenders gain the lead after the ♠A and ♠K have been cashed, they may be able to cash further rounds of the suit. Let us look at that in detail. We have six spades between us, leaving seven for the opponents. Now, if they split 4–3, we may lose two tricks; if they split 5–2, we may lose three tricks; if they split 6–1, we may lose four tricks and if they split 7–0, we may lose five tricks.

Let us consider this further. If they are 7–0, then East will show out on the first round and we shall be informed of the position immediately. That is most unlikely. With such a long suit, non-vulnerable, he almost certainly would have managed an overcall or pre-emptive call on the first round. Indeed, an overcall is likely even with a six-card suit and in that case, as he has failed to overcall, we can deduce that most if not all the remaining honors in the other suits are likely to be with East.

2   We can insist on four rounds of hearts, winning one and losing three. Again, if the opposing hearts are very unevenly distributed, we could lose up to six tricks in the suit.

3   We can insist on five rounds of diamonds, winning five and losing none. The only circumstance in which a trick could be lost arises if the suit breaks 6–0 (scarcely a 1 per cent chance), in which case a defender will be left with a long card after we have cashed our five winners.

4   We can insist on four rounds of clubs, and we shall certainly win one but a second trick is possible if the suit breaks 3–3. However, this will involve losing the lead twice to establish the long card. We shall lose at least two tricks, possibly more, according to the break.

5   With the opponents silent, we know little of the lie of the opposing cards except that, as explained above, very unbalanced hands are unlikely. However, as West has led the ♠Q, it is almost certain that he has the ♠J and probably the ♠10 or ♠9 or both. With ♠ Q J x x or Q J x x x, it is usual to start with the fourth highest. However, he would lead the queen from ♠ Q J x or (less likely) ♠ Q x, in an attempt to find his partner's long suit. This is on the principle of leading high from the short hand first to avoid blocking the suit.

We shall discuss this in more detail in a moment. Notice also that, by leading the ♠Q, West has informed his partner that he does not hold the ♠K. With both, he would have started with the king, playing the higher of touching honors.

6   Tallying up our winners, we have two in spades, one in hearts, five in diamonds and one in clubs to total nine.

7   Tallying losers, we have at least one in spades, three in hearts and at least two in clubs, i.e. at least six in all. So with the total of winners and losers coming to more than thirteen, the race is on and we must take our nine winners quickly before the opponents take more than four.

8   The four winners in spades, hearts and clubs are easily cashed; the only problem lies in diamonds, where the order of play is critical.

As indicated earlier, the guide (although never forget that it is no more than that – there are plenty of exceptions) is to play high cards from the shorter hand first and to ensure that the round on which that shorter hand runs out is won in the longer hand so that the suit may be continued without interruption. In this case, we shall play the ace first and then the low card to the board's king, after which the remainder can be cashed without difficulty. Satisfy yourself that, if you play low to the board first and then the second round to the ace in your hand, the suit will be blocked as you have no entry back to the board to enjoy the rest of the suit. You will now have to be content with only six tricks – down three!

9   The play goes:
          (i) Win the opening lead with ♠K.
          (ii) Cash ♢A.
     (iii)–(vi) Cash the other diamonds.
          (vii) Cash ♣A.
          (viii) Cash ♡A.
          (ix) Cash ♠K
     (x)–(xiii) Concede the last four tricks as there are no high
                cards left. You have thus made your contract
                exactly to score 100 under the line.

10   The defenders can do nothing to stop you although you
        should have noticed a couple of points. First, the order in
        which you cash tricks after the ♣A does not matter. More
        important, as the defenders attacked spades, where you
        have two stops, you are in control of all three non-diamond
        suits while running the diamonds. This means that at least
        one defender must keep a minimum of three clubs. If both
        of them come down to a doubleton or less, you will be able
        to give up a club and enjoy two long clubs to finish with
        two overtricks. This is a small point in this hand but it could
        be crucial in others and, in any event, later on in your career
        when you play tournament bridge with what is called
        'match-point pairs' scoring, overtricks (and preventing
        them) are critical to success. The defenders, of course,
        should realize that they have to keep clubs, having heard
        you bid them. They will be watching your own discards
        while you run the diamonds and will keep whatever you
        keep. Thus, if you choose to discard clubs, they will
        concentrate on keeping the majors.

Let us now juggle that diamond suit around. In the example hand
above, we had:

KQJ109
A 2

and we realized that we had to play the ace first and then the two
to the honors on the board to ensure running the suit. The same
principle applies if we have:

```
A Q J 10 9          A K J 10 9          A K Q 10 9
  K 2                 Q 2                 J 2
```

but note that there is a difference between the example hand and
the three below it. In the first case, it is critical to play the ace first
but with the others, as long as we do not win the second round in
the South hand, we have the option to reach the board twice. For
example, in the first of the three, we could play the two to any
card except the ace and then play the ace, underplaying the king,
before enjoying the rest of the suit; or we could start by playing
the king to the ace to enjoy the rest of the suit. This second entry
to the board is not needed in the example hand but could be
crucial in other situations where entries are valuable. The most
common arises where we need to take finesses. Let us introduce
the club suit and suppose we had this layout:

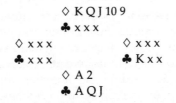

```
              ◇ K Q J 10 9
              ♣ x x x
  ◇ x x x                  ◇ x x x
  ♣ x x x                  ♣ K x x
              ◇ A 2
              ♣ A Q J
```

If we needed eight tricks in the two minor suits, we would be
disappointed. We could only get to the board once and take one
club finesse. But change the scene to:

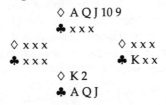

```
              ◇ A Q J 10 9
              ♣ x x x
  ◇ x x x                  ◇ x x x
  ♣ x x x                  ♣ K x x
              ◇ K 2
              ♣ A Q J
```

and now we have a chance. We overtake the ◇K with the ◇A
and play a small club to the ♣Q. Now we play the ◇2 to any
honor on the board, run the rest of the suit and then take another
club finesse.

I have given a very extensive analysis of this simple hand in
order to illustrate in detail how we are going to think about each
hand we play and defend. In many examples, I shall juggle

individual suits around to illustrate positions where similar plays
are appropriate, and also to point out differences. We are now
going to progress gradually to more complicated examples.

Hand No. 2
Dealer East
Both vulnerable

♠ J 6
♡ 9 8 7 2
◇ A K 6 5 2
♣ 6 4

W	N	E	S
		Pass	1♣
Pass	1◇	Pass	2NT
Pass	3NT	end	

```
        N
   W         E
        S
```

♠ A K 4
♡ A 6 5
◇ Q J
♣ A 8 5 3 2

After a pass by East (get into the habit of noting that this denies
values for an opening call), South opens 1♣, 3NT being favorite
as goal contract with 5♣ a possible outsider. West passes (again
note his failure to overcall) and North replies 1◇. South has 18
points (there is no need to devalue the doubleton diamond
holding as the honors are likely to be working in partner's bid
suit). The five-card club suit may provide long-suit tricks but it is
a poor suit and it is hardly appropriate to add a point for it. Also
for no trump, South is lacking in intermediates. He therefore
rebids 2NT, showing 18–19 points. Remember that this is a limit-
call and therefore non-forcing. North, with 8 points and a good
five-card suit, has no hesitation in bidding the no-trump game –
there is no point in considering any other contract.

With the auction having emphasized the minors, it is no
surprise that the lead is from a major suit (very common against
no-trump) and West leads the ♠10. Now before reading on, I
should like you to give a full analysis of the hand, answering the
same ten questions as before. Start your stop-watch. Time will
not matter too much for the moment but you should be aiming to
get well under one minute. At the table, it is not uncommon for
experts to think for up to two minutes or more over difficult
hands but, on the everyday hand, ten to fifteen seconds is the
norm. Let us go through it:

1 In spades we can have three rounds, either winning two and losing one or winning all three without loss. The opponents may have long cards.

2 In hearts we can have four rounds, winning one or two and losing at least two and possibly more long cards.

3 In diamonds five rounds are possible, but how many we will win depends on the break. However, we can certainly win at least three without loss.

4 In clubs there will be five rounds, with one definite winner, but further tricks depend on the break.

5 Regarding the lie of the cards we know little, but West has chosen to lead spades in preference to hearts, suggesting that he is at least as long in spades. He is likely to have the ♠9 but, at present, we do not know where the ♠Q is as he would lead the ♠10 from ♠ 10 9 or from ♠ Q 10 9.

6 We have four top winners outside diamonds in hand and therefore, if the diamonds are good for five tricks, that will complete nine.

7 The opponents may be able to set up long cards in hearts or spades and may well succeed if we try to get the clubs going, which will involve losing the lead at least twice before we can enjoy the long cards.

8 There are problems with the diamond suit. Unlike the previous example, the suit here is not completely solid and we shall need a 3–3 split. As with the previous example, we must ensure that the second round is won on the board as there are no outside entries. This means that, after cashing one of South's honors, we must overtake the other and cash the remaining honor on the board, hoping that both defenders will follow three times and that the board's last two cards will remain as masters.

9 Now for the line of play, and the first question is which card to play from the board at trick one. If West has the ♠Q, putting up the ♠J will gain us an extra trick. Playing low will only gain if East has the ♠Q singleton and it is worth noting that, should this be the case, the ♠J will remain on the board and will serve as an entry. That means that we can afford to cash the two diamonds in hand *without overtaking*, and then cross to

the ♠J to play the rest of the diamonds (unless they split 5–1 or worse). In any event, we shall make four diamond tricks, three spade tricks and the other two aces for the contract. So which is it to be? In practice, it is most unlikely that East has the ♠Q singleton. If he has, West must have a seven-card suit, most unlikely anyway but particularly so as he did not bid. So we play the ♠J and East covers with the ♠Q.

(i) It is wise to win, to avoid a heart shift and go for the diamonds.

(ii) Cash ♢Q – all follow.

(iii) Overtake ♢J with ♢A – all follow.

(iv) Cash ♢K.

Now, if all follow again, we can cash the other diamonds and complete five diamond tricks, two spades and the two other aces for nine tricks. If they don't, we will have to abandon the diamonds and shift to clubs but we are now unlikely to make the contract.

(vi) Suppose we play a low club from both hands, losing. The defenders will either continue spades or shift to hearts and ensure at least two tricks in one of the majors, at least two in clubs (even assuming a 3–3 break) and the outstanding diamond before we can establish the long clubs.

Let us replay the hand but this time, on trick one, assume the ♠J holds, West having started with the ♠Q. We still have the diamond option open but there is no rush. We can now make a more serious attempt at the clubs. At (ii) play a low club from both hands. Note the technique of losing tricks early to keep control. With at least two inevitable losers, the play costs nothing and the ace could be a disaster if there is a bad split against us. Let us see all four hands:

Suppose this is the distribution. If we play low from both hands on the first round, East can win and return the suit but now we are on play and can look elsewhere for tricks when

West reveals the bad break by showing out. If, on the other hand, we play the ace followed by another round, East can win and cash all his winners for four tricks (against only one the previous way) – a big difference. The defenders thus win the first round of clubs and now, if they continue spades, we can win with the ♠A and duck another round of clubs, once again better than the ace and another in case the layout is:

$$\clubsuit 6\,4$$

♣ 9 7   ♣ K Q J 10

$$\clubsuit A\,8\,5\,3\,2$$

Again the defenders win (they were due for two club tricks anyway but as we are still holding the ace, they cannot cash a third). They play another spade or shift to hearts.

At trick (vi), we now test the clubs with the ace and if all follow, we have had a 3–3 split in the suit; the remaining two are high and we are guaranteed three club tricks, three spades, one heart and at least three diamonds for ten tricks, scoring 100 under the line with 30 over. If the clubs fail to break, we can still fall back on the diamonds.

Now before reading on, I should like to go back over this hand and make double sure that you have understood everything I have said. Once you are completely satisfied, you can proceed to consider juggling the suits around. Let us first look at those diamonds in detail. The following positions would require similar handling to the one above:

A Q 6 5 2	K Q 6 5 2	A J 6 5 2	K J 6 5 2
K J	A J	K Q	A Q

but note the black sheep of the family:

Q J 6 5 2
A K

and, in this last case, the second honor in the South hand cannot be overtaken. Thus, if there is no entry to the board, the suit will provide two tricks and no more.

So let us now juggle that spade suit around and allow an entry to the board:

♠ K 6   or   ♠ A 6
♠ A J 4   ♠ K J 4

Now there are two changes: firstly, we are certain of three spade tricks, irrespective of who has the ♠Q. We play low from the board at trick one to keep the high honor there as entry to the diamonds. Secondly, we now no longer need the 3–3 diamond split. Even in the black-sheep case above, we can cash the two tops in hand, without overtaking, before crossing to the board's spade honor to take the rest of the diamonds for at least four tricks in the suit. Only a 5–1 or 6–0 split will prevent a fifth.

This highlights an important point. The more the combined high-card strength of a partnership is concentrated in one hand, the more difficult the play becomes. Lack of entries to the weak hand makes it awkward, if not impossible, to cash long-suit winners and to lead from weakness to strength. Thus, while 25 points may be enough for 3NT when the strength is balanced, once we get to 20 opposite 5 or more extreme, it will usually require 26 or even more points combined to make the game unless there is a long suit in the *strong* hand.

We have so far considered long suits which can be played from the top. We are now going to consider situations where opponents have high cards in our long suit which need to be knocked out. Consider this example:

Hand No. 3
Dealer West
N-S vulnerable

♠ A 7
♡ 8 6 4
◊ K Q J 10 3
♣ 7 3 2

W	N	E	S
Pass	Pass	Pass	1♣
Pass	2◊	Pass	3NT
end			

```
    N
W       E
    S
```

♠ K 8 2
♡ A K 3
◊ 6 5 4
♣ A 9 8 5

After three passes (so we shall note that, of the 15 points missing, they will be split 11–4 or more evenly between the two opponents), South opens 1♣ and North, considering that, by his initial pass, his hand is in the 0–11 range, has a very big hand with a solid suit which should prove useful in the likely goal contract of 3NT. He therefore jumps to 2◊, prepared to play in 3♣ if necessary. South, with 14 points and promised just under opening values, accepts with 3NT.

Again there was no attempt to play in a major suit and it is therefore no surprise that West attacks in one of them, actually leading the ♠Q. Now before reading on, answer the ten questions against the stop-watch.

From now on, instead of going through all the answers, one by one, I shall discuss the hand in the normal way of an experienced declarer, picking out the salient points, pointing out any problems and deciding how we are going to play the hand.

We have clearly two top winners in both spades and hearts. We can insist on five rounds of diamonds of which, barring an unlikely 5–0 split, we will win four and lose one. In clubs, we have the ace for one trick but, in order to set up a long card (which we can only enjoy if there is a 3–3 split), we would have to lose the lead twice, by which time the opponents will have set up several tricks in the majors, which, added to their two club tricks and ◊A will spell a certain set. So it appears we have nine tricks, only having to lose the lead once and, as we shall be in control of all three non-diamond suits when we lose it, there will be no danger of the opponents cashing five tricks first. The question arises as to whether there are likely to be any further problems.

This is a classic example of how easy it is to throw away a contract by hasty play to the first trick. We have three options: to win with the ace on the board; to win with the king in hand; or to duck in both hands in an attempt to exhaust East of spades and thus make it difficult for the opponents to set up the suit, notably if East has the ◊A.

Well, which option is it to be or do you think it doesn't matter? In fact, only the second option is correct. Let us play it showing you the full deal (overleaf):

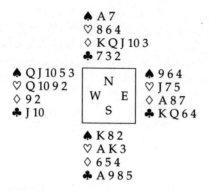

```
                    ♠ A 7
                    ♡ 8 6 4
                    ◇ K Q J 10 3
                    ♣ 7 3 2
♠ Q J 10 5 3                          ♠ 9 6 4
♡ Q 10 9 2         N                  ♡ J 7 5
◇ 9 2          W       E              ◇ A 8 7
♣ J 10             S                  ♣ K Q 6 4
                    ♠ K 8 2
                    ♡ A K 3
                    ◇ 6 5 4
                    ♣ A 9 8 5
```

The suit distributions are perfectly reasonable and yet, unless we win the first trick with the ♠K in hand, we will be set. Try winning the first spade with the ace on the board. We then play the ◇K and East holds up, trying to exhaust our hand of diamonds to stop our running the suit. We play low and West plays the nine. This is to show his partner an even number of cards in the suit. The information helps him hold up his ace the correct number of times, i.e. to win on the round when South plays his last card in the suit. A high card shows an even number so East realizes that his partner probably has a doubleton. It is usually clear in cases of this kind.

So East holds up his ◇A to the third round and resumes the spade attack. South cannot now reach his established diamonds. All he can take is seven tricks for down two and 200 above the line to East-West.

Try ducking the first spade completely – no better. West simply continues the suit and the ♠A is again knocked out too early. East holds up the ◇A twice as before and again we are held to seven tricks. Winning the first trick with the ♠K ensures the preservation of the board's entry and now, irrespective of when East takes his ◇A, we cannot be prevented from reaching the rest of the suit via the ♠A.

This hand illustrates the importance of preserving entries to long suits, and note that this can apply to both hand and dummy and to no-trump and suit contracts. Let us now juggle the hand around to see if you have understood this point.

Before presenting the next problem, be warned that it only takes a subtle change of one or two cards to alter the correct line of play. Here we shall have to make certain assumptions about the whereabouts of enemy forces.

♠ A 7 2
♡ 8 6 4
◇ Q J 10 9 7 3
♣ 7

Hand No. 4
Dealer South
Both vulnerable

W	N	E	S
			1♣
Pass	1◇	Pass	2NT
Pass	3NT	end	

```
        N
    W       E
        S
```

♠ K 8 6
♡ A K 10
◇ 6 5
♣ A K 10 6 2

After South has shown an 18–19 point limit-call, it is questionable whether North should bid the game. He should take the view that it will depend on the diamonds being brought in and that this is doubtful as there is only one side-suit entry. We consider the possible gains and losses in this light.

If 3NT is making, the score is $100 + 500$ (for the rubber) = 600. If we stop in a part-score, signing off in 3◇, the score is 60 for 3◇ $+ 50$ (for the part-score value) = 110. The loss for failing to bid the game is thus 480. If 3NT fails, say by two tricks, the loss for bidding it is 200, plus the value of the part-score, totalling 310. Thus it is worth bidding the game with odds of 2:1 when the chance of bringing the diamond suit in is probably nearer even money.

Note that a double (which could swing the odds towards the part-score) is most unlikely. Before reading on, can you say why?

The reason is that, while South has limited his hand, North is still unlimited and, for all the opponents know, could be near a slam try, i.e. up to about 14 points. Thus a double (which only gains a significant amount for a two-trick or heavier set) risks a redouble and/or overtricks which would easily outweigh the potential gain).

Please take careful note of the way this decision was analyzed. Many close bidding decisions depend on this kind of reasoning. Three questions should be considered:

1 What do you stand to gain?
2 What do you stand to lose?
3 What are the odds involved?

If you pay close attention to these considerations, you may not take the right decision on every individual case but you will certainly be showing a profit in the long term. If players ranging from beginners to world chapions did this more often, many bidding howlers at all levels would be avoided.

Having discussed the bidding in detail, let us turn to the play. The opening lead, once again, is the ♠Q. Start your stop-watch and give an analysis of the hand, in under two minutes if you can.

To give you a hint, you will again be faced with the decision of whether, and if so where, to win that first trick.

We have two top tricks in each of the non-diamond suits and therefore the long diamonds will have to be brought in if we are to have any chance. Again, therefore, it will be important to keep the solitary spade entry on the board as long as possible, particularly as the lead will have to be lost twice before the diamonds are established. Thus taking the first trick on the board is a non-starter. So it is a question of ducking the first trick or winning in hand. In order to decide, we need to look at those diamonds in closer detail.

Let us do our one-closed-hand exercise in that suit alone. We have eight between us, leaving five for the opponents, the ace, king and three low ones. A 3–2 split is most likely but it should be appreciated that, in this case, unless the ace and king are in the doubleton, the defenders can refuse to win the first round and South will be exhausted after the second. The board can be entered with the ♠A to set up the suit but there will be no further entry to cash the long winners. Thus we must assume that somebody has ◇ A K doubleton or that there is a 4–1 split with one of the honors as the singleton. In that case, they will have to win the first round. On winning that trick, they will surely continue spades, knocking out the ♠A on the board while their remaining diamond stopper remains intact, leaving us without hope.

Thus our only realistic hope is that a defender (and it will have to be East) has a singleton diamond honor and that, on taking the trick, he will be unable to persist with spades. To put it more clearly, we shall have to be optimistic and assume that the deal is something like this:

```
              ♠ A 7 2
              ♡ 8 6 4
              ◇ Q J 10 9 7 3
              ♣ 7
♠ Q J 10 5 4  ┌─────────┐  ♠ 9 3
♡ Q 2         │    N    │  ♡ J 9 7 5 3
◇ K 8 4 2     │  W   E  │  ◇ A
♣ J 5         │    S    │  ♣ Q 9 8 4 3
              └─────────┘
              ♠ K 8 6
              ♡ A K 10
              ◇ 6 5
              ♣ A K 10 6 2
```

Now we can try playing, 'seeing' all four hands. If we win the first spade in hand and play a diamond, East will win and play another spade. Now ducking on the board will not help as West will win this second round of the suit and play a third round to eliminate the board's ♠A too early, killing the diamonds. So we must duck the first trick and win the second spade in hand and only then play a diamond. East wins but is out of spades and must shift to clubs or hearts, which we can win in hand, keeping the ♠A on the board. Now we persist with diamonds to knock out the king and later enter the board with the ♠A to enjoy the rest of the diamonds. Our final tally will be two spade tricks, two hearts, four diamonds and two clubs for ten tricks, conceding a spade and two diamonds for 100 under the line, 30 for the overtrick above it and 500 for the rubber.

This was a very detailed analysis and I have proceeded very

slowly. I should like you to go over it all again until you have satisfied yourself that any other line of play fails with the deal as above and that, if the diamonds are distributed more equitably, say ◇ A x x opposite ◇ K x, the contract cannot be made. Set the cards out and play and replay the hand, over and over again if necessary, until you have completely absorbed and understood the considerations involved. Here we saw both sides, by the careful timing of winning tricks in the enemy's long suits, make life as difficult as possible for the opponents. Many no-trump contracts are decided in this way and the importance of understanding the principles cannot be overemphasized. I therefore urge you not to read on until you are fully conversant with the four problems we have discussed so far.

We now turn to a situation where there is a choice of suits on which to play – or is there? Again, you will have to count your tricks in each suit carefully and note the number of times you have to lose the lead to establish them. Also consider the number of tricks available to the opposition and the number of times *they* have to lose the lead to establish them.

Hand No. 5
Dealer East
Neither vulnerable

♠ K 7
♡ 4 3
◇ K J 7 6 3
♣ K 10 9 6

W	N	E	S
		Pass	1♣
1♡	2◇	Pass	2♠
Pass	3♣	Pass	3NT
end			

```
        N
   W        E
        S
```

♠ A Q 6 4
♡ A K
◇ Q 10 2
♣ K J 5 2

After East's initial pass, South opens 1♣. He intends to rebid 1♠ and then go up at least to 2NT with his 18 points, hoping to finish in 3NT, 4♠ or possibly 5♣.

Actually West overcalls with 1♡. This shows a good five-card or longer heart suit and a point-count a little short of an opening call or better. North is forced up to the two-level to bid his diamonds but, as he is easily strong enough to play in 3♣, he can comfortably bid 2◇ despite, strictly speaking, being a point short. South's rebid is forcing, with North having guaranteed another call. He gives preference to 3♣ and South signs off in 3NT.

West leads the ♡Q, obviously top of a sequence. Start your stop-watch and do a full analysis, trying to get under two minutes, before reading on.

In spades, we have three top tricks – satisfy yourself that, with all the intermediates missing, there is no distribution of opposing cards that would allow a fourth. In hearts, there are two top tricks. Note two points: first, that we have no option about when to take them – we have to win whenever West leads them; second, even if South had an extra heart, holding up, with a view to exhausting East, is unlikely to be beneficial. South has 18 points and North 10, totalling 28. That leaves 12 unaccounted for, making it almost certain that West has both minor aces to go with his advertised heart honors. It might be a different matter if East was likely to hold an ace.

That is all by the way (but note again the application of the one-closed-hand exercise). In diamonds, we are solid, apart from the ace, and can expect to win four tricks against one lost. In clubs, a similar situation exists, although this time we can only expect to win three tricks against one lost. So all told, we appear to have three spades, two hearts, four diamonds and three clubs, twelve tricks in all against the two aces. But now let us look at enemy plans. After winning the first heart, we shall attack one of the minors (note the spades are there on top and there is no rush to cash them – indeed to do so would achieve nothing but set up a trick for a defender). West will take his ace and play another heart. If we now try to knock out the other minor ace, West will win and cash at least three heart tricks (remembering that his bidding promised at least five to start with). That adds up to five tricks and a set.

So we must think again and recount our tricks in the knowledge that knocking out both aces is a non-starter. Can we make the contract if we knock out only one of the aces? Three spade tricks and two hearts are on top and so four diamonds will suffice to complete nine without touching the club suit. Thus, after

winning the first heart, we then play on diamonds, playing the
high cards from the South hand and keeping the ◇K on the
board so as to avoid blocking the suit. (Although, should
anything go wrong, the ♠K is available as entry.) West wins and
plays another heart. We cash the rest of the diamonds and then
the ♠K (high from the short hand first) before the ♠A and ♠Q
to complete nine tricks. After that, we play a club and West can
take his ♣A and two remaining hearts. Play the hand out and
satisfy yourself that he will have had to discard a winning heart
on the run of the spades.

Now, however, we are going to make a subtle alteration to the
hand and study the effect. Let us replace the ◇10 with the ◇4
and replay the hand. Does it make any difference? Start your
stop-watch and give another full analysis.

This time, if diamonds are breaking 3–2 (most likely), there is
still no problem and we can play as before. But they may be 4–1
as here:

◇ K J 7 6 3

◇ A 10 9 8   ◇ 5

◇ Q 4 2

If we start with the ◇Q, West will win and his remaining
trebleton will be solid against the king and jack and therefore
worth another trick. However, there is no need to start with the
queen. Even on the principle of playing high from the short hand
first to avoid a blockage, we can start with a low card towards the
board (intending to play the queen on the second round). On the
first round, if West rises with the ◇A, we shall be able to cash
four tricks in the suit anyway as the queen, king and jack will all
score separately. So West must duck, keeping his ace poised over
the queen.

Now, if we continue the suit with a low card to the queen,
West wins and has a second stopper as before. On the other hand,
if we cross to hand in spades and lead another low diamond,
West ducks again, leaving his ace and ten as masters and we will
not have time to set up another trick in the suit. How, therefore,
do we play now? Start your stop-watch and see if you can give a
revised line of play in under two minutes.

The crucial point to realize here is that, if West ducks the first round of diamonds, as we explained he must, we will have made a diamond trick *without losing the lead*. Thus our second heart stop has remained intact for the time being and we can recount our tricks. We have three spades, two hearts and one diamond, totalling six to date. So we only need three more and these are available from clubs (which are solid apart from the ace). Once the first diamond has held, we shift to clubs and ensure nine tricks.

Play the hand over for yourself and be sure that you are satisfied that this is the only line of play that guarantees the contract. Note the importance of leading from weakness through strength to strength in diamonds because that suit is *not solid*, but that we can start clubs from either hand because (apart from the ace) that suit *is solid*. This is a very simple example of what is called a lob (or in England, avoidance play), effectively inviting an opponent to win a trick with an ace 'beating air' rather than capturing another honor, or offering him the alternative of refusing to win, which may save a trick in the suit itself but costs a vital tempo needed to set up his own suit.

The subject of gaining or losing a tempo leads us conveniently to the next stratagem.

Hand No. 6
Dealer East
Neither vulnerable

♠ Q 7 3
♡ 4 3
◇ A Q J 7 6 3
♣ K 9

W	N	E	S
		Pass	1♣
1♡	2◇	Pass	2NT
Pass	3NT	end	

```
     N
  W     E
     S
```

♠ A K 6
♡ A J 5
◇ 10 9 4
♣ Q 5 4 2

After East's pass, South opens 1♣, intending to rebid 1NT over any one-level response and primarily looking for 3NT. West overcalls 1♡ and North forces with 2◇. South, with a good heart stop, rebids 2NT and North raises to game. West leads the ♡K. Start your stop-watch and plan the play.

We clearly will make three spades without loss, the ♡A, and certainly one club as the king and queen are solid against the ace. That implies that the diamond suit will have to be brought in. Let us look at it in detail. If West has the king (as is likely on the bidding), there will be no problem. We shall lead the high cards from South and take the finesse against him. That will give six tricks in the suit and the contract, probably with two over-tricks for 100 under the line, 60 over and the first game to us.

However, if the king is with East, we shall have to lose a trick to him and that will give the opponents a chance to continue hearts. With that in mind, how did you play to trick one?

The best way to illustrate the solution is trial and error. Let us look at the deal based on the auction and our assumptions so far:

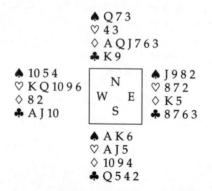

```
                    ♠ Q 7 3
                    ♡ 4 3
                    ◇ A Q J 7 6 3
                    ♣ K 9
      ♠ 10 5 4                      ♠ J 9 8 2
      ♡ K Q 10 9 6      N           ♡ 8 7 2
      ◇ 8 2         W     E         ◇ K 5
      ♣ A J 10          S           ♣ 8 7 6 3
                    ♠ A K 6
                    ♡ A J 5
                    ◇ 10 9 4
                    ♣ Q 5 4 2
```

Now observe the consequences of winning the first heart. We shall take the diamond finesse, losing to East, and he will now return a heart. That will give West four heart tricks and with the ♣A still to come, the opponents will take six tricks in all for down two and 100 to them over the line. But now let us try the effect of letting the ♡K hold. Now, all of a sudden, if West leads them again, we have a second stop in the suit. If he doesn't, our ace remains as a stop and we can knock out the ◇K without risk. The hold up with A J x against a strong suit bid on the left, from which the king is led, is known as the 'Bath Coup'. It was first reported in a whist game many years ago in the English spa town in the county of Somerset. Note that it does not work so effectively if the heart position is:

$$\heartsuit\ 4\ 3$$
$$\heartsuit\ K\ 10\ 9\ 8\ 6 \qquad\qquad \heartsuit\ Q\ 7\ 2$$
$$\heartsuit\ A\ J\ 5$$

The correct lead from West now is the ten (the higher card from the solid part of an internal sequence) and East plays the queen. Now, if South holds up, East is on play and can continue the suit profitably as it is now the defenders who are leading from weakness through strength to strength. Should South, then, win or duck in this situation? Well, it depends on a number of factors and there is no hard and fast rule. We are, therefore, going to look at some more situations of this kind and work out each case on its own merits. Let us first consider this:

Hand No. 7
Dealer South
N-S vulnerable

♠ A 6 5 3
♡ 4 3 2
◇ 10 9 4
♣ K J 9

	N		
W		E	
	S		

♠ 10 4
♡ A J 5
◇ A Q J 7 6
♣ A Q 5

W	N	E	S
			1◇
1♡	1♠	Pass	2NT
Pass	3NT	end	

The heart position has remained unaltered but the diamonds have exchanged places and you will see that this can be critical. After South's opening call, primarily looking for 3NT or possibly 5◇, West again overcalls in hearts but this time North bids 1♠. This is forcing and although, with a flat hand, 3NT will still be uppermost in his mind as goal contract, 4♠ is a possibility, should South turn up with four or more spades in a distributional hand and/or if he is unable to stop the hearts. After East's pass, South rebids 2NT, showing 18–19 points, at least one heart stop and denying four spades. North raises to game, having no other contract to discuss.

Once again, West leads the ♡K. Start your stop-watch and decide how you are going to play the hand and in particular, whether you are going to win or duck the first trick.

You have one spade trick, one heart and three clubs and therefore four diamond tricks will be sufficient – just as well as the diamond finesse is likely to be wrong. Now, if we duck the first trick, West cannot profitably continue hearts but this time . . . down one and 100 away. West will realize that, as far as hearts are concerned, the game is up and look elsewhere. A shift to spades now sets the contract as the defenders will make three spade tricks, the ◇K and the heart we have already given them. That applies irrespective of when we take the ♠A and it is instructive to note that, if we duck on the board at trick two, East has the option to carry on spades or shift back to hearts (from the right side of the table this time!) and now we actually lose six tricks and 200.

So this time, the Bath coup is a loser and we must win the first trick. The difference between this hand and the last hand lies in two factors.

First, if the diamond finesse has to be lost, it will be lost to West and he cannot effectively attack your ♡J whereas before, East could.

Second, there is the danger of a lethal shift if you duck the heart, whereas before, no such danger existed.

The deal:

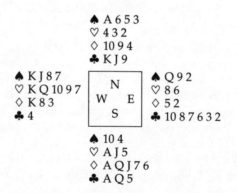

```
                    ♠ A 6 5 3
                    ♡ 4 3 2
                    ◇ 10 9 4
                    ♣ K J 9
  ♠ K J 8 7                         ♠ Q 9 2
  ♡ K Q 10 9 7        N             ♡ 8 6
  ◇ K 8 3          W     E          ◇ 5 2
  ♣ 4                 S             ♣ 10 8 7 6 3 2
                    ♠ 10 4
                    ♡ A J 5
                    ◇ A Q J 7 6
                    ♣ A Q 5
```

I hope that these two hands have adequately illustrated the hopelessness of trying to learn bridge by general rules and the vital importance of understanding what you are doing. I pushed this point continually in the beginners' book and this is yet another illustration. Practice makes perfect, so let us alter the hand again and see if you can decide the correct line of play. Start your stop-watch.

Hand No. 8
Dealer East
E-W vulnerable

```
                              ♠ K 7
                              ♡ 7 2
                              ◇ A J 9 7 4
                              ♣ K 9 3 2
                          ┌──────────────┐
W      N      E      S     │      N       │
              Pass   1NT   │  W       E   │
                          │      S       │
Pass   3NT    end         └──────────────┘
                              ♠ A 6 4 3
                              ♡ A J 5
                              ◇ Q 10 2
                              ♣ A 5 4
```

After East's initial pass, South opens 1NT, primarily looking for 3NT, although 4♠ is possible if partner has a spade suit. North has a slightly unbalanced hand but has more than enough, opposite a minimum of 15 points, to insist on game. It is now a question of whether to look for five of a minor or just punt 3NT. Particularly as there are clearly no singletons or voids in either hand, it is probably better to go for the no-trump game, hoping that partner has the hearts stopped and/or the opponents will not be able to take too many tricks in the suit.

West leads the ♡6, which may be read as fourth highest from a long suit. Let us apply the rule of eleven: $11 - 6 = 5$, i.e. there are five cards higher than the six in the three remaining hands. We can see two in hand and one on the board, leaving two more for East.

We also note that the ♡4 and ♡3 are missing; in other words, West has led from a four- five- or six-card suit, leaving East with four, three or two respectively. You play low from the board and East plays the king. This clearly denies the queen as, with both honors, he would have played the queen in third position. How do you play? Start your stop-watch.

We have four top tricks in the black suits plus the ♡A and so will require four tricks from diamonds. If the finesse has to be lost, it will be to East, and therefore he must be exhausted of hearts before that finesse is taken. Let us consider the heart suit in that light. If they are breaking 4–4, we will lose three tricks in the suit plus the ◊K at worst and there is no danger. If they are 5–3 or 6–2 and we win the first round, East will be able to push a second round through our jack to ensure four or five more tricks for his partner. To be safe, we should hold up our ♡A to the third round (note that we have a double stop in both black suits and therefore a shift to either cannot hurt us) and only then take the diamond finesse to ensure the contract against a layout like this:

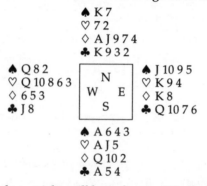

```
                    ♠ K 7
                    ♡ 7 2
                    ◊ A J 9 7 4
                    ♣ K 9 3 2
   ♠ Q 8 2                        ♠ J 10 9 5
   ♡ Q 10 8 6 3      N            ♡ K 9 4
   ◊ 6 5 3       W       E        ◊ K 8
   ♣ J 8             S            ♣ Q 10 7 6
                    ♠ A 6 4 3
                    ♡ A J 5
                    ◊ Q 10 2
                    ♣ A 5 4
```

Thus the first three tricks will be in hearts. We shall then pass the ◊Q to East's ◊K and he will presumably shift to the ♠J. We shall win and have four more tricks in diamonds, the two black aces and kings and the ♡A for the contract.

Now try this one:

Hand No. 9
Dealer East
Neither vulnerable

W	N	E	S
		Pass	1NT
Pass	3NT	end	

```
          ♠ A 7
          ♡ 7 2
          ◊ Q J 9 7 4
          ♣ A 9 3 2

              N
          W       E
              S

          ♠ K 6 3 2
          ♡ A J 5
          ◊ A 10 2
          ♣ K 5 4
```

Again, West leads the ♡6 to his partner's ♡K. Start your stop-watch and give a full analysis, clearly explaining why you intend to win or refuse the first trick. You should be experienced enough now to be able to give an answer in under thirty seconds.

Again, with four top tricks in the black suits and the ♡A, we need four out of the five diamonds for the contract and, if the finesse has to be lost, it will be to West, the man with the long hearts. Ducking, therefore, will not work. They will simply knock out our ace and, when West gets in with the ◇K, he will cash the remaining hearts for down one or two. (We will only escape if the suit breaks 4–4.)

However, if we win the first heart, the remaining holding of ♡ J 5 cannot be effectively attacked from the West side. Cross to one of the board's black winners, say the ♠A, pass the ◇Q (West can make life awkward without risk by ducking the first round) and then play low to the ◇10, losing to West. If he shifts to a club, we must be very careful to keep the ♣A on the board with the long diamonds and win in hand with ♣K. Now unblock the ◇A before returning to the board with the ♣A to enjoy the rest of the diamonds. Replay the hand yourself and make sure you understand that any other line endangers the contract.

We will now turn to other situations where the decision between winning and holding up is critical. Consider this problem:

Hand No. 10
Dealer East
Neither vulnerable

♠ A 7
♡ 6 2
◇ 10 7 4
♣ A J 10 9 7 6

W	N	E	S
		Pass	1NT
2♡	3♣	Pass	3NT
end			

```
      N
  W       E
      S
```

♠ K 6 3
♡ K Q 5
◇ A Q 9 2
♣ Q 8 4

After South's opening call and West's overcall, North forced with 3♣ and South rebid 3NT with a good heart stop.

West leads the ♡J, top of an internal sequence, and East plays low. How do you plan the play? Start your stop-watch, work out the positions of the critical cards and decide the best line in under two minutes.

We can count two tricks in spades, one in hearts and at least one in diamonds and therefore five tricks in clubs out of the six possible rounds will be enough. We can therefore afford to lose to the king, but that could be in the East hand and now he could return a heart through our remaining honor, allowing West to cash his hearts before we can enjoy the clubs. Let us consider the heart lay-out in more detail in that light. After the overcall, a 4–4 split is ruled out. If they are 7–1, we are not in danger as East is now exhausted of hearts. The critical cases are 6–2 and 5–3. If they are 5–3, the defence must prevail. We can try ducking the first trick but West simply leads another low heart and now our last honor remains unguarded while East still holds one card. In that case, the club finesse will have to be right. But if the hearts are 6–2, then ducking the first trick works even if the club finesse is wrong as East will be exhausted of hearts after the second round.

Play it through yourself with full deal on view:

```
                 ♠ A 7
                 ♡ 6 2
                 ◇ 10 7 4
                 ♣ A J 10 9 7 6
  ♠ Q 8 2                        ♠ J 10 9 5 4
  ♡ A J 10 9 8 3   ┌───────┐     ♡ 7 4
  ◇ K 6 3          │   N   │     ◇ J 8 5
  ♣ 2            W │       │ E   ♣ K 5 3
                   │   S   │
                 └───────┘
                 ♠ K 6 3
                 ♡ K Q 5
                 ◇ A Q 9 2
                 ♣ Q 8 4
```

You can see that, if we win the first heart and take the club finesse, East will win and return a heart, giving his partner five heart tricks for down two and −100. If we duck the heart, our stop remains intact and now no defence can prevent nine tricks.

It will be instructive to juggle that heart position around and set out situations requiring similar handling. For example, splitting the honors between North and South makes no difference:

$$\heartsuit \text{ K x (or Q x)}$$

$$\heartsuit \text{ A J 10 9 x x} \qquad\qquad \heartsuit \text{ x x}$$

$$\heartsuit \text{ Q x x (or K x x)}$$

Again, on the lead of the jack, South must duck in both hands if the lead in his long suit will have to be lost to East. The same applies here:

$$\heartsuit \text{ x x}$$

$$\heartsuit \text{ A 10 8 6 x x} \qquad\qquad \heartsuit \text{ J x}$$

$$\heartsuit \text{ K Q x}$$

This time, West leads his fourth-highest $\heartsuit 6$ to his partner's jack. On this occasion, the fact that East is now on play is irrelevant. South must still duck. And again here:

$$\heartsuit \text{ x x}$$

$$\heartsuit \text{ A 10 9 8 x x} \qquad\qquad \heartsuit \text{ Q x}$$

$$\heartsuit \text{ K J x}$$

This time, West leads the ten and East puts up the queen. If the trick in declarer's suit has to be lost to East, South must duck, leaving his king-jack solid against the ace. If the trick in his long suit has to be lost to West, South wins the first round and now the remaining J x cannot be profitably attacked from the West side.

This position, however, illustrates the advantage of having the short hand as declarer:

$$\heartsuit \text{ K x x (or Q x x)}$$

$$\heartsuit \text{ A J 10 x x x} \qquad\qquad \heartsuit \text{ x x}$$

$$\heartsuit \text{ Q x (or K x)}$$

Now South can win the first trick in hand and still have a second stop. This point is important enough to be taken into account in the auction. With holdings like Q x and K x, try to be declarer at no-trump. With K x x or Q x x it is less likely to be important.

You will already have appreciated the importance of losing tricks to one opponent or the other according to which hand is dangerous in defenders' suit. We are now going to extend that idea to other combinations. This kind of situation occurs regularly:

Hand No. 11
Dealer East
Both vulnerable

♠ Q 6
♡ Q 7 2
◇ K J 9 8 2
♣ 9 6 5

W	N	E	S
		Pass	2NT
Pass	3NT	end	

```
        N
   W         E
        S
```

♠ A K 4 2
♡ A 3
◇ A 10 3
♣ A J 7 2

After East's initial pass, South opens 2NT, showing 20–22 points, balanced. North knows that the partnership has no more than 30 points between them and, with a reasonably balanced hand, has little reason to consider any other contract than 3NT. West leads the ♡J. Start your stop-watch and decide how you would play.

We have three top spade tricks, at least one heart and one club. So, even if we fail to pick up the ◇Q (by finesse or drop), four tricks in diamonds should be sufficient. Where is the problem? The first question is: 'Who has the ♡K?' At present, we do not know, as West would have led the ♡J from ♡ J 10 9 x x or from ♡ K J 10 x x. In the latter case, we will have two stops in the suit as the queen is well placed over the king. But if it is with East, we could be in trouble as we can only hold up the ace for one round. The risk now is that we shall lose four heart tricks and one diamond. Let us look at those diamonds in more detail. With the ace and king in different hands, we are in a position to play either defender for the queen. In the dangerous case, where the ♡K is with East, West will be the dangerous hand and he, therefore, must be kept out of the lead. So we play the ♡2 from the board and win the first round with the ♡A in hand. Now follow with the ◇A and the ◇10, passing it to East. If West has the ◇Q, the finesse will work and we shall make at least ten tricks for 100 under the line, 30 over, the rubber bonus of 500 and 150 for four aces. If East has the ◇Q, he will take it but cannot profitably continue hearts.

Let us look at the full deal:

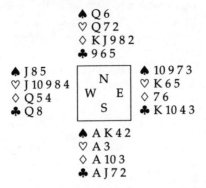

```
                 ♠ Q 6
                 ♡ Q 7 2
                 ◊ K J 9 8 2
                 ♣ 9 6 5
   ♠ J 8 5                      ♠ 10 9 7 3
   ♡ J 10 9 8 4      N          ♡ K 6 5
   ◊ Q 5 4      W        E      ◊ 7 6
   ♣ Q 8            S          ♣ K 10 4 3
                 ♠ A K 4 2
                 ♡ A 3
                 ◊ A 10 3
                 ♣ A J 7 2
```

The observant student will notice that, on this layout, the contract
can be made by ducking the first heart completely, winning the
second and taking the diamond finesse in either direction. East is
left with the ♡K; the suit is blocked and West can never get in to
cash the remainder. However, this would fail if West turned up
with the ♡K after all. On the above line, the contract is made
irrespective of the position of the ♡K. Let us turn the red suits
around and see if the finesse in diamonds is still appropriate.

Beginners are taught that, when you have eight cards between
you in a suit, playing for the drop offers a poorer chance than the
50 per cent available on the finesse. Similarly, with nine cards, the
drop offers a slightly better than that 50 per cent chance. Hence
the old dictum: 'With eight ever; with nine never.'

However, we have learnt by now that there are other matters
to be taken into account.

Hand No. 12
Dealer South
E-W vulnerable

```
                                ♠ Q 6 3 2
                                ♡ A
                                ◊ A K 10 9 3
                                ♣ 9 6 5

                                     N
                                W         E
                                     S

                                ♠ A K 4
                                ♡ Q 7 2
                                ◊ J 8 2
                                ♣ A J 7 2
```

W	N	E	S
			1NT
Pass	2♣	Pass	2◊
Pass	3NT	end	

South opens 1NT and North has easily enough to insist on game opposite a minimum of 15 points. 3NT, 4♠ and 5♦ are all possible candidates. A Stayman enquiry finds South without a major suit so North decides to go for no-trump game without further investigation.

West leads the ♡10. This places the ♡J with East, but the position of the ♡K is as yet unknown. Clearly, if it is with East, the contract is not in danger as the ♡Q will constitute a second stop. But if it is with West, then, if East is allowed to get on lead, we could lose four or more heart tricks.

We consider our line of play in that light. There are four top tricks in the black suits and the ♡A and so four tricks in diamonds will be sufficient.

How do we play the suit? If West has the queen, the contract is not in danger and so a successful finesse gains no more than an overtrick.

If East has the queen, it can only be caught as a singleton or doubleton and so we cash the ace and king to guard against this layout:

```
                    ♠ Q 6 3 2
                    ♡ A
                    ♦ A K 10 9 3
                    ♣ 9 6 5
  ♠ J 9                                ♠ 10 8 7 5
  ♡ K 10 9 5 4 3         N             ♡ J 8 6
  ♦ 6 5 4           W         E        ♦ Q 7
  ♣ Q 8                   S            ♣ K 10 4 3
                    ♠ A K 4
                    ♡ Q 7 2
                    ♦ J 8 2
                    ♣ A J 7 2
```

We shall only be in trouble if East has the ♦Q to three or more but in that case, she could never have been caught anyway, either by finesse or drop. When East does get in, we still have the chance that he had the ♡K all the time.

Let us now make a slight alteration. Suppose the diamond position had been:

$$\diamond \text{ A Q 10 9 3}$$
$$\diamond \text{ J 8 2}$$

How would you play now? Now the odds heavily favor taking a finesse, but still the ace first is the correct play. If West has the king, only the overtrick is lost. If East has him guarded, there is nothing to be done. The critical case arises when East has a singleton or *stiff* king. Now the play of the ace saves the contract.

Having seen how we can organize a possible second stop in opponents' long suit, we shall now look at another way of causing disruption – blocking. Try and place the opposing cards and find a successful line of play in this example. The auction and opening lead should give you enough information to reproduce the whole deal, after which you can play, effectively seeing all four hands, i.e. *double dummy*.

Start your stop-watch.

Hand No. 13
Dealer South
Neither vulnerable

♠ K Q 5 4
♡ A 7
♢ 7 5 4
♣ K Q J 8

N			
W		E	
S			

W	N	E	S
			1♢
1♡	1♠	Pass	2♢
Pass	2♡	Pass	2NT
Pass	3NT	end	

♠ J 6
♡ 10 9 6 4
♢ A K 9 8 6
♣ A 6

After South's opening call, orientated towards 4♡, 5♢ or 3NT, West came in with an overcall of 1♡ and North forced with 1♠. South made the normal rebid of 2♢ and now North bid 2♡. What does this call mean? Clearly with a five-card or longer heart suit advertised with West, North will not want to play the hand in hearts. In this type of situation, the bid of opponents' suit is referred to as a *directional asking bid* and effectively says: 'I am interested in playing no-trump but my heart holding (typically including one honor but no more) is not good enough to enable me to bid it outright – I need some help.' This normally implies that you are required to have at least a half-stop to bid no-trump. A half-stop is a holding like Q x, J x x, 10 x x x or better. These do not constitute stops on their own but two of them together will suffice. For example:

Q x
J x x

guarantees a stop if the opponents lead the suit. Just play low from the board when West leads it and East will either play low, allowing the jack to win, or if he plays an honor, South will play low and now the queen and jack will be solid against the defenders' remaining honor. In the example above, South's 10 9 x x is ample and North, with more than opening values, confidently bids the no-trump game.

West leads the ♡3. Start your stop-watch and this time, I should like you to do a full analysis, answering the questions overleaf as accurately as possible:

1 How many hearts has West and which ones?
2 How many hearts has East and which ones?
3 Where is the ♠A?
4 How many tricks are available in each of the four suits and how many losers?
5 How often will you have to lose the lead in order to set up a minimum of nine tricks?
6 How do you propose to play to trick one?
7 Will your play allow the defenders to cash five tricks first?
8 If so, is there a better line which will prevent this?

Let us work through the answers:

1 West bid hearts and then led the ♡3. In order to justify an overcall, he should have at least a five-card suit. He has led his fourth-highest, and as there is only one card lower than the three, he must have exactly five hearts, including the ♡3 and ♡2. We can go further. The ♡K, ♡Q and ♡J are all missing. If West had all of them, his exact holding would be ♡ K Q J 3 2

but in that case, he surely would have led the king. So clearly he does not hold all three honors and will probably have K Q x 3 2, K J x 3 2, or Q J x 3 2 (where x is the 8 or 5).

2 That leaves a doubleton honor with East, his small card being the 5 or 8, respectively.

3 The ♠A is almost certainly with West. This would be less clear if he had all the heart honors because, in that case, with such a good suit, he would need little more to justify a non-vulnerable overcall.

4 In spades, we have at least two certain tricks, against one loser to the ace. In hearts, we can only have one trick as the ace will drop on the second round; the opponents will know they do not have to play an honor as the ace is visible on the board. Potentially, therefore, the defenders may be able to take up to four tricks in the suit. In diamonds, we have two top tricks and given a reasonable 3–2 split, could set up two more. In clubs, we have four top tricks, remembering that, when we cash them, we shall play the ♣A first, to avoid blocking the suit. That all adds up to eleven winners, but there could be up to six losers, so the race is on.

5 Setting up tricks in both diamonds and spades will involve losing the lead twice, and by that time, the opponents will have enough heart tricks to set the contract, so this is out of the question. We must therefore consider choosing one or the other. If we go for the spades, we shall make two spades, a heart, two diamonds and four clubs – nine tricks. If we go for the diamonds, we get no spades, one heart, four diamonds and four clubs – also nine tricks, but here we are relying on the 3–2 break, likely but by no means certain. Thus it is better to go for the spades, which guarantees two tricks in all circumstances.

6 So we have decided on how we are going to set up nine tricks but even losing the lead once could be fatal if they can cash four heart tricks plus the ♠A. Suppose we duck the first heart. Then East will win and return the suit, knocking out the board's ace.

7 On gaining the lead with the ♠A, West cashes the rest of the hearts for down one and −50.

The deal:

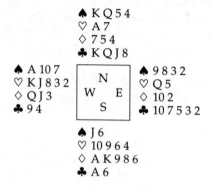

```
                    ♠ K Q 5 4
                    ♡ A 7
                    ◇ 7 5 4
                    ♣ K Q J 8
    ♠ A 10 7                         ♠ 9 8 3 2
    ♡ K J 8 3 2        N             ♡ Q 5
    ◇ Q J 3        W       E         ◇ 10 2
    ♣ 9 4              S             ♣ 10 7 5 3 2
                    ♠ J 6
                    ♡ 10 9 6 4
                    ◇ A K 9 8 6
                    ♣ A 6
```

Now let us try the effect of winning the first trick. East will play low. Now a low spade to our ♠J and West's ace and what is he to do? If he starts cashing hearts from the top, i.e. now plays ♡K, his partner's ♡Q will fall on the same trick and our ♡10 will be promoted to a stop. On the other hand, if he plays a low heart to his partner's queen, East will not have another one to return and our nine tricks will come in first. We can now see that, even with a 3–2 diamond split, playing on diamonds would not have worked. Let's try it: win the first heart with the ace and lose a diamond. Now the defenders cash the ♡Q and East is able to put his partner back on play with the ♠A to cash the rest of the hearts for down two and −100. Satisfy yourself that this is the case by playing the hand through.

This type of hand illustrates a useful guide (but be warned! – there are countless exceptions), namely that it is often advisable to lose tricks to cards which cannot be avoided in preference to those which can. Here, there is no way we can avoid losing to the ♠A but we can avoid losing a diamond by refusing to touch the suit. This, of course, contradicts the dictum commonly taught to beginners that: 'At no-trump, you always play on your longest suit.'

Let us juggle the heart suit around and observe that there are other situations where playing a high card on the first round can cause a blockage:

$$\heartsuit \text{ K x}$$
$$\heartsuit \text{ A J x x x} \qquad \qquad \heartsuit \text{ Q x}$$
$$\heartsuit \text{ 10 9 x x}$$

Here, you will have one stop whether you play the $\heartsuit$K first time or not, but the play of the $\heartsuit$K will give the opponents similar entry trouble to that in the example above.

Where you have 9 x x x in hand, a blockage is still possible if East has two honors in his doubleton, as here:

$$\heartsuit \text{ A x}$$
$$\heartsuit \text{ K Q x x x} \qquad \qquad \heartsuit \text{ J 10}$$
$$\text{9 x x x}$$

The ace will capture one of East's honors on the first round, after which West will have the choice of cashing the other or leading low and leaving his partner on play but now void of the suit. In that case, an entry in another suit will be needed in the West hand. Here is another example:

$$\heartsuit \text{ A x}$$
$$\heartsuit \text{ K x x x x x} \qquad \qquad \heartsuit \text{ Q x}$$
$$\heartsuit \text{ J 10 x}$$

Again, playing low is fatal, while putting up the ace gives East the choice of playing low and blocking the suit or playing the queen, leaving our $\heartsuit$ J 10 solid against the king, thereby forming a second stop. Of course, in this situation, South is faced with an awkward decision in that the actual layout could be:

$$\heartsuit \text{ A x}$$
$$\heartsuit \text{ K Q x x x x} \qquad \qquad \heartsuit \text{ x x}$$
$$\heartsuit \text{ J 10 x}$$

and now the ace is a losing play while playing low is a winner. How we decide which to go for will be learnt later on. The first step is to be aware of the various possibilities and how to handle them.

While a declarer can block opponents' suits in certain positions, he must be careful to avoid blocking his own. Sometimes it is worth giving up the chance of a finesse or even a trick to ensure that potentially inaccessible winners can be cashed. Let us start with this example:

Hand No. 14

Dealer South

N-S vulnerable

♠ A 8
♡ Q 4 3
◇ K J 10 8 2
♣ 7 5 3

W	N	E	S
			1♣
Pass	1◇	Pass	2NT
Pass	3NT	end	

```
      N
   W     E
      S
```

♠ K 7 2
♡ A J
◇ 9 6 4
♣ A K Q J 10

South opens 1♣, primarily looking for 3NT, 5♣ being an outsider. When North replies with a forcing 1◇, South knows that all the suits are well covered and it is a question of how many no-trump to call on his 18 points. 2NT is the standard limit-call but there is a good case for 3NT with those five solid clubs. Against that, if both king and queen of hearts are in enemy hands, the ♡J will not be pulling its full weight. Despite this, the hand is probably worth a direct game call, but South decides on 2NT and North has more than enough to raise to game.

West leads the ♠Q. Start your stop-watch and see if you can find a line of play that guarantees the contract, irrespective of the opponents' defence and distribution.

We have five solid club tricks, two top spades and one heart at least to give eight tricks and it seems no problem to set up further tricks in diamonds. However, this may involve losing the lead twice and in the meantime, the defenders may be able to set up three or more spade tricks to go with their ace and queen of diamonds.

Let us therefore look at the heart suit in more detail. With only the king missing, we can set up two tricks for one lost but we must be careful, in that case, not to touch diamonds at all for fear of losing the lead too often.

How do we play the hearts? We can, in fact, take two tricks without losing the lead by taking a finesse through East. Suppose we win the opening lead on the board and play a heart immediately. If the jack holds, we have nine tricks on top and can try the diamonds for overtricks.

But if the finesse loses, we are likely to be set. West will win and play another spade, which we can only win in hand. We can cash the ♡A but the ♡Q is stranded on the board and we cannot reach her, even if we guess the diamond position correctly, before the defenders have taken their five tricks – three spades (unless we are lucky enough to find them with a 4–4 split) the ♡K and the ◇A.

The guide of keeping an entry with the long suit applies here even though the 'long' suit is only ♡ Q x x. Win the first spade in hand. (Note that ducking completely is no good as the second round will force the ace before the king.) Now play the ace and jack of hearts while the ♠K remains on the board. When the defenders win and play another spade, we shall be on the board to cash the ♡Q for our ninth trick.

The deal:

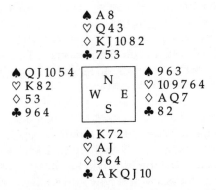

```
              ♠ A 8
              ♡ Q 4 3
              ◇ K J 10 8 2
              ♣ 7 5 3
♠ Q J 10 5 4        N        ♠ 9 6 3
♡ K 8 2                      ♡ 10 9 7 6 4
◇ 5 3        W       E       ◇ A Q 7
♣ 9 6 4            S         ♣ 8 2
              ♠ K 7 2
              ♡ A J
              ◇ 9 6 4
              ♣ A K Q J 10
```

The student who plays the hand out will observe that, on this lie of the cards, the contract can also be made by winning the first or second spade on the board, crossing to hand in clubs and playing on diamonds, but that line will fail if we swap the positions of the ♡K and one of the diamond honors and South mis-guesses on the first round of diamonds. West is unlikely to have the ♡K and the ◇A with that spade suit when he did not make a non-vulnerable overcall at the one-level.

Let us now strengthen the diamonds and weaken the clubs to highlight further the importance of preserving entries.

```
                                    ♠ 7 5 2
                                    ♡ Q J 6
Hand No. 15                         ◇ K Q J 10 5 3
Dealer East                         ♣ 7
E-W vulnerable
                                  ┌──────────┐
                                  │    N     │
W        N        E        S      │  W    E  │
                  Pass     1NT    │    S     │
                                  └──────────┘
Pass     3NT      end
                                    ♠ A K 3
                                    ♡ A 5 3
                                    ◇ 6 4
                                    ♣ A J 9 6 4
```

After East's initial pass, South opens 1NT, primarily angling for 3NT. North sees that this is one of those hands where all hangs on whether the diamonds come in or not and decides to punt 3NT straight away. It is possible that 5◇ is on but that is two tricks more and unlikely to be right on an aceless hand. West leads the ♡4, which you may assume is fourth-high. How do you play the hand? I shall give you the free piece of information that, if you play a heart honor on the first trick, East will play low. Start your stop-watch. By this stage, you should be doing your full analysis in under ninety seconds.

Given a free finesse in hearts, you have four tricks in the majors and one in clubs so that the diamonds will have to provide the other four required. A singleton ace is most unlikely so the defenders are likely to hold it up to the second round, after which a side-suit entry will be needed to enjoy the rest of the suit. That can only be in hearts, and now you realize that your ace is a liability rather than an asset. Suppose we play an honor from the board, winning trick one. Now we attack diamonds, losing the second round, whereupon the defenders shift to spades. We win in hand and now what? Unless East has the ♡K, now alone, we cannot reach the board.

The deal:

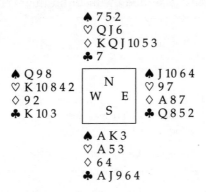

```
                    ♠ 7 5 2
                    ♡ Q J 6
                    ◇ K Q J 10 5 3
                    ♣ 7
    ♠ Q 9 8              N        ♠ J 10 6 4
    ♡ K 10 8 4 2                  ♡ 9 7
    ◇ 9 2          W       E      ◇ A 8 7
    ♣ K 10 3             S        ♣ Q 8 5 2
                    ♠ A K 3
                    ♡ A 5 3
                    ◇ 6 4
                    ♣ A J 9 6 4
```

Let us go through the play in detail:

(i) West leads ♡4 to ♡Q, ♡9, ♡3.

Note that East gives the count in this position. It is obvious that, as he cannot beat the ♡Q, the encouragement/discouragement position is clear and it is important for him to tell his partner whether or not South's ♡A is going to fall on the next round.

(ii) North leads ◇K to ◇7, ◇4 and ◇9.

Note again, West gives count. Encouragement/discouragement is again irrelevant in a suit which is opponents' principal source of tricks and it is crucial for East to know how long to hold up his ace. As explained before, a high card tries to show an even number. It cannot be four (or else South is void) so it must be two.

(iii) North plays the ◇Q.

Now you would expect East to win this time, but he ducks again. Before reading on, can you say why? If that nine is, in fact, from a doubleton, East could safely win now but for all he knows, it could be a singleton, leaving South with three. It is worth investing a trick to be safe in this kind of situation as East knows that the contract depends on bringing the diamond suit in.

(iv) North plays ◇J to East's ◇A, South discards ♠3 and West the ♣3.

(v) East returns a heart and the heart position is now:

$$\heartsuit \text{J } 6$$
$$\heartsuit \text{K } 10\ 8\ 2 \qquad \heartsuit 7$$
$$\heartsuit \text{A } 5$$

There is nothing South can do to get to the board. Note that, had West held the $\diamondsuit$ A, he would simply have got off play or *exited* with a spade, leaving South to play hearts; again the board cannot be reached.

South is held to seven tricks for -100, and that was only because East held up his $\diamondsuit$ A once too often. It could well have been -150.

What went wrong? Hasty play to trick one – the cause of so many unnecessary sets. The heart position was typical of the sort of three-card position discussed at great length in the beginners' book:

$$\heartsuit \text{Q J x}$$
$$\heartsuit \text{K x x} \qquad \heartsuit \text{x x x}$$
$$\heartsuit \text{A x x}$$

Actually in the above problem, East only had a doubleton, but that is of little relevance. Insisting that West leads, it is clear that N-S will win two tricks and lose one unless West leads them twice. What is less clear is whether North or South will win the two tricks and when. With a big diamond suit at stake, this is crucial. We have just seen that, if North wins the first trick for his side, South will have to win the second, but why not let *South* win the first round and keep the two honors on the board, solid against the king? Nothing now can prevent declarer from reaching the board and the established diamonds. Effectively, we are down to the two-card position:

$$\heartsuit \text{Q J}$$
$$\heartsuit \text{K } 10 \qquad \heartsuit \text{x x}$$
$$\heartsuit \text{x x}$$

Now it is one trick each, but the N-S trick is won by North. Thus the correct line of play is for the board to play low at trick one, spurning the free finesse, and for South's ace to win. Now knock out the ◇ A and use the heart entry at the proper time to reach the rest of the diamonds. Opponents will, of course, realize what is going on and can establish a couple of tricks by shifting to clubs (although, in practice, on the bidding they are more likely to shift to spades). We, however, cannot be denied at least nine out of ten tricks (five diamonds, two hearts, two spades and the ♣A.)

I hope this hand has impressed upon you the importance of studying the two- and three-card positions in the beginners' book. This kind of problem occurs hand after hand and familiarity, preferably without having to think too long about it, is invaluable. Note that, if East had the suit (say he had overcalled) and West led it in this layout:

$$♡ \; Q \, J \, 6$$
$$♡ \; 9 \, 7 \qquad\qquad ♡ \; K \, 10 \, 8 \, 4 \, 2$$
$$♡ \; A \, 5 \, 3$$

precisely the same play would be required even though the finesse is known to be right. Put up an honor on trick one and East will simply play low. The board will never be reached again as East will shift to a black suit when in with the ◇ A. It will be worth juggling that heart suit around.

Let us give the jack to South:

$$♡ \; Q \, x \, x$$
$$♡ \; K \, 10 \, x \, x \, x \qquad\qquad ♡ \; x \, x$$
$$♡ \; A \, J \, x$$

Still assuming that an entry to the board is needed, South's ace must be played at trick one. Give the jack to the defenders and the same applies:

$$♡ \; Q \, x \, x$$
$$♡ \; K \, J \, 10 \, x \, x \qquad\qquad ♡ \; x \, x$$
$$♡ \; A \, x \, x$$

As you become more advanced, you will learn that sometimes spectacular sacrifices need to be made:

$\heartsuit$ J 10 x

$\heartsuit$ K 9 x x x x $\heartsuit$ A

$\heartsuit$ Q x x

West leads low to his partner's ace and the South must play the queen now.

$\heartsuit$ J 10 x

$\heartsuit$ Q 9 x x x x $\heartsuit$ A

$\heartsuit$ K x x

Again West leads low to his partner's ace and South must drop the king! Note there is no cost: N-S were only ever going to take one trick in the suit. West will not touch it again when he sees that his partner is unable to return it.

We are going to conclude this section on no-trump declarer play with some miscellaneous test examples which I should like you to do against the stop-watch. At the table, you will be expected to play within a few seconds of the dummy going down but if you can give a full analysis in under ninety seconds, that will be ample for the time being. In each case, I should like you to answer the ten questions set out earlier in the section and arrive at a reasoned line of play which will guarantee the contract or at least give you the best chance. Take no credit for good guessing. Be satisfied only if you made every point I give in the solutions.

Problem 1

Hand No. 16
Dealer South
Neither vulnerable

$\spadesuit$ A 8 3
$\heartsuit$ Q 6 5
$\diamondsuit$ K 2
$\clubsuit$ A 10 9 7 6

W	N	E	S
			1NT
Pass	3NT	end	

```
      N
  W       E
      S
```

$\spadesuit$ K 6 4
$\heartsuit$ A 2
$\diamondsuit$ A 8 7 3
$\clubsuit$ K J 5 3

West leads the $\heartsuit$J.

Problem 2

Hand No. 17
Dealer North
E-W vulnerable

♠ K 7 3
♡ A
◇ K 7 2
♣ A J 10 9 7 6

W	N	E	S
	1♣	Pass	1◇
Pass	3♣	Pass	3NT
end			

```
        N
    W       E
        S
```

♠ A 6 4
♡ J 7 2
◇ A 8 4 3
♣ Q 8 4

West leads the ♡K.

Problem 3

Hand No. 18
Dealer East
Both vulnerable

♠ J 10 2
♡ K 9
◇ A Q 7 2
♣ J 10 4 2

W	N	E	S
		Pass	1NT
2♡	3NT	end	

```
        N
    W       E
        S
```

♠ A Q 8
♡ J 7 4
◇ K 4
♣ K Q 9 7 6

West leads the ♡6.

Problem 4

Hand No. 19
Dealer South
E-W vulnerable

♠ J 3
♡ 8 6 5
◇ K Q 7
♣ A J 10 4 2

W	N	E	S
			1NT
Pass	3NT	end	

```
        N
    W       E
        S
```

♠ A 6 5
♡ A 4 3
◇ A J 6 5
♣ Q 9 8

West leads the ♠2. As he might have led from the king and queen, it costs nothing for you to play the ♠J. However, East covers with the ♠Q.

Problem 5

Hand No. 20
Dealer East
N-S vulnerable

W	N	E	S
		Pass	1NT
3NT	end		

♠ K 4 2
♡ Q J 6
◇ K 6 5
♣ J 10 5 3

```
      N
  W       E
      S
```

♠ A 8 6 5
♡ K 7 2
◇ A Q 7 4
♣ Q 9

West leads the ♡10 to his partner's ♡A and East returns the ♡4.

Solutions

Problem 1

We have two top tricks in spades and another two in diamonds plus the ♡A, to total five so far. So, even if we cannot catch the ♣Q, four out of five possible club tricks will suffice. If West has the ♡K, there can never be any problem as the ♡Q will constitute a second stop. So we must assume that it is with East and in that case, should West gain the lead, another heart through could result in the loss of four heart tricks which, added to the ♣Q, would spell a set. Therefore, to be safe, we must take the club finesse through West to ensure that, if a trick has to be lost in the suit, it will be to East, who can do no damage. Play low from the board at trick one and win in hand with the ace. Cash the ♣K (in case there is a singleton queen, after which no finesse will be necessary) and then a low club from South, ducking if West plays low. Good technique is rewarded with an overtrick.

The deal:

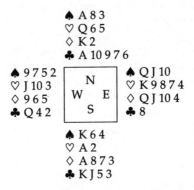

```
              ♠ A 8 3
              ♡ Q 6 5
              ◇ K 2
              ♣ A 10 9 7 6
  ♠ 9 7 5 2      ┌─────────┐    ♠ Q J 10
  ♡ J 10 3       │    N    │    ♡ K 9 8 7 4
  ◇ 9 6 5        │  W   E  │    ◇ Q J 10 4
  ♣ Q 4 2        │    S    │    ♣ 8
                 └─────────┘
              ♠ K 6 4
              ♡ A 2
              ◇ A 8 7 3
              ♣ K J 5 3
```

Note West's carefully thought-out lead. Knowing his opponents had at least 25 points between them, he realized that the bulk of the remaining strength was with his partner. He therefore tried to find his partner's suit rather than concentrate on his own, very poor spades. North-South had shown no interest in a major-suit game and so hearts were the best chance. Note that the 'eight ever, nine never!' specialists would have failed in this contract.

Problem 2

Here again, we have two top tricks each in spades and diamonds plus the ♡A, totalling five so far. There is a possibility of an extra diamond trick, should the suit break 3–3, but we will not come near to the contract without bringing in the clubs, so let us concentrate on them. We can insist on six rounds, of which we shall win at least five easily enough for the contract. However, we may have to lose the lead to the ♣K to set up the long cards and now we are in danger of losing at least four heart tricks. A 5–4 split in the suit is the best we can hope for and it is clear from the lead that the ♡Q is badly placed over our jack. For this reason, we must make every possible effort to keep East off play. If he has the ♣K protected, there is nothing we can do. If West has the ♣K, we can happily allow him to have a trick as a heart from his side is not dangerous. The critical case thus arises when East has the ♣K as a singleton and, to cover that position, we should, after winning the ♡A on the board perforce at trick one, cash the ♣A at trick two.

The deal:

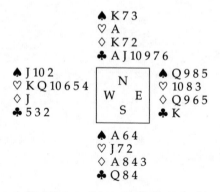

Again, our good technique is rewarded with eleven tricks instead
of the seven we would have had if we had taken the 'percentage'
play of the club finesse.

Problem 3

We have at least one spade trick and can ensure one heart by
playing low from the board at trick one. There are three diamond
tricks and thus four of the five rounds of clubs will suffice for
nine in total. The problem lies in the fact that we have only one
certain stop in hearts and that we shall have to give up the lead
once to establish the long clubs. The auction marks West with at
least five hearts and most, if not all, of the outstanding points. Is
there, therefore, any hope at all? It is clear that, if West has both
ace and queen of hearts, there is nothing to be done. Equally if
East has the ♡A the position is hopeless unless it is a singleton, in
which case the contract can never be in danger, irrespective of
how we play to the first trick. The critical case arises where East
has the ♡Q in a doubleton as in the layout opposite:

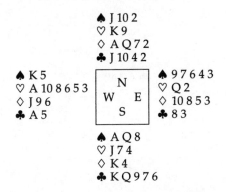

♠ J 10 2
♡ K 9
◇ A Q 7 2
♣ J 10 4 2

♠ K 5
♡ A 10 8 6 5 3
◇ J 9 6
♣ A 5

♠ 9 7 6 4 3
♡ Q 2
◇ 10 8 5 3
♣ 8 3

♠ A Q 8
♡ J 7 4
◇ K 4
♣ K Q 9 7 6

Now the play to trick one is critical. If we play low, East will win and return the suit. We shall be allowed one trick, but once West takes the ♣A, he can cash all his hearts for down two. However, if we put up the ♡K, the suit is blocked. When West takes his ♣A, he can either put his partner in with the ♡Q, after which East will have to shift to allow us to take nine tricks first, or he can hold the lead by playing the ♡A, but this crashes his partner's ♡Q, after which our ♡J becomes a second stopper.

Problem 4

The opening lead is probably fourth-highest, which means that we will lose three tricks in the suit and win one. As the suit is evenly divided between the two opponents, there is nothing to be gained by ducking and indeed, if we do, East may realize that, if he continues spades, the best he can hope for is three spade tricks and the ♣K to total four, not enough to set the contract. He should thus appreciate that his best chance is to shift to hearts. Now, if the club finesse fails, we will lose three heart tricks, the club and one spade to go down one. We should therefore win the first spade and take the club finesse immediately, ensuring four tricks in each of the minors and the two major aces for ten in total.

The deal:

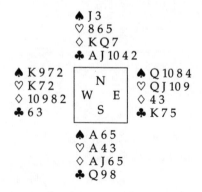

♠ J 3
♡ 8 6 5
◇ K Q 7
♣ A J 10 4 2

♠ K 9 7 2
♡ K 7 2
◇ 10 9 8 2
♣ 6 3

♠ Q 10 8 4
♡ Q J 10 9
◇ 4 3
♣ K 7 5

♠ A 6 5
♡ A 4 3
◇ A J 6 5
♣ Q 9 8

Problem 5

We have two top spade tricks, two in hearts and three in diamonds to total seven. There are two lines of play for the other two. One is to hope that the diamonds are breaking 3–3. In that case, we give up an early spade trick and hope that this suit splits evenly too. This involves giving up the lead only once, in which case the opponents can set up their heart winners but cannot cash them. The other line is to play on clubs, knocking out the ace and king to leave us with two top winners, irrespective of distribution. This involves losing the lead twice and the possibility that we could end up losing three heart tricks as well to total five – down one.

When two lines of play are available in situations like these, it is wise to calculate the percentages involved. The chance of two suits breaking 3–3 is just under 13 per cent in principle and here it is less when it is considered that we are working on the assumption that the hearts are breaking 5–2. (If they are 4–3, we *can* afford to give up the lead twice in clubs). The chance of the hand with the long hearts having only one or neither of the club honors is about 80 per cent – clearly better. (Remember that a club honor in the hand with the short hearts is no danger as the defender has no heart left to play). So on winning the second heart, we should play on clubs, observing the principle of losing inevitable tricks rather than those which could be avoided.

The deal:

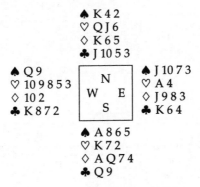

```
                    ♠ K 4 2
                    ♡ Q J 6
                    ◇ K 6 5
                    ♣ J 10 5 3
   ♠ Q 9              N          ♠ J 10 7 3
   ♡ 10 9 8 5 3   W     E        ♡ A 4
   ◇ 10 2            S           ◇ J 9 8 3
   ♣ K 8 7 2                     ♣ K 6 4
                    ♠ A 8 6 5
                    ♡ K 7 2
                    ◇ A Q 7 4
                    ♣ Q 9
```

You are strongly urged to replay all the hands in this no-trump declarer-play section until you are completely satisfied that you understand everything and can produce solutions to the test examples in under thirty seconds, something approaching the speed expected at the table. Notice particularly that the bulk of the work was done before a single card was played at trick one – viz. counting of tricks in each suit, counting of tricks available to declarer and defenders and attempting to place enemy cards, notably when they had made a call.

Note also that similar situations in a given suit had to be handled differently according to circumstances when a hand was considered as a whole. It is crucially important to appreciate these points before proceeding further because now we are going to introduce the trump suit and matters can only become more complicated.

SECTION 2:

Basic Plays at Trump Contracts

The introduction of a trump suit brings in a large number of complexities and so there is far more to discuss. Trumps are primarily used to override opponents' winners but, of course, that works both ways. For that reason, many schools teach beginners that the first job, when declaring a trump contract, is to pull opponents' trumps and indeed, that is very often good advice. However, even now, a number of questions need to be answered.

1 How do we pull opponents' trumps?
2 Do we pull *all* their trumps?
3 What happens afterwards if
   a We do indeed pull all the trumps?
   b We leave one or more trumps at large?

In *The Expert Beginner* we set out a number of suit combinations and learnt how to play them. This will be an excellent opportunity to revise them and learn more. The play in a given suit can vary according to how many tricks are needed. Consider this example:

♠ Q 10 9 6 5
♠ A 7 4 3 2

The spades are trumps and with eight solid tricks in the side suits, you are playing a small slam. How would you pull trumps to ensure four tricks? The first job is, of course, the one-closed-hand exercise on this suit. The king, jack and eight are missing.

Clearly, if they split 2–1, the ♠A will capture two of them, leaving only one outstanding, and we can never lose more than one trick. So we must consider the possibility (admittedly less likely) that all three spades will be in one hand, i.e. visualize the full layout as:

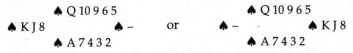

The question arises as to whether there is a play to cater for either contingency. The rule of leading from weakness through strength to strength applies. Clearly, playing out the ♠A will be good enough in the first layout because, when East shows out, we can play a low card through West's king to the board's queen, losing just the one trick. However, the play loses in the second layout because now the enemy K J stands as a tenace over the board's queen, so we must think again.

A low card towards the board's ♠Q is sufficient in either case. In the first layout, if West plays low, the board's ♠Q will hold, the ♠A will pull a second round and only one trick will be lost. In the second layout, West will show out and the ♠Q will lose to the ♠K, but now we are effectively left with this two-card position:

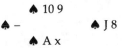

We cross to the board in a side-suit and run the ♠10, the finesse being clearly marked by West's failure to follow to the first round.

That play will be good enough but it can be improved slightly. Try the effect of starting with the ♠10 from the board. Now, if East shows out, we simply take the ♠A and lead low towards the ♠Q, conceding the ♠K only. If East follows with the ♠J, we can take the ♠A and will only lose to the ♠K. If East plays the ♠8, we play low and now, if West wins, there has been a 2–1 split; if he shows out, we cash the ♠A and concede to the ♠K only. This play has two slight advantages in that, if East has a singleton ♠K, we make an overtrick, and that the play of low card towards the

♠Q not only guarantees to lose one trick but gives the defenders the option to take the first round, after which there could be a ruff if there is an unbalanced split in a side-suit. Passing the ♠10 also carries this risk but a trick will be lost to the first round in far fewer cases and so the risk is less serious.

But now let us consider the play if our ambitious partner puts us into a grand slam. Clearly now, a 3–0 split leaves us with a certain loser and we must hope for the more likely 2–1. We have to choose between passing the ♠Q, which works in this layout:

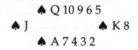

```
            ♠ Q 10 9 6 5
   ♠ J                    ♠ K 8
            ♠ A 7 4 3 2
```

or cashing the ♠A, which works if either defender holds the ♠K singleton.

The second line works in two layouts:

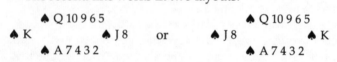

```
      ♠ Q 10 9 6 5                    ♠ Q 10 9 6 5
 ♠ K             ♠ J 8     or    ♠ J 8             ♠ K
      ♠ A 7 4 3 2                    ♠ A 7 4 3 2
```

against only one for the first line, and therefore is twice as good a play.

For our second example, let us consider this:

```
            ♠ A 9 8 7
            ♠ K Q 6 5 2
```

That leaves the ♠ J 10 4 3 missing and, unless they are all in one hand, we can pull them without loss. Thus we must consider the 4–0 splits:

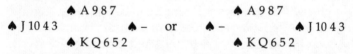

```
      ♠ A 9 8 7                       ♠ A 9 8 7
 ♠ J 10 4 3          ♠ –     or   ♠ –          ♠ J 10 4 3
      ♠ K Q 6 5 2                     ♠ K Q 6 5 2
```

On the left-hand side, there is no chance. If we play a low card from hand towards the ♠A, West will put in an honor, forcing the ♠A, to leave:

```
            ♠ 9 8 7
   ♠ 10 4 3              ♠ –
            ♠ K Q 6 5
```

and now, unless West can be forced to lead the suit, the ♠10 cannot be caught. On the right-hand side, however, we have two honors over the ♠ J 10 and as we have 9 8 7 as well, we can take a double finesse. The correct play, therefore, is the ♠A first, so that South's two honors are kept intact. When West shows out, we follow with the ♠9, forcing East to cover. We win and then return to the board in a side suit and follow with the ♠8 and East's remaining honor is caught. Play it over yourself and ensure that you understand the reasoning behind it.

For our third example, we will consider a position in which even 'good' players often go wrong.

♠ 8 7 6 5

♠ A Q 10 4 3

The ♠K, ♠J, ♠9, and ♠2 are thus missing. First of all, let us consider the play if we need all five tricks in the suit. The ace first will win in one situation only:

♠ 8 7 6 5

♠ K   ♠ J 9 2

♠ A Q 10 4 3

The king will drop and after that, we can return to the board in a side suit and take the marked finesse against the ♠J. A much better chance is to assume that East holds the ♠K. In that case, we will lead a low card from the board and if East plays low, we have the choice of finessing the ten or queen. Finessing the ♠10 gains in these two positions:

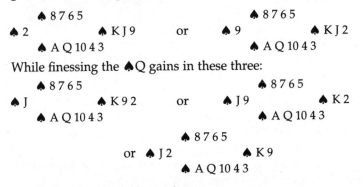

♠ 8 7 6 5   ♠ 8 7 6 5

♠ 2   ♠ K J 9   or   ♠ 9   ♠ K J 2

♠ A Q 10 4 3   ♠ A Q 10 4 3

While finessing the ♠Q gains in these three:

♠ 8 7 6 5   ♠ 8 7 6 5

♠ J   ♠ K 9 2   or   ♠ J 9   ♠ K 2

♠ A Q 10 4 3   ♠ A Q 10 4 3

♠ 8 7 6 5

or   ♠ J 2   ♠ K 9

♠ A Q 10 4 3

and therefore is the better line.

However, where only four tricks are needed, the first priority is to avoid losing two tricks and now we can cater for more situations. If both ♠K and ♠J are with West and accompanied by one or both low cards, there is nothing we can do. But if either or both are with East, the play of the ace first will ensure four tricks. Many players like to take a finesse on the first round but, irrespective of whether they try the ♠Q or ♠10, they run an unnecessary risk. If the ♠Q loses to the ♠K and East follows low to the next round, you will sit there wondering whether to play for the finesse or drop against the ♠J; the same applies if you try the ♠10 on the first round and it loses to the ♠J, which may be stiff or doubleton with the ♠K. Play the ace first time and if an honor drops on your left, you will be saved a guess at the cost of a possible overtrick.

You should have got the idea by now. Can you give an analysis of this position in under sixty seconds. Start your stopwatch and try to make five tricks here:

♠ J 8 7 6 5
♠ A Q 9 4 3

Again the finesse is clearly preferable to cashing the ace, as the latter play only gains in the one position where West has a stiff ♠K. The finesse gains in the following layouts:

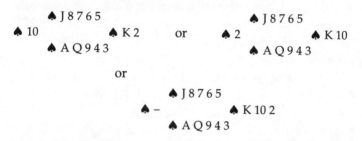

In the first two of these three cases, we can start with the ♠J or play low to the ♠Q; it does not matter. But in the third case, we must start by passing the ♠J. East will cover and we win with the ♠A. After that, we must return to the board in another suit and take another finesse against the ♠10. Observe what happens if we start by playing low to the ♠Q. That will leave:

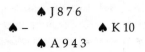

♠ J 8 7 6

♠ –   ♠ K 10

♠ A 9 4 3

Now the ♠ K 10 form a tenace over the ♠J and cannot be caught.

Let us consider one more example:

♠ A 10 6

♠ K 8 5 4 3 2

Four cards are missing: ♠ Q J 9 7. If we need five tricks in the suit, we can afford one loser – what is the best play? It is clear that, if the suit breaks 2–2 or 3–1, the ♠A and ♠K will capture all, or all but one, of the outstanding cards and thus we need only consider a 4–0 split. Let us show the two layouts:

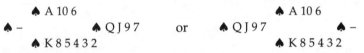

♠ A 10 6   ♠ A 10 6

♠ –   ♠ Q J 9 7   or   ♠ Q J 9 7   ♠ –

♠ K 8 5 4 3 2   ♠ K 8 5 4 3 2

In the left-hand case, there is no hope and two tricks must be lost. In the right-hand case, however, we can play a low card from the South hand. Now, if West plays low, we put in the ♠10. If that loses, we have had, at worst, a 3–1 break and only one trick will be lost. But in the actual layout, the ♠10 will hold and we can cash the ♠A and ♠K to leave one loser only. Alternatively, West may play an honor. Now the ♠A wins and East shows out. We are left with:

♠ 10 6

♠ J 9 7   ♠ –

♠ K 8 5 4 3

but must still be careful.

We return to hand in another suit and lead a low spade towards the board. If West plays low, the ♠10 will win and we cash the ♠K to leave just the one loser. If West rises with the ♠J, we will later cash the ♠10 and return to hand in another suit to cash the ♠K. Play the combination over yourself to ensure that you understand that no other line works and note that three side-suit entries are needed to the South hand to pull trumps completely. Where we need six tricks in the suit, a 2–2 or certain 3–1 splits are needed. The correct procedure is to leave the ♠ A 10 holding intact and start with the ♠K. If both defenders follow with low cards, the ♠Q and ♠J are still outstanding and we must cash the ♠A, hoping for a 2–2 split. If West follows with an honor on the first round, we shall have to hope that he started with both honors, doubleton, and cash the ace as before.

A more interesting position arises if West plays low on the ♠K and East produces an honor. Now there is a choice. We are left with:

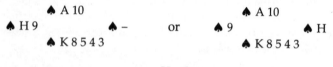

$$H = honor$$

so that, when we play another low card and West plays low again, we can take the finesse or play for the drop. The decision rests on a slightly advanced concept of the *principle of restricted choice*, which was mentioned briefly in the beginners' book. Say East played the ♠J on the first round. Did he start with ♠ Q J or ♠J, singleton? With the singleton, he would have to play the ♠J every time while, with the doubleton, the jack and queen are equals and he could play either with impunity. It is therefore reasonable to assume that he would play the ♠J half the time and the ♠Q half the time. Thus, in cases where he plays the ♠J, it is twice as likely that we are in the position where he has the singleton and therefore the finesse is the correct percentage play. That, indeed, was the purpose of leaving the ♠ A 10 intact and starting with the ♠K.

Alter our position to:

♠ A 10 6
♠ K 9 5 4 3 2

and we can now start with either ♠A, intending to take a finesse against East if West drops an honor; or ♠K, intending to take a finesse against West if East drops an honor.

In these five examples, we have studied some fairly difficult plays. My prime concern is that you should understand how to work out the correct procedure in each case, appreciating that the number of tricks you need in the suit (or, in other words, how many you can afford to lose) can be critical. To complicate matters further, I have to remind you that the technically correct play in a single suit may not be correct in the context of a whole hand. A number of factors, including the auction or early play which may suggest a skew distribution, lack of entries and the reluctance to lose a trick to a particular defender, could swing your decision to a different line. That, however, would be running before you can walk. The first step is to learn the correct plays in a single suit without such hindrances.

In the following sections, we are going to demonstrate the various ways in which trumps can be used, illustrating the advantages over the no-trump denomination. Let us start with setting up a long side-suit. Consider this position:

♣ A K x x x x
♣ x x

With this club suit, we see that, if there were no-trump, we could make five tricks against one lost, if the suit breaks 3–2; four tricks against two lost, if the suit breaks 4–1; three tricks against three lost, if the suit breaks 5–0. But let us allow spades to be trump and now we can set up the same number of winners, according to the break as above, but *without loss*. The ♣A and ♣K will account for the two low ones in hand and any more can be ruffed by South.

So provided we have entries to the board after the suit has been established and the opponents' trumps are pulled (otherwise, with the defenders also exhausted of the suit, they could ruff our winners) we can cash the established low cards as if we were in a no-trump contract. Let us start with a simple example – a grand slam.

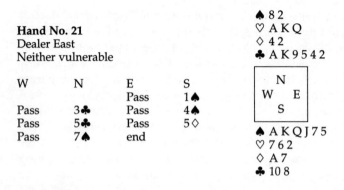

Hand No. 21
Dealer East
Neither vulnerable

♠ 8 2
♡ A K Q
◇ 4 2
♣ A K 9 5 4 2

W	N	E	S
		Pass	1♠
Pass	3♣	Pass	4♠
Pass	5♣	Pass	5◇
Pass	7♠	end	

♠ A K Q J 7 5
♡ 7 6 2
◇ A 7
♣ 10 8

The auction merits some discussion. After East's pass, South opens 1♠, primarily looking towards 4♠. North jumps to 3♣. This is forcing to game and shows a good, one-suited hand. With the partnership now committed to game, it is preferable to have as long a discussion as possible. So there is little point in South's jumping to 4♠, which costs a round of bidding *unless the call carries a very clear message*. Here South shows a solid suit, i.e. one he is prepared to have as trump, even without support from partner. This sets the trump suit and now every subsequent suit call is a *cue-bid* rather than showing a suit. The cue-bid is new to you and will be discussed in more detail in the bidding section later. For the moment, it will suffice to say that it shows first-round control, i.e. ace or void (obviously the ace in a bid suit!) or, if that has already been denied (or promised by partner), second-round control (king or singleton).

North thus bids 5♣, showing the ♣A. Notice that North does not use Blackwood. If he did and found his partner with one ace (obviously the ♠A on the promise of a solid spade suit), he would not know what to do as the ace and king of diamonds could still be missing. South bids 5◇, showing the ◇A and North can confidently bid the grand slam. The only danger lies in the possibility of South turning up with three small clubs but even then, there is the chance of a 2–2 split (about 40 per cent).

West leads the ◇K. Start your stop-watch and work out how to play the hand, preferably in under a minute.

Barring an unlikely 5–0 split in trump, we have six top tricks there, plus three in hearts, one in diamonds and two in clubs to total twelve. The thirteenth can only come from setting up long cards in those clubs. So we win the first diamond and pull trumps, taking four rounds if necessary. On the third and fourth round, we discard the remaining diamond and a low club from the board. Now cash the ace and king of clubs. Notice that we do *not* touch those hearts. They are top tricks and can be cashed at any time. It may be essential to keep them on the board as entries to the clubs. If both defenders follow to both rounds of clubs, then the suit has broken 3–2 and one more round, which we will ruff in hand, will clear the way for the remainder. We now return to the board in hearts and cash a long club, on which we discard our losing diamond and are now home with a trick to burn.

The deal:

```
                    ♠ 8 2
                    ♡ A K Q
                    ♦ 4 2
                    ♣ A K 9 5 4 2
   ♠ 10                          ♠ 9 6 4 3
   ♡ 10 9 8 5 3       N          ♡ J 4
   ♦ K Q J 8 3    W     E        ♦ 10 9 6 5
   ♣ 6 3             S           ♣ Q J 7
                    ♠ A K Q J 7 5
                    ♡ 7 6 2
                    ♦ A 7
                    ♣ 10 8
```

First of all, notice that in no-trump, twelve tricks are the limit. Second, let us replay the hand, exchanging the defenders' ♦5 and ♣3 so that now the clubs are breaking 4–1. Again, we win the first diamond and pull trumps. Now we cash the ace and king of clubs and ruff a third round. We then return to the board in hearts and play a fourth round, ruffing again. The last club is now high and we return to the board in hearts again to cash it for the diamond discard.

Let us replay it a third time but replace the ♡Q with a low card. Again, both black suits will break 4–1. We win the first diamond and pull trumps, being careful to discard the board's low heart and the diamond, which are both potential losers, as opposed to the low clubs which are potential winners. Now ace, king and a third club, ruffed. Return to the board with a heart and ruff a fourth club to establish the suit. Return to the board again in hearts to enjoy the last two clubs, on which we discard our losing diamond and losing heart. Any comment on that? So important were those heart entries that, in this layout, a heart lead, removing one of them prematurely, would have defeated the contract. Indeed, West, on hearing the auction, might well have realized that this was the case and found that decisive lead.

Let us now consider the next use of trumps – as ruffers for our own losers. This usually means ruffing on the board (the hand that is shorter in trump).

As we learnt in the beginners' book, ruffing in the long hand achieves little, except, as in the above case, if it is done to establish long cards or if ruffing results in declarer's hand becoming shorter in trump than the board's.

Let us start with another grand slam.

Hand No. 22
Dealer West
Both vulnerable

♠ Q J 10 5
♡ 2
♢ K 7 3 2
♣ A K 9 5

W	N	E	S
Pass	1♣	Pass	2♠
Pass	3♠	Pass	4♢
Pass	5♣	Pass	5♡
Pass	5NT	Pass	7♠
end			

```
      N
  W       E
      S
```

♠ A K 7 6 4 3
♡ A 7 6
♢ A 4
♣ 4 2

After North's opening call and South's game force, note that, as explained in the last hand, there is no need to rush, the partnership being in a game-forcing situation, unless there is a specific message to send. A quiet raise to 3♠, to agree the suit as trump, is all that is required at this stage.

Now the partnership can discuss the possibility of a slam. South's 4♢ is a cue-bid, promising first-round control (ace or void) in diamonds but, at the same time, denying first-round control in clubs by virtue of having failed to bid 4♣.

Note this *negative inference*. These are vitally important in both the auction and play. Detective story fans will remember that Sherlock Holmes used to point out that the dog who does nothing might be telling you just as much as his kennel-mate who barks and/or wags its tail! Note again that South does not use Blackwood. If he did and his partner produced no ace, he would have little idea as to whether the ♣K was missing as well. His partner could quite easily have an opening call despite missing both top clubs.

North now cue-bids 5♣, promising first-round control in clubs and denying first-round control in hearts by virtue of having by-passed 4♡. South now shows his heart control with 5♡ and North, well equipped with second-round controls in all three suits, need only check up on the top trumps with 5NT, another new convention, the *grand-slam force*. It asks partner to bid the grand slam with two of the top three honors. South duly obliges.

West leads the ♡K. Start your stop-watch and work out your line of play.

We have six top spade tricks plus three aces and two kings in the side suits to total eleven in all. The other two can only come from heart ruffs on the board. We win the heart lead in hand and pull trumps, which break 2–1. We now ruff a heart on the board, return to hand with the ◇A and ruff our last heart on the board. The ◇K and ♣ A K look after our other losers and the rest of our hand is trump. We have thus effectively taken eight trump tricks and five tops outside to make the grand slam for 210, 1500 vulnerable grand slam bonus and 500 for the rubber, 2210 in all. Notice that, in no-trump, eleven tricks, not even the small slam, are the limit.

The deal:

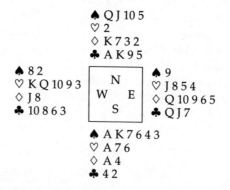

```
                    ♠ Q J 10 5
                    ♡ 2
                    ◇ K 7 3 2
                    ♣ A K 9 5
 ♠ 8 2                             ♠ 9
 ♡ K Q 10 9 3        N            ♡ J 8 5 4
 ◇ J 8          W         E       ◇ Q 10 9 6 5
 ♣ 10 8 6 3          S            ♣ Q J 7
                    ♠ A K 7 6 4 3
                    ♡ A 7 6
                    ◇ A 4
                    ♣ 4 2
```

But let us make a small alteration, exchanging the positions of the ♡9 and ♠9 so that now the trumps are breaking 3–0. Start your stop-watch again and state what difference that would make to your line of play and indeed why the line I suggested above is not actually the best.

We have to be careful not to pull all the trumps immediately. If we do, there will only be one trump left on the board and we cannot ruff two hearts. So we can only afford to pull two rounds of trumps before taking our heart ruffs and again, we must be careful. If we pull the first two rounds with the ace and king of trumps, one of which will capture the ten, and then take our ruffs with the remaining queen and jack of trumps, the nine will be left as master.

The safest line is, after winning the first heart in hand, to ruff a heart immediately with the ♠10, return with a low spade to the ♠K and ruff our last heart with the ♠J. We now cash the ♠Q, exhausting the board of trumps, and then we return to hand with the ◇A to pull the last trump with the ♠A and claim the remaining tricks on top. If we play in any other order, we could run into trouble if the minor suits are breaking badly, as at the top of the next page:

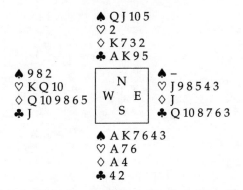

```
                    ♠ Q J 10 5
                    ♡ 2
                    ◇ K 7 3 2
                    ♣ A K 9 5
♠ 9 8 2                            ♠ –
♡ K Q 10        N                 ♡ J 9 8 5 4 3
◇ Q 10 9 8 6 5  W   E             ◇ J
♣ J                 S             ♣ Q 10 8 7 6 3
                    ♠ A K 7 6 4 3
                    ♡ A 7 6
                    ◇ A 4
                    ♣ 4 2
```

Try replaying it the way suggested the first time. If we win the first heart and take two rounds of trumps with the ♠ 10 and ♠ A, ending in hand, and then ruff a heart, return to the ◇ A to ruff the last heart, we now have to find a way back to hand to pull the last trump. On the above deal, it is actually safe to cash the ◇ K and then ruff a diamond in hand, but it could just have easily been:

```
                    ♠ Q J 10 5
                    ♡ 2
                    ◇ K 7 3 2
                    ♣ A K 9 5
♠ 9 8 2                            ♠ –
♡ K Q 10        N                 ♡ J 9 8 5 4 3
◇ J             W   E             ◇ Q 10 9 8 6 5
♣ Q 10 8 7 6 3      S             ♣ J
                    ♠ A K 7 6 4 3
                    ♡ A 7 6
                    ◇ A 4
                    ♣ 4 2
```

and now the ◇ K will be ruffed for one off and 2310 points chucked. The only safe way back to hand now would be the ace and king of clubs, followed by a club ruff, failing on the previous layout. Yes, it would be very unlucky to find such unbalanced breaks, but this hand has been included to illustrate that you cannot be too careful. Indeed, it usually pays to think twice before pulling trumps if ruffs need to be taken on the board. Here is another case in point.

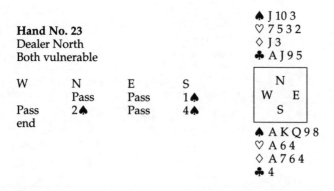

Hand No. 23
Dealer North
Both vulnerable

♠ J 10 3
♡ 7 5 3 2
◇ J 3
♣ A J 9 5

W	N	E	S
	Pass	Pass	1♠
Pass	2♠	Pass	4♠
end			

♠ A K Q 9 8
♡ A 6 4
◇ A 7 6 4
♣ 4

In response to South's opening call, North makes the limit, non-forcing raise to 2♠.

West leads the ♡K. Start your stop-watch and plan your line of play in under two minutes.

You have five top trump tricks and three aces outside and, at the moment, little else barring the very unlikely event of the ♣ K Q being a doubleton. The other two tricks will have to come from ruffing diamonds on the board. Looking at that diamond suit in closer detail, we see that after the ace, we shall have to lose the lead once before we can get those ruffs going. For that reason, we cannot afford to touch trumps at all and even one round would be premature, as we shall see in a moment. We must win the first heart, cash the ◇A and play a second diamond. The defenders will win and, realizing that we are threatening ruffs on the board, will, after cashing their two established heart tricks, undoubtedly play trumps themselves. We win in hand and ruff a diamond on the board, cash the ♣A and return to hand by ruffing a club (note that is the only way to get back to hand; to play a trump would remove the board's last trump). We now ruff our last diamond and the remainder of our hand is high trumps. Altogether, we have taken seven trump tricks (five tops and two ruffs on the board) plus the three side aces.

The deal:

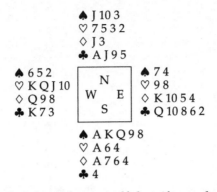

```
                    ♠ J 10 3
                    ♡ 7 5 3 2
                    ◇ J 3
                    ♣ A J 9 5
   ♠ 6 5 2                        ♠ 7 4
   ♡ K Q J 10      N              ♡ 9 8
   ◇ Q 9 8      W     E           ◇ K 10 5 4
   ♣ K 7 3         S              ♣ Q 10 8 6 2
                    ♠ A K Q 9 8
                    ♡ A 6 4
                    ◇ A 7 6 4
                    ♣ 4
```

Replay the hand and satisfy yourself that, if you play so much as one round of trumps (bearing in mind that the defenders will play another one when they get in with the second round of diamonds), you will finish up a trick short. Also note that an initial trump lead would have set the contract. The defenders are now a move ahead and when they gain the lead in diamonds, a second round of trumps leaves only one on the board available for ruffing.

There is another point about this hand worthy of study. Let us look at that heart position in closer detail:

```
                ♡ 7 5 3 2
    ♡ K Q J 10              ♡ 9 8
                ♡ A 6 4
```

The ♡K was led. Did you consider holding up the ace? There are situations where it could be right to do so. If the defenders' hearts broke 3–3, it would cost nothing but here, where they are 4–2, there could be a positive gain. If you could arrange that any subsequent lost tricks would be to East, then, by taking the second round of hearts, we could exhaust East of the suit. Now, if we have a long suit on the board on which to discard South's losing heart, we could reduce our heart losers from two to one. This could mean the difference between failure and success. On this occasion, we were right not to hold up for fear of a trump shift. However, keeping that heart position unaltered, let us juggle the rest of the hand to reconsider this point.

♠ A 10 4 3
♡ 7 5 3 2
◇ J
♣ A J 10 9

Hand No. 24
Dealer East
N-S vulnerable

W	N	E	S
		Pass	1♠
Pass	2♣	Pass	2♠
Pass	3♠	Pass	4♠
end			

```
        N
   W         E
        S
```

♠ Q J 9 8 7
♡ A 6 4
◇ A 7
♣ Q 5 4

After East's initial pass, South opens 1♠, primarily angling for 4♠ or 3NT. Once North has bid 2♣, South can bid game confidently in the knowledge that his ♣Q is a working card.

Again, West leads the ♡K. Start your stop-watch and decide how you are going to play – in particular, what you are going to do on trick one. No credit without a full discussion of the pros and cons of winning or holding up.

Even if both black kings have to be lost, we have four spade tricks, three club tricks, two red aces and a diamond ruff on the board, totalling ten. However, we might have to lose the lead twice to establish those black-suit tricks. Now, if we count losers, we see that the contract is in danger if indeed East has both the black kings. In addition to those two tricks, we could lose two heart tricks to total four for down one and −100. If the hearts break 3–3, there is nothing we can do but, if they are 4–2 with West having the length as before, holding up the first trick exhausts East on the second round. We then have time to pull trumps and set up a long club on which we discard our last losing heart.

The deal:

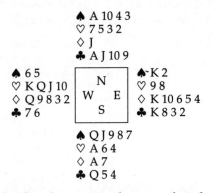

```
                    ♠ A 10 4 3
                    ♡ 7 5 3 2
                    ◇ J
                    ♣ A J 10 9
    ♠ 6 5                           ♠ K 2
    ♡ K Q J 10      N               ♡ 9 8
    ◇ Q 9 8 3 2   W   E             ◇ K 10 6 5 4
    ♣ 7 6           S               ♣ K 8 3 2
                    ♠ Q J 9 8 7
                    ♡ A 6 4
                    ◇ A 7
                    ♣ Q 5 4
```

So we refuse the first heart, win the second and take a trump finesse, ensuring that East, if anyone, gets the lead. Note that, this time, the diamond ruff can wait. Only one needs to be taken and, if we take it immediately, the board would now be left on play. Anything now could be fatal. A black suit (now played from the wrong side) could result in an unnecessary loss to the king in the West hand, after which he could cash his hearts. A heart would give him his tricks immediately – precisely what we have tried to avoid.

So East takes his ♠K and returns a diamond, which we win with the ◇ A. We complete the pulling of trumps (still no rush for the diamond ruff) and run the ♣Q, taking a second finesse if East ducks. He wins the first or second round of the suit and plays a diamond, which we can ruff on the board. We now cash the winning clubs, discarding our losing heart while a frustrated West can do no more than watch.

One final point you should have noted is that if the hearts actually split 5–1, holding up the first round could be fatal, as East would ruff the second round and still have his two black kings to come. In that event, as East is exhausted of hearts after the first round, the winning play is to take the first trick. In answer to that, it should be pointed out that a 4–2 split is about three times as likely as a 5–1, even more so as with ♡ K Q J 10 x, West may well have overcalled, being non-vulnerable against vulnerable opponents. Indeed, if he had overcalled, winning the first round is a must, as a 5–1 split is a virtual certainty.

Let us now switch the heart position and give the length (announced by an overcall) to East and see if that makes any difference.

Hand No. 25
Dealer South
N-S vulnerable

♠ A 10 4 3
♡ 7 5 3 2
◇ A
♣ Q J 10 9

W	N	E	S
			1♠
Pass	2♣	2♡	2♠
Pass	3♠	Pass	4♠
end			

```
        N
   W        E
        S
```

♠ Q J 9 8 7
♡ A 6 4
◇ J 7
♣ A 5 4

The positions of the minor-suit aces have been switched over but apart from that, the hand is similar to the previous one.

West leads the ♡8, this time a clear-cut singleton. Start your stop-watch and work out your plan of campaign.

Again there are four potential losers, two hearts and the two black kings.

As before, we can discard one of our losing hearts on the fourth round of clubs, but not before trumps are pulled and the ♣K knocked out. There will be no danger if the ♣K is with East (as is likely on the bidding), as it is now finessable, so we must assume it is with West. Now how about the trump king? If it is protected with East, there is nothing we can do. If it is with West, it can be caught by a finesse, but as long as East is kept out of the lead, we do not mind losing a trick to West. The critical case, therefore, arises when East has the ♠K singleton, in which case we must play for the drop. We therefore win trick one – holding up is fatal as another heart will be returned and our ace will be ruffed – and play a spade to the ace, guarding against the following type of layout:

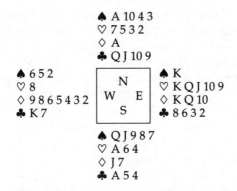

```
                      ♠ A 10 4 3
                      ♡ 7 5 3 2
                      ◇ A
                      ♣ Q J 10 9
     ♠ 6 5 2                        ♠ K
     ♡ 8            ┌─────────┐     ♡ K Q J 10 9
     ◇ 9 8 6 5 4 3 2│    N    │     ◇ K Q 10
     ♣ K 7         │ W     E │     ♣ 8 6 3 2
                    │    S    │
                    └─────────┘
                      ♠ Q J 9 8 7
                      ♡ A 6 4
                      ◇ J 7
                      ♣ A 5 4
```

Satisfy yourself that this is the best line and that, if you try changing the positions of the black kings around (there are obviously four possible combinations), this line of play will never cost more than an overtrick.

We turn to the use of trumps as 'stoppers' against defenders' side-suit winners. Where you are short of a suit (doubleton, singleton or void) you can prevent defenders from taking tricks by ruffing, provided, of course, you have trumps available. Often you have to arrange to be short of a suit so that you can ruff, i.e. by discarding losing cards on other side-suit winners. Let us start with this simple example:

Hand No. 26
Dealer East
Neither vulnerable

```
                                        ♠ 4 3
                                        ♡ J 10 9 3 2
                                        ◇ A Q 7
                                        ♣ 9 6 2
W        N        E        S          ┌─────────┐
                  Pass     1♡         │    N    │
Dbl      3♡       Pass     4♡         │ W     E │
end                                   │    S    │
                                      └─────────┘
                                        ♠ K J 7 2
                                        ♡ K Q 8 7 5
                                        ◇ K 2
                                        ♣ A 8
```

After East's initial pass and South's good opener, West showed just under an opening call or stronger (no upper limit) and ideally a three-suited hand with shortage in hearts. North's raise to 3♡ is pre-emptive and as he is primarily trying to keep East out of the bidding, he bids one more than he would have done otherwise. It is therefore questionable whether South should go on to game. With the bulk of the outstanding strength behind him, and particularly as a take-out double of a major suit suggests a possible interest in the other major, he could take the view that both his spade honors are badly placed and that the same could apply to the ◇K.

Rightly or wrongly, however, he decides to bid game and West leads the ♣K. Start your stop-watch and decide how you are going to take your ten tricks in under two minutes.

Out of five rounds of hearts, we have four top winners, losing the ace, three top diamonds and the ♣A to total eight. However, if we lose two rounds of spades (we must be prepared for the ♠ A Q to be badly placed on the auction) then we can ruff the other two on the board to total ten. (That applies even if it takes three rounds to pull trumps, as there will still be two trumps left on the board). However, looking at enemy plans, we are in danger of losing two spade tricks and the ♣Q in addition to the inevitable ace of trumps – four in total for down one and −50. The spade losers cannot be avoided but we can save the club if we play three top diamonds, discarding the ♣8 from hand. That will have to be done before trumps are pulled as this would involve the loss of the lead immediately. Thus the order of play is:

1 Win the first trick with ♣A.
2 Cash ◇K; note that we play high from the short hand first to avoid blocking the suit. Satisfy yourself that, if you play either of the other honors first, you cannot make the contract because you cannot cash all three in quick succession.
3 Cross to the ◇A or ◇Q.
4 Cash the remaining diamond honor, discarding the remaining club.
5 Now, and only now, start pulling trumps.

Later, we can return to the board in trumps and try the spade finesse in case East has the ♠Q. We will then make an overtrick for 120 under the line and 30 over. Probably it will fail and we will lose two spade tricks, but no more as the two low spades can be ruffed on the board.

The deal:

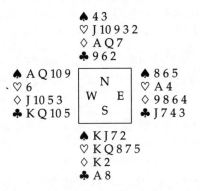

```
                     ♠ 4 3
                     ♡ J 10 9 3 2
                     ◊ A Q 7
                     ♣ 9 6 2
   ♠ A Q 10 9                    ♠ 8 6 5
   ♡ 6              N            ♡ A 4
   ◊ J 10 5 3    W     E         ◊ 9 8 6 4
   ♣ K Q 10 5       S            ♣ J 7 4 3
                     ♠ K J 7 2
                     ♡ K Q 8 7 5
                     ◊ K 2
                     ♣ A 8
```

Note, in particular, that we gain nothing by discarding a spade in preference to a club. Let us look at that spade position in close detail:

♠ 4 3

♠ K J 7 2

On the likely assumption that the ♠A and ♠Q are unfavorably placed with West, the first two rounds of the suit are losers. But with plenty of trumps on the board, the third and fourth rounds can be ruffed for positive gain and are thus effectively *winners*. Thus, by discarding a spade on the third diamond, we are effectively discarding a winner. (It might be a different matter if there was a desperate trump shortage on the board).

Notice also that there is everything to gain and nothing to lose by the early discard on the diamonds. It might be argued that, with our postponement of pulling trumps, the third round of diamonds may be ruffed.

Let us juggle the hand round to illustrate this point. Suppose that West had bid 2♣ in preference to a double and we switch two low diamonds from his hand with two low clubs from East's so that the full deal was as shown overleaf:

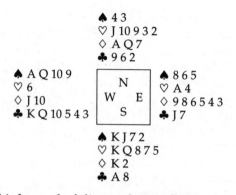

```
                    ♠ 4 3
                    ♡ J 10 9 3 2
                    ◇ A Q 7
                    ♣ 9 6 2
   ♠ A Q 10 9         ┌─────────┐      ♠ 8 6 5
   ♡ 6                │    N    │      ♡ A 4
   ◇ J 10             │ W     E │      ◇ 9 8 6 5 4 3
   ♣ K Q 10 5 4 3     │    S    │      ♣ J 7
                    └─────────┘
                    ♠ K J 7 2
                    ♡ K Q 8 7 5
                    ◇ K 2
                    ♣ A 8
```

Now the third round of diamonds is ruffed but we could never have made the contract anyway. What we have effectively done is to trade a club loser for a diamond loser, gaining and losing nothing. But even with this diamond distribution, we could still gain. Just exchange the ♡A for the ♡6 in the above diagram and now, if West ruffs, it is with a card which was his trick anyway and therefore, in effect, he has ruffed his own club winner with his trump winner, coalescing two tricks into one. The play also gains if West started with a void of trump. The only time this line of play is a loser (when the contract could be made) arises when East has the ♠Q and the diamonds break 7–1 or 8–0 and the hand with the shortage has at least one low trump.

Sometimes, we have to lose an early trick in order to arrange to discard and shorten ourselves in the dangerous side-suit. Let us juggle the above hand around a little to illustrate this point.

Hand No. 27
Dealer East
Neither vulnerable

```
                              ♠ 4 3
                              ♡ J 10 9 3 2
                              ◇ Q J 7
                              ♣ K 9 2
                           ┌─────────┐
                           │    N    │
                           │ W     E │
                           │    S    │
                           └─────────┘
                              ♠ K Q 7
                              ♡ K Q 8 7 5
                              ◇ K 2
                              ♣ A 8 3
```

W	N	E	S
		Pass	1♡
Dbl	3♡	Pass	4♡
end			

The auction is unchanged from last time but the lead is the ♣Q. We have three aces to lose and a potential club, unless our club can be discarded quickly. Start your stop-watch and decide your line of play, in under ninety seconds this time, explaining with good reason where you intend to win that first trick.

We are noticeably short of aces and, every time we lose the lead, the defenders are going to persist with clubs. We can only discard our losing club on the third round of diamonds and as there is no time to lose, the pulling of trumps must again be delayed and we must attack diamonds at once. As we have an excess of diamonds on the board, that must be considered the 'long' suit and we must observe the principle of keeping an entry with the 'long' suit. Thus the ♣K must be kept on the board and the first round must be won in hand. Now again, we play high from the short hand in diamonds to avoid the blockage, starting with the ◇K. The spotlight now turns on West. If he wins and continues clubs, life is easy for us. We win on the board and play two more diamonds, discarding our last club, and pull trumps, quietly conceding the ♠A later. If he ducks, we have to play a second diamond and West wins now and continues clubs. Now we appreciate the importance of having kept the ♣K on the board at trick one.

Had we won the first trick with it, we would now have to win this second round of clubs in hand and would have no quick way to reach our established diamond. We would have to play a trump and now the defenders are in time to cash their club to add to their three aces.

The deal:

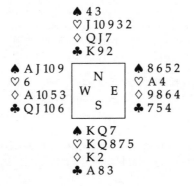

```
                    ♠ 4 3
                    ♡ J 10 9 3 2
                    ◇ Q J 7
                    ♣ K 9 2
    ♠ A J 10 9                    ♠ 8 6 5 2
    ♡ 6             N             ♡ A 4
    ◇ A 10 5 3    W   E           ◇ 9 8 6 4
    ♣ Q J 10 6       S            ♣ 7 5 4
                    ♠ K Q 7
                    ♡ K Q 8 7 5
                    ◇ K 2
                    ♣ A 8 3
```

Notice that it is most unlikely that ducking the first round of diamonds will cost West a trick. We discussed this point in detail in the beginners' book. Just exchange the positions of the ◇2 and ♣4 in the above deal so that the ◇K is stiff. Yes, West loses his diamond trick, but still gets a club and two major aces. If he wins the first diamond, he enables us to discard two losing clubs in the South hand on the two diamond honors on the board. Thus, at worst, he breaks even, and he sets the contract in the case where, having started with a doubleton diamond, we erroneously win the first club on the board.

In our next example, an 'unnecessary' finesse may have to be taken to achieve the discard. Look back to Hand 26 and give North the ◇J in exchange for the ◇Q so that the diamond position looks thus:

$$◇ A J 7$$
$$◇ K 2$$

We can easily make two diamond tricks without loss by cashing the ace and king, but taking the finesse against West gives us the opportunity to discard our losing club and save the contract. This is in the knowledge that, if the diamond finesse loses, we will probably go down two instead of down one. So let us consider the consequences in terms of the score.

Non-vulnerable: The potential loss is 50; the potential gain is 50 + 420, i.e. the saved undertrick + value of non-vulnerable game. We are therefore talking about 50 v 470 on a 50:50 bet. Thus even forgetting that, in view of the auction, West is more than 50 per cent likely to hold the ◇Q, it must be right to take the finesse.
Vulnerable: The potential loss is 100; the potential gain is 720. This reduces the gain from over 9:1 to just over 7:1, but still it is overwhelmingly right to take the finesse.

(The above calculations have been done on duplicate scoring 'break-up' game values (300 non-vulnerable, 500 vulnerable); at rubber bridge the odds are slightly different, dependent on the opponents' vulnerability, but you can see the point!)

Still on the above diamond situation, there are many occasions where the finesse is available free of charge in that, if it loses, a

discard of a loser in another suit can be made on the remaining
honor.

Hand No. 28
Dealer East
Neither vulnerable

♠ 4 3 2
♡ Q J 10 2
◇ A J 7
♣ 6 5 2

W	N	E	S
		Pass	1♡
Dbl	3♡	Pass	4♡
end			

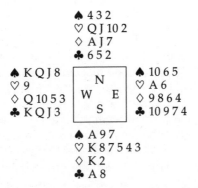

♠ A 9 7
♡ K 8 7 5 4 3
◇ K 2
♣ A 8

West leads the ♣K. This time, you should be able to give a line of
play in under thirty seconds.

We have five heart tricks out of six possible rounds and, as
North has no ruffing values, two black aces and two top
diamonds. The tenth can only come from a successful diamond
finesse and note that, this time, it costs nothing to take it. If it fails
and the opponents cash their club, we can always discard an
inevitable spade loser.

The deal:

♠ 4 3 2
♡ Q J 10 2
◇ A J 7
♣ 6 5 2

♠ K Q J 8   ♠ 10 6 5
♡ 9   ♡ A 6
◇ Q 10 5 3   ◇ 9 8 6 4
♣ K Q J 3   ♣ 10 9 7 4

♠ A 9 7
♡ K 8 7 5 4 3
◇ K 2
♣ A 8

Note that the diamond finesse must be tried before trumps are
pulled. If we try to pull trumps, the opponents can cash their club
and shift to spades and now, if the diamond finesse does fail, the

defenders can cash two more spades (before we can take our discard) to take the contract down two instead of one.

Having considered positions in which our trumps can stop defenders from cashing their winners, we must now look at those where opponents' trumps can stop us from enjoying our winners. Often when we pull trumps, we have to consider what to do if opponents hold a master trump. It may or may not be right to pull it. There are two considerations: on the one hand, we will have to lose the lead to do so and it will cost two trumps; on the other, if we do not, it may appear at an embarrassing moment. Let us start with this example.

Hand No. 29
Dealer South
Both vulnerable

♠ 10 7			
♡ J 6 4			
◇ 9 5 2			
♣ A K J 8 6			

W	N	E	S
			1♠
Pass	INT	Pass	3♠
Pass	4♠	end	

N
W   E
S

♠ A K 6 5 3 2
♡ 5 3
◇ A Q 8
♣ Q 5

South opens 1♠, primarily angling for 4♠. North replies with 1NT, showing 6–10 points and primarily angling for 3NT, possibly 5♣. South, with 15 points, knows that the partnership is in the game zone. He makes the very invitational but non-forcing call of 3♠. With a maximum in 6–10 range, North accepts and, in the knowledge that the partnership has at least a 6–2 spade fit, he signs off in 4♠. Note that he prefers 4♠ to 3NT as he has little or no stop in either red suit and he hopes that partner's spades will act in that capacity – they cannot do so unless they are trumps!

West leads the ♡K. His partner encourages with the ♡8, whereupon he plays the ♡Q and follows with the ♡10 to the ♡J and East's ♡A, which you ruff. You cash your ace and king of trumps. Both defenders follow but the ♠Q remains at large. How do you continue? Start your stop-watch and give a reasoned line of play in under two minutes.

Allowing for the spade loser, we have five spade tricks, five clubs and a diamond for eleven in total and that doesn't consider the possibility of a successful diamond finesse. Regarding losers, we have the two hearts already lost and the trump, which we cannot avoid, to total three. So there appears to be no problem except that we cannot cash all the clubs until the trump has been eliminated. With the board completely devoid of entries, if the second or third round of clubs is ruffed, we shall not be able to return to the board to enjoy the rest of the suit or even try the diamond finesse (which may not work anyway). Only in the case where the defender holding the trump has at least three clubs will we be able to play four rounds of clubs uninterrupted, discarding our two diamond losers on the third and fourth rounds. A defender can ruff the fourth round if he pleases but then the rest of our hand is high and we shall have made six trump tricks, three clubs and the ◇ A.

The safe line, therefore, is to pull the trump now. We still hold the ◇ A and the defenders cannot make a fourth trick quickly before the whole club suit comes in. In the end, we have a trick to burn.

The deal:

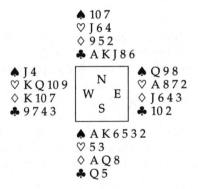

```
              ♠ 10 7
              ♡ J 6 4
              ◇ 9 5 2
              ♣ A K J 8 6
♠ J 4                        ♠ Q 9 8
♡ K Q 10 9       N           ♡ A 8 7 2
◇ K 10 7     W     E         ◇ J 6 4 3
♣ 9 7 4 3        S           ♣ 10 2
              ♠ A K 6 5 3 2
              ♡ 5 3
              ◇ A Q 8
              ♣ Q 5
```

Do not read on until you have satisfied yourself that, if you do not pull the trump before playing on clubs, the contract cannot be made.

But now let us alter the hand slightly and consider this arrangement:

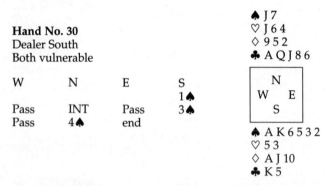

Hand No. 30
Dealer South
Both vulnerable

♠ J 7
♡ J 6 4
◇ 9 5 2
♣ A Q J 8 6

W	N	E	S
			1♠
Pass	INT	Pass	3♠
Pass	4♠	end	

♠ A K 6 5 3 2
♡ 5 3
◇ A J 10
♣ K 5

We have traded the ◇Q for the jacks in diamonds and spades but the defence is going to be less friendly. Again West cashes the ♡K and his partner encourages with the ♡8. However this time West's second heart is the ♡2 (clearly original fourth-high), so that, when East wins with the ♡A, he knows that there are no more hearts to cash. He therefore shifts to a low diamond. How do you play this time?

Start your stop-watch – having read and understood the last example, you should be an expert in this kind of situation by now and be able to produce a full analysis of the hand in well under thirty seconds.

This time, the defenders are a move ahead. If we clear trumps completely so that the clubs can be enjoyed uninterrupted, the defenders will win the third round and cash two diamonds for −200.

This time, therefore, the two diamond losers will have to be thrown on the clubs without the lead being lost and we shall have to assume not only a 3–2 trump split but also that the hand with the long trump can follow clubs at least three times and therefore cannot ruff in before the fourth round, as follows:

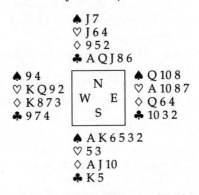

```
            ♠ J 7
            ♡ J 6 4
            ◇ 9 5 2
            ♣ A Q J 8 6
♠ 9 4                      ♠ Q 10 8
♡ K Q 9 2      N           ♡ A 10 8 7
◇ K 8 7 3   W     E        ◇ Q 6 4
♣ 9 7 4        S           ♣ 10 3 2
            ♠ A K 6 5 3 2
            ♡ 5 3
            ◇ A J 10
            ♣ K 5
```

We must win the diamond shift immediately, cash two top
trumps as before and start on the clubs, the king first so as not to
block the suit. We throw one losing diamond on the third round
and the other on the fourth, whether East ruffs or not. Apart from
the trump, the rest of the hand is high.

You should satisfy yourself that, on Hand 29, had East won the
second heart and attacked diamonds from his side of the table,
you could not have made the contract. In any event, you would
have been faced with the decision of whether to try the diamond
finesse (a 50 per cent chance) or (less likely) rely on the hand
holding the long trump also having at least three clubs.

We have already emphasized the importance of keeping
entries alongside long suits on the board. Sometimes a trump will
serve this purpose, at the same time keeping control of an enemy
side-suit. Try this illustration:

Hand No. 31
Dealer East
Both vulnerable

```
            ♠ 9 8 7
            ♡ 2
            ◇ J 5 2
            ♣ A K J 10 8 5

                 N
            W         E
                 S

            ♠ A K 5 3 2
            ♡ Q 8 7 5
            ◇ K 8
            ♣ Q 3
```

W	N	E	S
		Pass	1♠
Pass	2♣	Pass	2♡
Pass	2♠	Pass	3♠
Pass	4♠	end	

Strictly, as we learned earlier, North should have 11 or more points for a two-over-one call but the spade opening improves his hand considerably. With the ♣Q known to be working, South invites game, and North accepts.

West leads the ♡A and shifts to the ♣4. Start your stop-watch and decide how you would play. You should be aiming for under sixty seconds.

There could be a number of heart ruffs on the board, but to be realistic, the contract is unlikely to be made unless that club suit can be brought in. For this reason, there should be no attempt to ruff hearts as the one thing declarer does not want to do is weaken the board's trumps. We win the club in either hand and cash two top trumps, hoping for a 3–2 split. Now, leaving the outstanding master trump alone, we continue clubs, discarding a diamond on the third round, forcing the defenders to ruff, sooner or later. Now we can ruff their second diamond in hand and return to the board with a heart ruff to enjoy the rest of the clubs, completing five club tricks and six trump tricks. In fact, there will probably only be ten in total as they can cash one heart, one diamond and one spade first. However, if the defender with the long trump has three or more clubs, we can discard both our diamonds before being interrupted and now we do take eleven tricks.

The deal:

```
                    ♠ 9 8 7
                    ♡ 2
                    ◇ J 5 2
                    ♣ A Q J 10 8 5
        ♠ J 6 4                      ♠ Q 10
        ♡ A K J 9         N          ♡ 10 6 4 3
        ◇ A 7 4 3      W     E       ◇ Q 10 9 6
        ♣ 4 2            S           ♣ 9 7 6
                    ♠ A K 5 3 2
                    ♡ Q 8 7 5
                    ◇ K 8
                    ♣ K 3
```

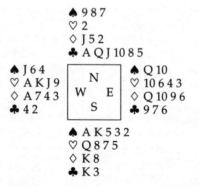

Now let us introduce a couple of variations. Suppose West, instead of shifting to a club, had persisted with the ♡K, forcing the board to ruff. How would you have played now?

Start your stop-watch and, as you are now an accomplished connoisseur of these situations, produce an answer in under thirty seconds.

Our entry to the clubs has now been removed, but the ♡Q is a master so there is no danger of any further immediate losers and we can revert to the other approach of pulling trumps completely. If West produces the length, as in the layout above, he cannot profitably attack diamonds and the contract is safe. If East has the length and plays a low diamond, you will have to guess which way round the honors are; playing low is the winner in this case.

Let us now try one further variation, exchanging South's ♡Q for West's ♡J. The bidding has now become a little optimistic but we are here to discuss the play. West cashes the ♡A and plays the ♡K, which is ruffed on the board. How would you continue this time?

Start your stop-watch and see if you can give an answer in under ninety seconds.

This time, we have the worst of both worlds. No longer in control of hearts, we cannot pull trumps completely, but equally, if we just pull two rounds in clubs, the defenders will ruff in at the earliest opportunity and will be able to cash at least two more red-suit winners. The solution involves a new technique – ducking to keep control. We do have to pull trumps but, if we lose the first round, we can keep a trump on the board to look after the hearts. Thus, having ruffed the second round of hearts, we play a low spade from both hands. If East wins and pushes a diamond through, we shall have to guess well but, if West wins, the diamond position cannot profitably be attacked from his side.

This example makes an excellent introduction to the broader subject of trump control and indeed, it is often good tactics to lose tricks early – sometimes even apparently 'unnecessarily' – to achieve this, as in the example overleaf.

Hand No. 32
Dealer West
E-W vulnerable

♠ 5 3
♡ 6 2
◇ K 9 8 6
♣ K Q J 10 8

W	N	E	S
1♡	2♣	2♡	4♠
end			

```
        N
    W       E
        S
```

♠ A K Q J 10
♡ J
◇ A 10 7 5
♣ 9 3 2

After West's opening call, North's non-vulnerable overcall is primarily based on playing strength (almost certainly four playing tricks in his trump suit plus a king in a long side-suit) rather than on points. When East raises, South has something of a problem of what to bid. It is clear that, with some club support, a solid suit and a useful singleton in hearts, he will insist on game, but it is very much a question of 4♠ or 5♣. Indeed, the latter could very easily be the better contract. However, with solid spades and a trick less needed for game, he tries 4♠.

West starts with two top hearts. Start your stop-watch and decide your line of play in under two minutes, clearly indicating the problem on the hand and what you propose to do about it.

We have five top spade tricks and four club tricks out of five rounds, as well as the two top diamonds for eleven in total. Against those, there is a top heart loser and the ♣A. Any diamond losers on the third and fourth rounds of the suit can be discarded on the long clubs. So, at first sight, it appears to be plain sailing, but a closer look at the trump situation reveals a chink in the armoury. We have only seven between us. A 3–3 break is easily handled but, if they are 4–2, we could lose trump control. If we ruff this second round of hearts, pulling trumps will run us out of the suit and, on losing to the ♣A, the defenders will be able to run the rest of their hearts.

The solution is to set up the clubs before trumps are pulled. This might involve sustaining a ruff but, if the defenders try to force us again with a heart, we can ruff on the board, keeping our long trumps intact.

The deal:

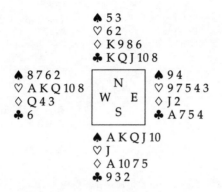

An alternative line would be to refuse to ruff the second heart. Then any further force can be taken on the board, our five trumps remain intact and we can pull trumps with a trump to spare. However, in the above layout, this line of play fails when West shifts to a club and collects a ruff to complete the first four tricks for −50.

It is instructive to note that in 5♣, the heart forces can be taken in the short hand and the contract is made comfortably with four top clubs, one ruff, two diamonds and the five top spades, losing two aces. Also, were the vulnerability reversed, it would be worthwhile for East-West to sacrifice in 5♡; they make nine tricks (losing the four tops in spades and diamonds) to leave us with +300 rather than the more valuable vulnerable game. The sacrifice would even be worthwhile at love all or game all, conceding 500 in the latter case.

Sometimes, it only needs a singleton trump to control a side suit but, in that case, the timing of losing the lead is often critical. The next example is an excellent illustration.

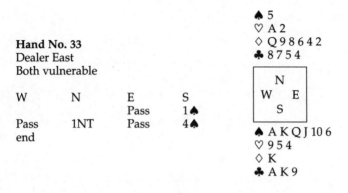

Hand No. 33
Dealer East
Both vulnerable

♠ 5
♡ A 2
◇ Q 9 8 6 4 2
♣ 8 7 5 4

W	N	E	S
		Pass	1♠
Pass	1NT	Pass	4♠
Pass			
end			

♠ A K Q J 10 6
♡ 9 5 4
◇ K
♣ A K 9

On this occasion, North-South are playing weak twos so South, not strong enough for an outright game force with 2♣, opens at the one-level, hoping that his partner can reply. North's promise of 6–10 points is all South needs to bid a game. West leads with ♡K.

Start your stop-watch and decide how you would arrive at ten tricks in under two minutes.

There are clearly eight top tricks in the black suits in hand, plus the ♡A on the board. A tenth trick could be established for the ◇Q but, with the heart lead, there is going to be problem reaching it. Meanwhile, on the debit side, we shall certainly lose a heart and the ◇A. If we cannot reach the ◇Q, we will have nothing on which to discard our losing club and will lose a trick there as well. There is also the danger of losing a second heart trick, to complete four losers in all. What is to be done? We could try for a heart ruff by winning the first trick and returning the suit immediately but the defenders will obviously realize what is going on and play a trump to remove the ♠5 from the board in good time. The board will never be reached again and is said to be *dead*.

The only solution is to reverse the order of play. Instead of winning the first heart and returning the suit, we should refuse the first round. Now the defenders are caught between the devil and the deep blue sea. If they persist with hearts, we win, cross to hand in clubs and take the heart ruff. If they shift to trumps, then the heart ruff is off but the ♡A remains intact and can be used as entry for the ◇ Q. So we pull trumps and play the ◇ K, losing to the ◇ A. Whatever they return, we have time to cross to the ♡ A and cash the ◇ Q, discarding our losing heart or club, later conceding one further trick, in the suit from which we did not discard, but no more.

The deal:

```
                    ♠ 5
                    ♡ A 2
                    ◇ Q 9 8 6 4 2
                    ♣ 8 7 5 4
      ♠ 8 7                          ♠ 9 4 3 2
      ♡ K Q 10         N             ♡ J 8 7 6 3
      ◇ A J 10 7   W       E         ◇ 5 3
      ♣ Q 10 6 3       S             ♣ J 2
                    ♠ A K Q J 10 6
                    ♡ 9 5 4
                    ◇ K
                    ♣ A K 9
```

You should satisfy yourself that no other play guarantees the contract. During our discussions of no-trump contracts, emphasis was placed on losing tricks to the correct hand. The same applies with equal force to trump contracts. A couple of examples will illustrate.

Hand No. 34
Dealer East
E-W vulnerable

♠ Q 7 2			
♡ K 6			
◇ A 4			
♣ K J 10 9 7 3			

W	N	E	S
		1◇	1♠
Pass	4♠	end	

```
        N
    W       E
        S
```

♠ K J 10 5 4 3
♡ J 7
◇ 9 3
♣ A Q 6

After East's opener, South's overcall promised a five-card suit and North has little reason to investigate any other contract than 4♠.

West leads the ♢2. Start your stop-watch and decide on a line of play in under two minutes.

We have plenty of winners. Five trumps out of six, six top clubs and the ♢A totals twelve, even assuming that (as is probable) the ♡A is unfavorably placed over the king. We can discard our red-suit losers on the long clubs, but not before trumps are pulled. That will involve losing the lead so it will be advisable to consider enemy plans. They have one diamond trick and the ♠A and possibly two hearts. This implies that West will get on play and that East has both ace and queen of hearts. Could this possibly happen? If West has the trump ace, there is little we can do. We shall have to hope that he also has the ♡Q and play low on his heart shift. However, if East has the trump ace, there is a better chance. The only way he could get his partner in is with a diamond, so let us consider the diamond position in more detail. The ♢2 has been led – probably from three or four to an honor. If we win now and start pulling trumps, East will win and put his partner in with a diamond for a heart shift, and we shall be set if the layout is as follows.

The deal:

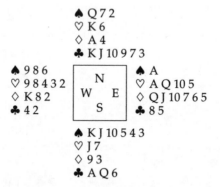

```
              ♠ Q 7 2
              ♡ K 6
              ♢ A 4
              ♣ K J 10 9 7 3
♠ 9 8 6                       ♠ A
♡ 9 8 4 3 2      N            ♡ A Q 10 5
♢ K 8 2       W     E         ♢ Q J 10 7 6 5
♣ 4 2            S            ♣ 8 5
              ♠ K J 10 5 4 3
              ♡ J 7
              ♢ 9 3
              ♣ A Q 6
```

The way to avoid this mishap is to ensure that the diamond trick is lost to East, in other words play low on this first trick. West will never get on play again and we shall lose the two major aces but no more. Indeed, on taking his ♠A, East will have to cash the ♡A to avoid conceding an overtrick.

You should have noticed that an initial heart lead would have set the contract. East cashes his two heart tricks and shifts to a diamond and there is nothing now that declarer can do. In other words, the diamond, which could be attacked from either side, can wait; the heart, which can only be attacked from the West side, cannot. However, particularly with such an uninviting heart holding, West had little or no reason to ignore his partner's call.

The timing of losing tricks is also illustrated here:

Hand No. 35
Dealer East
E-W vulnerable

♠ 9 4 3
♡ A Q 7 5
◇ Q 8 4 2
♣ K J

W	N	E	S
		Pass	1◇
Pass	1♡	Pass	2♣
Pass	3◇	Pass	3♠
Pass	4◇	Pass	5◇
end			

```
        N
   W         E
        S
```

♠ A 8
♡ 6 3
◇ K J 10 7 6
♣ A Q 6 5

South's 3♠ was a directional asking bid, asking his partner for help, typically a half-stop, in spades for no-trump. When North failed to oblige, South tried for the minor-suit game.

West leads the ♡2. Start your stop-watch and decide how you would play in under two minutes.

We have four out of five trump tricks, four top club tricks and the two major aces to total ten, while the opponents have the ◇ A and possibly a spade and a heart, so all seems to rest on the position of the ♡K. If it is with West, then the finesse will work and we shall have eleven tricks. If it is with East, our only hope is to be able to discard two spades on the clubs and thus avoid the spade loser. However, we will not be able to cash four clubs without pulling trumps and that will involve losing the lead.

It is therefore important that we should not lose the lead twice, so that our ♠A can be kept intact. The contract can be assured if we forget about the heart finesse and concentrate on avoiding that spade loser. We should win the first heart with the ♡A and attack trumps. The defenders will presumably win and attack spades. We win with the ♠A, cash the board's two club honors and then complete the pulling of trumps in hand. We now cash South's two remaining club honors, discarding the board's two remaining spades, and concede a heart quietly at the end.

The deal:

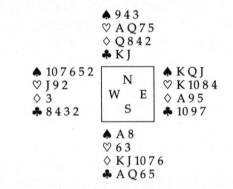

```
                    ♠ 9 4 3
                    ♡ A Q 7 5
                    ◇ Q 8 4 2
                    ♣ K J
   ♠ 10 7 6 5 2            ♠ K Q J
   ♡ J 9 2        N        ♡ K 10 8 4
   ◇ 3         W     E     ◇ A 9 5
   ♣ 8 4 3 2      S        ♣ 10 9 7
                    ♠ A 8
                    ♡ 6 3
                    ◇ K J 10 7 6
                    ♣ A Q 6 5
```

Note that trying the heart finesse costs the contract. East wins and shifts to spades at once (there is obviously no future in hearts with the ♡A still on the board). Now, on regaining the lead with the ◇A, he can cash another spade trick for down one. Note that, were the contract 6◇, we should have no alternative but to assume that the heart finesse is right and play the ♡Q at trick one, being prepared to go down two if it fails.

In this last example, we eventually ruff South's ♠8 on the board. Sometimes more than one loser has to be ruffed and then the timing and manner of pulling trumps can be critical. Let us consider the next deal, showing all four hands from the start.

Hand No. 36
Dealer East
Game All

```
                                    ♠ 9 7 6 3
                                    ♡ A 8
                                    ◇ A 7 6 3
                                    ♣ Q 9 5
W     N     E     S
            Pass  1NT   ♠ K Q 5            ♠ J 10
                       ♡ J 9 7 5 3    N    ♡ Q 10
Pass  2♣    Pass  2♠   ◇ K 10      W    E  ◇ Q 9 8 4 2
Pass  4♠    end        ♣ 8 7 3       S    ♣ J 10 4 2
                                    ♠ A 8 4 2
                                    ♡ K 6 4 2
                                    ◇ J 5
                                    ♣ A K 6
```

After South opens 1NT, North makes a Stayman enquiry, looking for 4♠ as a possible alternative game to 3NT. Many players, including a number of recognized experts, are not in favor of using Stayman on such hands, arguing that the spades are very weak, the hand is relatively balanced and that, in order to show a profit by preferring the trump contract, there must be a two-trick advantage. On top of that, if a Stayman sequence is used and 3NT becomes the final contract, a large amount of information has been given to opponents which is likely to help them in respect of opening lead and defence. A straight raise in no-trump would have left them relatively in the dark.

It has to be admitted that the anti-Staymanites have a good case, but I would stand by Stayman on the North hand. Without being 'wise afterwards' the hand is nothing but aces and a king – *quick* as opposed to *slow* tricks, which are better suited to trump contracts. As you see on the full deal, there is little hope for more than eight tricks in no-trump.

Anyway, we shall be discussing bidding in detail later on; we are here to make the contract after West's lead of the ♣8. Seeing all four hands, can you find a solution in under a minute? Start your stop-watch.

We have three top club tricks, two hearts and the ◇A to total six, implying the need for four in trumps. With a certain diamond loser, there will be little hope if the trumps fail to break 3–2 but, even if they do, three rounds of trumps will leave one in each hand to make separately. In addition to the ♠A, that gives us three trump tricks against two lost, which is insufficient. This means we must resort to ruffing before trumps are pulled and there are two possible approaches. One is to give up an early diamond and try to ruff two diamonds in hand. West can overruff, but it does not hurt us because, having the long trumps, he is overruffing with a trick which was going to be his anyway. We are then in a position to pull the rest of the trumps in two rounds and ruff the remaining diamond later. The alternative is to play on hearts. Unfortunately, East is able to overruff the third round with a trick which was *not* going to be his anyway and now we lose three trump tricks and a diamond to go down one.

So it would appear that playing on diamond ruffs works,

while playing on heart ruffs fails. However, there is no reason why East should not have had the longer trumps, and now playing on diamonds fails while playing on hearts works.

Are we therefore to assume that we are on a guess, or is there a line to cater for either contingency? The answer lies in pulling two rounds of trumps only and then proceeding to take the ruffs. The defender with the outstanding trump can interfere when he pleases but that will be his trick anyway and we shall make three of our four remaining trumps for the contract. The question therefore arises as to whether there is a problem of pulling exactly two rounds of trumps. If we play the ♠A and another, West can win and pull a third round. The way to organize exactly two rounds is to ensure that *we* win the second. The play is as follows:

   (i) Win the first club on the board.
  (ii) Play a low spade from both hands, i.e. lose the first round.
 (iii) Win presumed club return in hand.
 (iv) Cash ♠A.
  (v) Cash ♡A. (Note high from the short hand first.)
 (vi) Cash ♡K.
(vii) Ruff a heart on the board.
(viii) Cross to hand in clubs.
 (ix) Ruff the last heart on the board.
  (x) Cash ◇A.

We are now left with two trumps and a losing diamond. We will have to concede one of the trumps and the losing diamond, but no more, and you should satisfy yourself that, even if the ◇A had been ruffed, it would have made no difference to the final result. However, we shall learn later that there are situations where it has to be cashed early.

In this line, we played on ruffing hearts on the board in preference to ruffing diamonds in hand. Now before reading on, can you confirm that we could just as easily have played on diamonds or might that have made a difference?

In fact, on the above layout, we could indeed have played on diamonds, but note the order of play. We have to concede a trump and a diamond early to set up a safe position to ruff and unlike the hearts, that involves losing the lead twice. If we duck the trump first, they can return a trump and then play a third round when in with the diamond. We must therefore duck the diamond first and the trump later. However, the deal could have been like this:

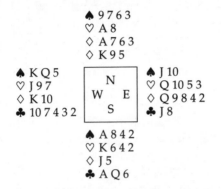

```
                    ♠ 9 7 6 3
                    ♡ A 8
                    ◇ A 7 6 3
                    ♦ K 9 5
        ♠ K Q 5                  ♠ J 10
        ♡ J 9 7        N         ♡ Q 10 5 3
        ◇ K 10     W     E       ◇ Q 9 8 4 2
        ♣ 10 7 4 3 2   S         ♣ J 8
                    ♠ A 8 4 2
                    ♡ K 6 4 2
                    ◇ J 5
                    ♣ A Q 6
```

Playing on diamonds now fails. We win the club lead and duck a diamond. We win the club return and duck a trump, but now a third round of clubs is ruffed by the *short*-trump hand, leaving us with one more trump trick to lose and defeat. (It would not matter if the third round were ruffed by the long-trump hand; the contract will still be made.)

I have gone into great detail on this hand and I hope that it drives home the importance of the close study of 'Who wins tricks and when?' on which we spent so much time in the beginners' book. The whole of advanced play depends on it and therefore complete familiarity and understanding is beyond price, and the earlier the better.

In the above hand, we looked at the possibility of ruffing side-suit losers in either hand and we are now going to extend this idea to ruffing in both hands – the *crossruff*. Let us start with a simple example:

Hand No. 37
Dealer West
E-W vulnerable

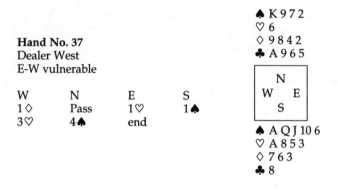

♠ K 9 7 2
♡ 6
♦ 9 8 4 2
♣ A 9 6 5

W	N	E	S
1♦	Pass	1♡	1♠
3♡	4♠	end	

♠ A Q J 10 6
♡ A 8 5 3
♦ 7 6 3
♣ 8

After West's opening and East's reply, South enters the auction with an overcall. He has a very good suit and favorable vulnerability and it is therefore safe to enter the auction. After West's raise to 3♡, North's jump to game is good tactics. He has little idea of whether the contract will be made or not, but in this kind of situation it is best to pre-empt as far as possible. On his hand, it is well on the cards that 4♡ is on for the opposition, so 4♠ is likely to be a worthwhile sacrifice, particularly at this vulnerability.

West cashes three top diamonds, his partner following with the ♦J and ♦5 to indicate a doubleton, and then shifts to a trump.

Start your stop-watch and see if you can plan your play in under two minutes.

We have the two side-suit aces and a trump trick already won to total three so far and the rest can only come from the trump suit. Fortunately, the hand is a *perfect fit* and we are in a position to make our seven remaining trumps separately. We cash the ♣A and ♡A, ruff a heart on the board, ruff a club in hand and repeat the process up to trick twelve, when we are left with the last diamond on the board and a high trump in hand. The defenders still have their two remaining trumps.

The deal:

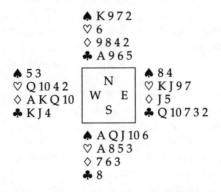

```
              ♠ K972
              ♡ 6
              ◇ 9842
              ♣ A965
♠ 53                           ♠ 84
♡ Q1042         N              ♡ KJ97
◇ AKQ10     W       E          ◇ J5
♣ KJ4           S              ♣ Q10732
              ♠ AQJ106
              ♡ A853
              ◇ 763
              ♣ 8
```

With the favorable spade break and club situation, 4♡ (which may well not have been bid anyway) can be heavily set, but that is purely of academic interest.

Actually, if the opposing spades are 4–0, 4♠ can be made by exactly the same line of play, and this time 4♡ is also likely to be made.

We now complicate the picture by introducing side-suit winners. How would you play this one?

Hand No. 38
Dealer West
E-W vulnerable

♠ AJ72
♡ Q
◇ K85
♣ AJ732

W	N	E	S
Pass	1♣	Pass	1♠
Pass	3♠	Pass	4◇
Pass	5♣	Pass	6♠
end			

```
        N
    W       E
        S
```

♠ KQ10086
♡ A953
◇ A42
♣ 6

After spades have been agreed, South cue-bids the ◇A, at the same time denying the ♣A, and North confirms his ♣A. With his wealth of top controls, South bids the slam. West leads the ♠5. Start your stop-watch and give a line of play in under two minutes.

West has done well to lead a trump. Clearly, he has suspected that we intend to take a lot of tricks by ruffing. There is an inference to be taken from that. The only other suit bid was clubs and North has clearly shown a club-spade two-suiter. West would only fear ruffing if he were confident that the club suit was not going to be brought in for tricks. It is therefore likely that he has the clubs heavily stacked or (less likely) is very short and has reason to believe that East has them stacked against us.

I am keen that you should get into the habit of picking up these inferences. They all assist in placing cards you cannot see – the essence of expert bridge. The books I have written for tournament players are packed full of examples of this kind.

Let us count our tricks. We have the ♡A, two top diamonds and the ♣A to total four. There is a possibility that we can set up a long club, but the lead suggests that this is unlikely. In any case, we could never enjoy it without pulling trumps and that would still imply the need for two heart ruffs on the board. A better chance is to crossruff the whole hand, in an attempt to make eight trump tricks to add to the four outside tops.

However, before starting the crossruff, another little task has to be fulfilled first. Suppose the full deal is like this:

```
                    ♠ A J 7 2
                    ♡ Q
                    ◇ K 8 5
                    ♣ A J 7 3 2
    ♠ 5                             ♠ 9 4 3
    ♡ J 2          N                ♡ K 10 8 7 6 4
    ◇ J 9 7 6 3  W   E              ◇ Q 10
    ♣ K 10 8 5 4    S               ♣ Q 9
                    ♠ K Q 10 8 6
                    ♡ A 9 5 3
                    ◇ A 4 2
                    ♣ 6
```

and we play as follows:

(i)   Win the first trump.
(ii) Cross to ♣A.
(iii) Ruff a club.
(iv) Cash ♡A.

(v) Ruff a club. East is now also out of the suit so he discards a diamond.

(vi) Ruff a heart.

(vii) Ruff a club. East discards another diamond.

(viii) Ruff a heart. West discards a diamond.

(ix) Ruff the last club. East discards a heart.

(x) Ruff the last heart.

We are now left with three diamonds in each hand and East still has two trumps and a heart and he takes the rest for down two and −100. What went wrong? We never took our two top diamonds. When a crossruff is planned, it is almost invariably right to cash side-suit winners before the defenders have the opportunity to discard their losers in the respective suits. Let us replay the hand and see the difference:

(i) Win first trump in hand.

(ii) Cash ◇K.

(iii) Cash ◇A.

(iv) Cash ♣A.

(v) Ruff a club.

(vi) Cash ♡A.

(vii) Ruff a heart on the board.

(viii) Ruff a club. East discards a heart.

(ix) Ruff a heart.

(x) Ruff a club. East discards a heart.

(xi) Ruff a heart.

(xii) Lead the last club and East, down to two trumps, has to ruff it; we overruff.

(xiii) Concede the last trick in diamonds to West's ◇J and East's trump.

We have taken the first twelve tricks, leaving the defenders to win the last in crushing style! But we chalk up 180 + 500 for the slam and have won a game.

That is enough on declarer play for the time being. We are going to conclude this section with some test examples which I should like you to do against the stop-watch. In each case, it will largely be a question of recognizing which of the techniques we have studied is required. You will be expected to give a full analysis, stating clearly where you expect your tricks and enemy tricks to come from, where you think the twenty-six unseen cards are lying, or where you are prepared for them to lie, and how you expect the play to go right from the lead up to trick thirteen. Up to now, I have usually set two minutes as solving time. You should be aiming to get your time down to well below sixty seconds, as will normally be expected at the table.

Problem 1

Hand No. 39
Dealer East
Both vulnerable

♠ 7 6 5 4 2
♡ A J
◇ 10 7 6 4
♣ A 2

W	N	E	S
		Pass	1♠
Pass	3♠	Pass	4◇
Pass	4♡	Pass	4♠
Pass	5♣	Pass	6♠
Pass	end		

```
        N
    W       E
        S
```

♠ K Q J 10 8
♡ Q
◇ A K Q J 3
♣ 7 3

West leads the ♣K.

Problem 2

Hand No. 40
Dealer North
E-W vulnerable

♠ J 9 4
♡ A Q 10 7 6
◇ 6 4
♣ A 5 2

W	N	E	S
	Pass	Pass	1♠
2◇	3♡	Pass	4♠
end			

```
        N
    W       E
        S
```

♠ A Q 10 8 7
♡ K J 8
◇ K 5 3
♣ 7 3

Having already passed, North's 3♡ call indicates the biggest hand possible in the 0–11 point-range, with support for spades;

i.e. willing to play 3♠. South chooses the spade game in preference to the heart game. He wishes to be declarer to protect the position of his ◇K. West leads the ♣K and, irrespective of your play from the board, East plays the ♣J.

Problem 3

Hand No. 41
Dealer West
E-W vulnerable

♠ J 10 8 3
♡ A 9 6 3 2
◇ K 7 2
♣ 8

```
        N
    W       E
        S
```

♠ K Q 9 4 2
♡ 7
◇ 6 4
♣ A 9 6 4 3

W	N	E	S
1♡	Pass	2♣	Pass
2◇	Pass	2♡	2♠
3◇	4♠	end	

You have taken something of a risk in coming into the auction, as West's shape might have been 4540. A double now could have cost you a great deal. Against that, East has almost certainly denied four spades and there could well be a fit with North. Partner is also likely to produce some points as both opponents, notably East, have limited their hands. On this occasion, you seem to have lit partner's blue paper and West leads the ♠A. All follow and he shifts to the ♣Q.

Problem 4

Hand No. 42
Dealer East
Neither vulnerable

♠ J 6 4
♡ 6 2
◇ A Q J 10 5 2
♣ A 9

```
        N
    W       E
        S
```

♠ A 5 3 2
♡ A K 9 8 7 5
◇ K
♣ J 8

W	N	E	S
		Pass	1♡
Pass	2◇	Pass	2♠
Pass	3♣	Pass	3♡
Pass	4♡	end	

Partner's 3♣ call was fourth-suit forcing, asking for a further description of your hand, primarily looking for 3NT if you had a half-stop or more in clubs. West leads the ♣K. You win and play two top trumps, all following. How do you continue?

Problem 5

Hand No. 43
Dealer East
Both vulnerable

♠ 7 2
♡ 6 2
◇ A Q J 10 5 2
♣ A 9 2

W	N	E	S
		Pass	1♡
1♠	2◇	Pass	3♡
Pass	4♡	end	

```
        N
   W         E
        S
```

♠ K 5 3
♡ A K Q 8 7 5
◇ K
♣ 8 4 3

West leads the ♣K and you win on the board. You start pulling trumps but, on the second round, West discards the ♣5. How do you continue?

Problem 6

Hand No. 44
Dealer East
N-S vulnerable

♠ 6 4
♡ 4 3
◇ A 8 6 5 4 3
♣ A 3 2

W	N	E	S
		Pass	2♣
Pass	3◇	Pass	4♡
Pass	5♣	Pass	5♠
Pass	6◇	Pass	6♡
end			

```
        N
   W         E
        S
```

♠ A Q
♡ A K Q J 10 8
◇ 9 7
♣ K Q 4

After your game-forcing 2♣, North replied positively with 3◇. You showed your solid heart suit and cue-bidding followed. West leads the ♣J. On the second round of trumps, he discards a spade.

Solutions

Problem 1

We have four trump tricks out of five, five top diamond tricks and the two other aces to total eleven. A twelfth could theoretically come from ruffing a club on the board, having first played all the diamonds to discard the board's ♣2. We cannot, however, cash the diamonds without first pulling trumps. That would involve losing the lead, enabling the defenders to cash their established club trick, so this approach is ruled out. (Note, however, that it would have been correct on any other lead.) The club loser will have to be discarded immediately and that can only be done on hearts. This implies crediting West with the ♡K and taking the finesse to set up a second heart trick. Even now, our problems are not over. We will have to lead the ♡Q from hand and we can only reach her quickly with a diamond. So after a diamond to hand at trick two, we pass the ♡Q and it holds. We now have to return to the board to cash the ♡A, on which we will discard the club loser in hand. Again, that can only be done in diamonds. We must, therefore, assume that the suit breaks 2–2 and play a second round to the board's ◊10. After the ♡A, we can start pulling trumps, conceding the ♠A as our only loser.

The deal:

```
                    ♠ 7 6 5 4 2
                    ♡ A J
                    ◊ 10 7 6 4
                    ♣ A 2
      ♠ 9 3                          ♠ A
      ♡ K 9 4 3         N            ♡ 10 8 7 6 5 2
      ◊ 8 5         W       E        ◊ 9 2
      ♣ K Q 10 9 4      S            ♣ J 8 6 5
                    ♠ K Q J 10 8
                    ♡ Q
                    ◊ A K Q J 3
                    ♣ 7 3
```

Problem 2

In the likely event that the ♠K is badly placed, we have four trump tricks out of five, five heart tricks and the ♣A to total ten.

Against that, four tricks may be available to the defenders in the form of two diamonds, the spade and a club. In order to take those two diamond tricks, however, East will have to lead the suit. Our efforts must therefore be directed towards avoiding this contingency. Remember that we have already moved in that direction by electing to play in spades in preference to hearts to ensure that West was on lead. (Had East bid diamonds and the ◇K been with North, we would have preferred the heart contract.)

How could East win a trick? Only in clubs. Note his play of the ♣J on trick one. This is to inform his partner that he has the ♣10 but not the ♣Q. We learnt the rule of going as near to the card led as possible to show solid sequences like this in the beginners' book and this is a good illustration of its application. If we win the first trick on the board, West, on gaining the lead with the ♠K (and we cannot discard losers on the hearts until trumps have been pulled), can confidently underlead his ♣Q to his partner's ♣10, after which a diamond from East will seal our doom.

The way to avoid this is to arrange to lose our club trick to West, i.e. play low from the board to the first trick. We can win the second round but South is now exhausted of the suit and we can pull trumps and cash the hearts quietly without risk of East gaining the lead. We will thus restrict our losses to a club, a diamond and the ♠K.

The deal:

```
                    ♠ J 9 4
                    ♡ A Q 10 7 6
                    ◇ 6 4
                    ♣ A 5 2
    ♠ K 5                           ♠ 6 3 2
    ♡ 3 2              N            ♡ 9 5 4
    ◇ A Q 9 8 7 2   W     E         ◇ J 10
    ♣ K Q 8            S            ♣ J 10 9 6 4
                    ♠ A Q 10 8 7
                    ♡ K J 8
                    ◇ K 5 3
                    ♣ 7 3
```

Problem 3

We are grateful that West has not led a second trump and it will pay to ask ourselves why. Clearly he doesn't have one. This ties in with the auction. He certainly has five hearts and we noticed that he competed further in diamonds, indicating another five-card suit. This was to cover the case where his partner had given false preference with two hearts and three diamonds. We can thus reconstruct the full hand as something like this:

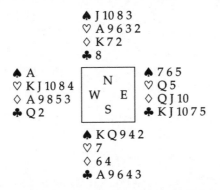

```
              ♠ J 10 8 3
              ♡ A 9 6 3 2
              ◇ K 7 2
              ♣ 8
♠ A                         ♠ 7 6 5
♡ K J 10 8 4     N          ♡ Q 5
◇ A 9 8 5 3   W     E       ◇ Q J 10
♣ Q 2            S          ♣ K J 10 7 5
              ♠ K Q 9 4 2
              ♡ 7
              ◇ 6 4
              ♣ A 9 6 4 3
```

Note the choice of the trump lead. Being rich in the red suits, knowing that his partner had bid clubs and that the E-W partnership had the balance of the points between them, West realized that it was almost certain that our only hope lay in making our trumps separately. So let us count our tricks. We have the aces of hearts and clubs and, if we can ruff three clubs on the board, seven trump tricks to total nine so far. The tenth can only come from the ◇K, which may well be favorably placed over the ace. The order of play is important in that we must set up that diamond trick early. If we go for the crossruff first, East will be able to discard diamonds on the third and fourth round of hearts and then ruff our ◇K. We should thus play a diamond at trick two, win whatever West returns and then go for the crossruff. As the cards lie, we can actually get away with taking one club ruff and one heart ruff before playing a diamond but establishing side winners first is a good habit to acquire.

Problem 4

We have five heart tricks out of six, the ♣A, the ♠A and at least four diamond tricks to total eleven. However, the lead has removed our only entry to the board and the diamonds can only be cashed by overtaking the ◊K with the ◊A. In that event, unless we clear the trumps completely, we could lose the contract if the diamonds were badly split as here:

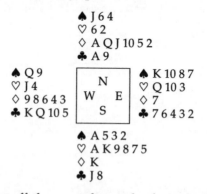

```
              ♠ J 6 4
              ♡ 6 2
              ◊ A Q J 10 5 2
              ♣ A 9
  ♠ Q 9                          ♠ K 10 8 7
  ♡ J 4          N               ♡ Q 10 3
  ◊ 9 8 6 4 3  W   E             ◊ 7
  ♣ K Q 10 5      S              ♣ 7 6 4 3 2
              ♠ A 5 3 2
              ♡ A K 9 8 7 5
              ◊ K
              ♣ J 8
```

Now East can ruff the second round, after which the board is dead. To prevent this, we must play a third round of trumps immediately. They could only win one club trick and we have first-round control of the spades. Note the importance of winning the first trick. Holding up, with a view to keeping the entry to the diamonds, would allow a spade shift and the defenders might be able to set up two spade tricks to add to their club and heart for down one.

Problem 5

Here we have a similar diamond situation and again an inevitable trump loser but the position in the black suits has altered to the extent that we cannot afford to lose the lead now for fear of losing up to five tricks in those suits immediately. The only hope now rests in assuming that East can follow diamonds at least three times. Thus, after the third high trump, we can play four rounds, discarding losers. He will ruff the fourth with his master trump (to prevent a fifth round), but that will leave us with six trump tricks, three diamonds and the ♣A for the contract.

The deal:

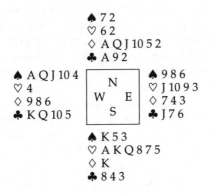

```
                  ♠ 7 2
                  ♡ 6 2
                  ◊ A Q J 10 5 2
                  ♣ A 9 2
   ♠ A Q J 10 4   ┌─────────┐   ♠ 9 8 6
   ♡ 4            │    N    │   ♡ J 10 9 3
   ◊ 9 8 6        │  W   E  │   ◊ 7 4 3
   ♣ K Q 10 5     │    S    │   ♣ J 7 6
                  └─────────┘
                  ♠ K 5 3
                  ♡ A K Q 8 7 5
                  ◊ K
                  ♣ 8 4 3
```

If East has four diamonds, we will make an overtrick, but if he has two or fewer, there is no chance.

Problem 6

We have six top trump tricks, three clubs and the other two aces to total eleven. There are two possible approaches for the twelfth trick. One is simply to take the spade finesse – a straight 50 per cent chance. The other is to go for a 3–2 diamond split – a superior 68 per cent chance. However, we shall see that good technique may allow us to have our cake and eat it. There is no hurry for the spade finesse.

We should observe the usual guide of keeping entries with the long suit so the ♣A must be preserved for the time being. We should thus win the opening lead in hand and then pull trumps. Now, we must take great care regarding what we discard from the board on the third and fourth rounds. The guide is: 'Discard losers, keep winners' – but here we must re-define what we mean by losers and winners. The only obvious winners on the board are the two minor aces, but we may also define any card which is covered by a winner in hand as a winner.

Let's go through the hand on the board. In spades, we have two low cards. One will definitely be covered by the ace and therefore may be considered a winner. The second may lose to the king (i.e. should the finesse be wrong) and is thus a possible loser. So there is absolutely nothing to be gained by discarding both spades, but we may discard one. Indeed, on this occasion, it may be crucial to keep one card in the suit to enable us to take the finesse. In clubs, there are two low ones on the board but they are covered by the ♣K and ♣Q and may therefore be considered winners. Indeed, it will be fatal to discard either as we must keep the ♣A on the board for as long as possible as entry to the long diamonds. Looking at those diamonds, we can again analyze the winners and losers. Assuming a reasonable 3–2 break, the second and third diamonds are losers while the ace and the other three are winners. On a 4–1 split, the second, third and fourth diamonds are losers, while the ace and the other two are winners. However, with eleven tricks already available, we only need one extra winner and so the sixth card is not required. The correct discards on the third and fourth hearts are a spade and a diamond, and you are strongly advised to reread this paragraph until you fully understand the argument. Countless contracts are thrown away by failure to adhere to this guide and it will apply with even greater force and wider application in defence. Here careless discarding presents declarer with millions of points (I am not exaggerating) annually through allowing unmakeable contracts to succeed. Even top-class players are regular offenders in this respect.

Having pulled trumps, we now consider the diamonds in more detail. With only one side entry, we see that, if they break 4–1 or worse, there is no way of setting up long winners. However, on the more likely 3–2 split, we have a chance but must still be careful. If we play the ace and then another, we shall need the ♣A as entry to ruff out the third round, but will then have no further entry to cash the established winners. We must thus arrange to play three rounds before disturbing that ♣A. The only way to achieve this is to duck the first round with a view to winning the second round with the ◊A and then playing the third round. The basic guide, when we have a suit with the ace and little else, is to play the ace on the last card in the opposite hand so that we can have another round 'free of charge'. Thus with

A x x x x
x x x

we play the ace on the third round.

Now much depends on what happens when we duck that first diamond. If East wins it, he will know that we have the ♣Q (because his partner led the ♣J, denying the ♣Q, and he has not got it himself) and will realize that the entry on the board cannot be attacked. He will thus have no alternative but to attack spades. In that event, we will have to play with the odds, refusing the finesse and winning with the ♠A. We now play a diamond to the ◇A, ruff a diamond to establish the suit and return to the board with the ♣A to enjoy the established diamonds, on which we discard our losing ♠Q.

The deal:

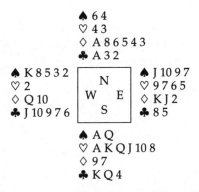

However, if West wins the first diamond (he might have started with ◇ K Q doubleton or East may fail to overtake in the above layout) he cannot profitably attack spades and must try to knock out the board's club entry prematurely, i.e. before the diamonds are established. So he leads another club. Now the importance of keeping both low clubs on the board becomes apparent. We again win in hand and play another diamond to the ◇A. If both opponents follow, we ruff out the suit and return the ♣A to cash the winners as before. But if someone shows out, we can now try the spade finesse as the only hope. We should succeed if the deal were like this:

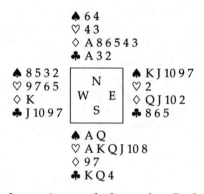

That completes the section on declarer play. I advise you to go over the problems again and again, including the variations which result in a set, until you are completely familiar with each example and the logic behind the recommended line of play. The importance of this cannot be overemphasized because, in the next section when we discuss defence, we shall spend a great deal of the time creeping into the mind of the declarer in an attempt to establish what he is trying to do. Only then can we have any reasonable idea of how to combat his plans.

I suggest you redo all examples in both no-trump and trump contracts until you can produce answers with fully analyzed reasons in well under thirty seconds. Once you can do that, you will be well placed to start the section on defence, which is complicated by the fact that you have a fallible human partner and, as we briefly mentioned in the beginners' book, there are ways of imparting information to him. Rather than play to parrot-type rules, we are going to work out every hand in detail and hopefully reach a much higher standard of defence.

SECTION 3:

Defence against No-trump Contracts

Defence is generally accepted to be the most difficult part of the game and there is little doubt that, while most of it is conducted with twenty-six cards on view, the opening lead, chosen when looking at only thirteen, is the most difficult part of defence.

Teachers and bridge schools give their students long lists of rules to guide them and I tabulated some of them in *The Expert Beginner*. Frankly, that was already once too often! I have only one rule: 'Work the hand out.' It is in this part of the game, more than any other, that the extension of the 'one-closed-hand' exercise to two hands is going to be put to use and, as we place the twenty-six cards we cannot see, you will appreciate that the ability to play 'seeing' all four hands rather than only two represents the difference between success and failure.

As I have already emphasized many times, the parrot rules commonly taught have so many exceptions that it is almost better not to know them in the first place. In any case, it is vital to understand the logic behind them in order to appreciate their limitations and to be able to recognize the countless situations in which they have to be broken.

In no-trump, as we have already seen, the play usually constitutes a race between declarer and defenders to see who can establish their long suit first. In the declarer section, we learnt that, rather than being a straight track event, there are obstacles like holding up stoppers to exhaust one hand of a suit and disrupt communications. We shall be looking at those in more detail from the defenders' point of view.

We shall also spend a lot of time considering what to discard once the declarer has established his long suit and starts cashing his winners because, as already indicated, this is a very neglected part of the game, particularly at lower standards of play, and the losses are incalculable.

In my experience I have found that one of the major causes of error is loss of interest by defenders who hold very poor cards and resign themselves, not only to the fact the declarer is going to make his contract with ease but (far worse) that there is nothing the defenders can do about it. Many of them seem to forget that they have a partner who may have better cards. Thus care taken to hold on to the correct spot cards can very often make all the difference. Yes, it does mean making an effort to count and place partner's and declarer's forces, but that is why we spent such a long time on the appropriate exercises in the beginners' book.

Anybody can make tricks by cashing aces, kings and queens. The winning player, however, is the one who makes tricks with the more modest members of the deck.

Let us start with the opening lead. There are two things to decide:

1 Which suit do we select?
2 Once we have selected the suit, which card do we choose?

Most teachers say 'Lead the fourth highest of your longest and strongest suit.' They recommend attacking the suit which is most likely to win tricks, which means using your discretion in situations like this, where you are on lead against 3NT and hold:

♠ A K Q J 10; ♡ 5; ◊ 6; ♣ 9 8 7 5 4 2.

You are expected to lead a spade rather than the ♣5! Remembering that common sense is the overriding priority in all bridge situations, I am still unhappy about the teachers' advice. What do they mean by the word 'your'? In practice, the student looks at his hand and selects from his longest suit; with two suits of equal length, he goes for the stronger. The fact that there is a partner, keen to contribute to the fray, sitting opposite, is completely forgotten. The attack should be made in the longest suit *of the partnership*. 'But how does one know,' I hear you cry, 'what partner has got?' A good question – but very often the answer can be worked out, if only we are prepared to make the effort. The auction, including passes, very often gives a mine of information; all we need to do is tap it.

Let us list the fragments of evidence likely to be provided by the auction:

1 Which suits, if any, have been bid by opponents? These are suits where they are likely to be long and are probably best avoided. Also which suits did they *not* bid?
2 Did partner bid a suit? If so, he is likely to be long in it and if it is obvious that he has the bulk of the defenders' points, he will have the bulk of the entries and that suit is likely to be our principal source of tricks.
3 Did the auction suggest that they will make their contract without breathing hard or did they struggle up there with the bare minimum of values? In the former case, desperate measures are justified; a poor lead will, at the worst, give away unnecessary overtricks which are of piffling value compared with that of the contract we are trying to set. (This particularly applies if a game or slam is at stake.) In the latter, your aim will probably be to avoid giving unnecessary tricks away and let declarer do his own work unassisted.
4 How are the points likely to be distributed between declarer and the board? If declarer has most of the points, you will probably be leading round to strength (i.e. to his advantage). If the big hand is likely to be on the board, then you are likely to be leading through strength, probably to your advantage. This could be an important consideration.
5 Same question regarding the division of points between you and your partner – who is likely to have the entries?

The best way to illustrate these considerations is to do some exercises. To begin with, allow yourself plenty of time, we shall say two minutes per example. In each case, I shall give you your hand (West) and the auction and I should like you to give a full analysis of the hand, including every piece of information available from the auction (including passes, remember) by answering the above questions. Then give the card you propose to lead. Start your stop-watch.

(1)   On each of the following, South deals at love all and opens 1NT. North raises to 3NT, you and your partner being silent. What do you lead from:

    (a) ♠ K Q J 5 3   (b) ♠ K J 10 7 5
         ♡ 10 8   ♡ 4 2
         ◊ K 5 2   ◊ 6 5 2
         ♣ 7 6 5   ♣ A 10 7

    (c) ♠ K 7 6 4 2   (d) ♠ 10 7 6 5 3
         ♡ 6 5   ♡ 8 6
         ◊ A 6 3   ◊ 8 6 4 3
         ♣ Q 6 5   ♣ 9 8

    (e) ♠ 10 3   (f) ♠ J 10 9 8 7 5
         ♡ A Q J 10 8   ♡ A 2
         ◊ 7 5 2   ◊ 6 5 2
         ♣ 8 6 5   ♣ A 10

    (g) ♠ 9 8 7 6 4 2   (h) ♠ 10 7 6 5 3
         ♡ 6 5   ♡ 8 6
         ◊ A 6   ◊ K Q J 10
         ♣ A 6 5   ♣ 8 5

(2)   On each of the following, South deals at love all and opens 1NT; his partner raises to 2NT and South bids 3NT. What do you lead this time?

    (a) ♠ 10 9 8   (b) ♠ 10 9 8 7 5
         ♡ A Q 10 8   ♡ Q 2
         ◊ 7 5 2   ◊ A 6 5 2
         ♣ 8 6 5   ♣ K 10

    (c) ♠ 6 4 2   (d) ♠ 10 7 6 5 3
         ♡ K 5   ♡ 8 6
         ◊ 10 6 3 2   ◊ K J 10 8
         ♣ J 7 6 5   ♣ 8 5

    (e) ♠ 10 3   (f) ♠ 7 5
         ♡ K J 9 7   ♡ A 2
         ◊ K J 5   ◊ Q 10 7 6 5 2
         ♣ Q 10 6 5   ♣ A 10 3

(g) ♠ 7 6 4
♡ 6 5
◇ Q 10 7 6 3 2
♣ 6 5

(h) ♠ 10 7 3
♡ 8 6
◇ Q J 10 9 8
♣ 8 5 2

(3) On each of the following, South deals at love all and opens 1♠ and the auction goes:

1♠	2♣
2NT	3NT

with you and your partner silent. What do you lead?

(a) ♠ 10 3
♡ A J 10 8 5
◇ 7 5 2
♣ 8 6 5

(b) ♠ Q J 10 9 7 5
♡ A 2
◇ 6 5 2
♣ A 10

(c) ♠ 6 4 2
♡ 6 5
◇ A 10 9 6 3
♣ A 6 5

(d) ♠ 10 7 6 5 3
♡ 8 6
◇ Q 10 7 5 3
♣ 8

(e) ♠ 10 3
♡ 4 3
◇ 7 5 2
♣ K Q J 10 7 5

(f) ♠ 8 7 5
♡ A 10 7 2
◇ A 10 7 2
♣ Q 10

(g) ♠ 9 4 2
♡ Q 10 7 6 5 4
◇ 6 3
♣ 6 5

(h) ♠ 10 7
♡ 8 6 5 4 2
◇ Q J 10 9
♣ A 5

(4) On each of the following, South deals at love all and the auction goes:

W	N	E	S
			1♠
Pass	2♣	2♡	2NT
Pass	3NT	end	

What do you lead this time?

(a) ♠ 10 3
♡ K
◇ Q 7 5 2
♣ 10 8 6 5 4 3

(b) ♠ K J 10 9 7 5
♡ Q 2
◇ 6 5 2
♣ 10 7

(c) ♠ 6 2
♡ Q 6 5
◇ A 9 8 6 4 3
♣ 6 5

(d) ♠ 5 3
♡ J 8 6 2
◇ 10 7 6 5 3
♣ 8 2

(e) ♠ 8 3
    ♡ A 8 2
    ◇ Q 7 5 2
    ♣ 8 6 5 4

(f) ♠ K Q J 10 9 7
    ♡ 4 2
    ◇ 6 5 2
    ♣ 10 7

(g) ♠ 7 6 5 4 2
    ♡ 5
    ◇ 6 3 2
    ♣ A 6 5 4

(h) ♠ 7 6 5 3
    ♡ 8 6
    ◇ A
    ♣ Q J 10 9 8 7

Let us work through the answers.

(1)   Here South has limited his hand to 15–17 points but North is only limited to the degree that he did not try for a slam. Thus he could have up to 15 points. Note also that North did not try Stayman or attempt to consider any other contract, which suggests that his hand is, if anything, orientated to the minor suits. South also has almost certainly denied a five-card major but he will have at least a doubleton in all four suits. It is clear, therefore, that desperate measures are called for and we must concentrate on trying to run a long suit even if it means leading from an embarrassing holding:

(a) No problem here: we have a long solid holding and we lead the top of a sequence – the ♠K.

(b) Again our longest and strongest suit is spades and we have the bonus of a side entry in the ♣A. From a semi-solid honor holding, we lead the top card of the solid part, i.e. the ♠J. In bridge parlance, this is referred to as *top of an interior sequence*.

(c) Again we have a five-card major and no reason to ignore it. Where we have only one or two honors in the suit, we hope to find partner with some help. He will probably be short in the suit and we observe the guide of leading high from the short hand first. So we start with a low card towards his presumed honor. The usual card is the fourth highest, here the ♠4. Note that, even if partner turns up with only low cards in the suit, what we are effectively doing is ducking the first round – usually good to preserve communications. We learnt that in the declarer section when we studied positions like A x x x x opposite x x x.

(d) Another five-card major but a poor one and we do not hold a single point. Assuming we are to have any reasonable chance of beating this contract, partner will have to be credited with at least an opening call. He will therefore have the entries and it is his suit that we must attack. Of course, he could have a spade fit with us, but that implies that both opponents are very short and might well at least have investigated the possibility of 4♡ or five of a minor. Far more likely, as Stayman was not used, is that partner's suit is hearts. We lead the higher from a doubleton – the ♡8.

(e) We have a very good five-card major but no entry outside. In order to keep communication with partner, we must try to lose a trick to the ♡K early. Again, we lead the top of the interior sequence, this time the ♡Q.

(f) The long solid major is lacking tops but partner may be able to help and there is always the possibility that enemy forces may fall together in layouts like this:

```
              K x
J 10 9 8 7 5              x x x
              A Q
```

In addition, we have two certain outside entries in the two aces, so we lead the normal, top-of-a-sequence ♠J.

(g) The same applies, this time leading the ♠9.

(h) Here we have to choose between a five-card major and a four-card minor but the diamonds guarantee three tricks while the spades may yield nothing. It is possible, of course, that the number of diamond tricks can be reduced by declarer's being able to hold up the ◇A long enough to exhaust partner and thus take advantage of our lack of side entries. In any event, however, leading the top-of-a-sequence ◇K is most unlikely to give anything away.

(2) In this sequence, both opponents have defined their point-counts fairly accurately. South will have a good 16–17; North 8–9. We can thus predict partner's hand more accurately. Furthermore, as the opponents have crawled up to what might well be a dubious game contract, passive defence is in order, the emphasis being placed on avoiding giving anything away rather than on rushing to set up long suits.

(a) Here a solid ♠10 would give nothing away, while touching that heart holding could easily do so. As it is only four-card, the gain from leading it is a trick less than that from the five-card suits in the examples above.

(b) Here we lead the solid ♠10 in all circumstances. It is our longest suit and we certainly do not want to touch any of the others.

(c) Here partner has most of the points and, against a confidently-bid game, a good case could be made for the ♡K, in an attempt to find his suit. Now, however, it is best to be passive and a spade is least likely to do any damage.

(d) Again we should lead a spade but, as we want to pursue diamonds in the later play, it may be better not to lead the fourth-highest but the ♠7. On seeing the board and his own hand, partner should be able to work out that this is not our fourth-highest but a card led on the *attitude* principle which will be explained in more detail later. For the time being, it will suffice to explain that, when leading spot cards, the higher the card led, the less interested is the leader in the suit and vice versa.

(e) We have 10 points, leaving partner with about 5, and again the aim should be to give away as little as possible. We have broken holdings in three suits and thus the spade lead, top of a doubleton ♠10 seems the safest.

(f) With a six-card suit and two side entries, the fourth highest diamond is probably still the best lead. Clubs and hearts are best not touched and a spade might well ruin partner's holding. We lead the fourth-highest ◇6 and if partner can manage the ◇J, there could be a heavy set.

(g) This time, there are no outside entries and there is little point in leading a diamond away from Q 10. Partner will be near an opening call and it is best to try and find his suit, hearts being the favorite – we lead the top-of-a-doubleton ♡6.

(h) This time the diamonds are solid and thus the ◇Q is best. We have little hope of bringing the suit in for lack of entries but it is certain that the lead will give nothing away – our principal concern.

(3) This time, two suits have been bid by opponents. North-South are unlimited except to the degree that they made no attempt to investigate a slam. Positive defence is therefore in order.

(a) Here we have a good five-card suit which was not bid although South is likely to have at least a stop. We lead the top-of-an-interior-sequence ♡J, keeping the ♡A over South to cover situations like:

$$\begin{array}{c}
♡ \text{ x x} \\
♡ \text{ A J 10 8 5} \qquad\qquad ♡ \text{ x x x} \\
♡ \text{ K Q x}
\end{array}$$

If we can get partner on lead for the second round, we have a tenace position and can run the rest of the suit.

(b) We have solid spades and two certain entries and know that partner is unlikely to have very much. Thus we must try to set the contract in spades and lead the top-of-a-sequence ♠Q which will, in any case, give nothing away. South will need to have ♠ A K 8 x x to stop us.

(c) Here, we have a good unbid diamond suit and a certain outside entry and we lead the top-of-an-interior-sequence ◇10. If partner can produce anything at all, we shall be well placed in these positions (overleaf):

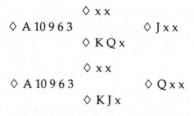

◇ x x

◇ A 10 9 6 3   ◇ J x x

◇ K Q x

◇ x x

◇ A 10 9 6 3   ◇ Q x x

◇ K J x

(d) Here we have only two points and our lack of entries gives little chance of that diamond suit being brought in. If there is to be any chance of setting this contract, partner will have to be near an opening call and his long suit is likely to be hearts. We lead the top-of-a-doubleton ♡8.

(e) This time, the clubs are solid and the lead of the top-of-a-sequence ♣K will give nothing away. No doubt, the ♣A will be held up to make sure that we cannot bring the whole suit in for lack of a side entry. However, declarer will not know how long to hold up and we are bound to win one or two tricks. Meanwhile, we can look at the board and will have more information on which red suit to attack later.

(f) This time, the red suits are identical and it appears to be a toss of a coin on which one to lead. In this kind of situation, it is usually better to prefer a major to a minor. An opponent might have suppressed a minor suit on the way to 3NT but is less likely to suppress a major as 4♡ may be a better contract. South is a case in point. Bearing in mind that, in reality, the difference is a small one, if there is nothing else to go on, the guide of preferring to attack a major suit against no-trump is as good as any.

(g) A case can be made for either red suit here. One approach is to take the view that there is little hope unless partner can produce three hearts and the opponents have two each, in which case the set could be heavy following the fourth-high lead of the ♡6. The other is that partner has the bulk of the points and that his suit is likely to be diamonds and therefore the ◇6 is better. I prefer the latter view as the chance of a heart miracle is very small.

(h) Having read the last paragraph, one would think that a five-card major suit should take precedence over a four-card minor but in view of the solidity of the latter and the presence of a certain outside entry, the top of a sequence ◇Q should be preferred. Even if both ◇A and ◇K are against us, we shall set up two tricks to add to the ♣A. If partner has 8 points, probably the best we can hope for, he may have two more. If we preferred hearts, partner will probably need to have at least a couple of honors and even then, it will take a long time to set up our tricks. Meanwhile, declarer may well run home in the black suits.

(4) Here the opponents' bidding is unchanged, except that partner has bid a suit. Let us consider that in detail. He has bid at the two-level despite both opponents having bid and is taking a considerable risk in the knowledge that we could well have nothing. (Remember South has only limited his hand to the extent that he failed to open at the two-level; i.e. he can have up to 19 points and North, having made a forcing call, is completely unlimited). The overriding requirement for partner is a good five-card suit at the very least. He is risking a considerable penalty and the opponents have, as yet, neither bid nor made game. South's 2NT should guarantee at least one good heart stop (not an absolute requirement in the absence of the overcall). In these examples, we shall almost certainly be leading partner's suit.

(a) We have a pleasant surprise for partner in the king of his suit and we have no hesitation in leading it. If it is allowed to hold, we shall have to shift but then, at least, we shall have seen the board.

(b) Another pleasant surprise in a heart honor and from a doubleton, we lead the honor to avoid blocking the suit, i.e. we observe the principle of leading high from the short hand first – lead the ♡Q.

(c) This is better still but this time, we lead low from three to an honor. The ♡5 works well in this kind of position:

$$\begin{array}{ccc} & \heartsuit\, x & \\ \heartsuit\, Q\,6\,5 & & \heartsuit\, A\,10\,9\,8\, x\, x \\ & \heartsuit\, K\,J\, x & \end{array}$$

South is likely to finesse on the second round, after which we can clear the suit. If there is a danger of a blockage, as here:

$$\begin{array}{ccc} & \heartsuit\, x\, x & \\ \heartsuit\, Q\,6\,5 & & \heartsuit\, A\,J\,10\,9\, x\, x \\ & \heartsuit\, K\, x & \end{array}$$

we can always throw in the ♡Q on the second round.

(d) This is also an excellent holding and we lead the normal fourth-high ♡2. Again, we may have to throw the potentially blocking ♡J on the third round in this kind of position:

$$\begin{array}{ccc} & \heartsuit\, x & \\ \heartsuit\, J\,8\,6\,2 & & \heartsuit\, A\,10\,9\,8\,7 \\ & \heartsuit\, K\,Q\, x & \end{array}$$

(e) Again we lead low from three to an honor, keeping our ♡A over South's holding at least for the time being. The ♡2 works well in these layouts:

$$\begin{array}{ccc} & \heartsuit\, x & \\ \heartsuit\, A\,8\,2 & & \heartsuit\, J\,10\,9\,7\, x\, x \\ & \heartsuit\, K\,Q\, x & \end{array}$$

or

$$\begin{array}{ccc} & \heartsuit\, x & \\ \heartsuit\, A\,8\,2 & & \heartsuit\, Q\,10\,9\,7\, x\, x \\ & \heartsuit\, K\,J\, x & \end{array}$$

where South's apparent double stop is reduced to a single stop if partner leads the second round. Should there be a danger of a blockage as in:

$$♡ x$$
$$♡ A 8 2 \qquad\qquad ♡ Q J 10 x x x$$
$$♡ K x x$$

we can always play the ♡A on the second round. The guide to prevent such blockages occurring is to avoid being left with nothing but an honor; always keep one small card.

(f) This is the one exception. Despite partner's call and our lack of side entries, the rock solid spades should be attacked. South is bound to hold up at least once and having pinched a trick (possibly two if North is void of spades) we can then shift to hearts. We lead the top-of-a-sequence ♠K.

(g) Here there is nothing to think about. We lead our partner's suit – the ♡5.

(h) This looks more debatable in view of the solid clubs and certain side entry. It will pay to work this out in detail. We have 7 points and opponents have promised something like 25 between them. That leaves only 8 for partner, which means his suit must be very good and most, if not all, of his points must be in it. Thus the first thing to realize is that it is most unlikely that he has either missing club honor and that it will therefore be impossible to bring our club suit in for lack of a second entry.

The only realistic hope of setting the contract is that South has one stop only and that it can be knocked out on the first round. Then we can cash out before South runs home with one heart trick, two clubs and six more in spades and diamonds. Thus we have to hope that the heart position is something like this:

♡ x x x

♡ 8 6   ♡ A Q J 10 x x

♡ K x

or

♡ x x

♡ 8 6   ♡ A K J x x x

♡ Q 10 x

In these cases, partner can duck the first trick, forcing South to use his stop immediately or not at all. When we get in with the ◊ A, we can run the rest of the heart suit. Note that there would be a much stronger case for a club lead if we had a singleton heart. Now the heart plan is off and the only realistic hope is that partner has bid on a much longer but weaker heart suit and does, after all, have one of the club honors.

To conclude this section, we must consider the effect, if any, of partner's doubling the final contract. The basic guides are generally accepted:

1 If partner has bid one suit and neither you nor he has bid another, then he is asking for the lead of his suit. He will probably be confident of establishing it while he has side entries, probably in opponents' long suit.

2 If you have bid one suit and neither you nor he have bid another, then he is expecting you to lead your suit, not worrying about the fact that declarer has promised at least one stop.

3 If neither of you have bid a suit, then there are two possibilities:

   a If opponents have mentioned any suits, partner is asking for the lead of the *first suit bid by the dummy hand*.

   b If opponents have not bid any suits, e.g. 1NT 3NT, then partner is telling you that he has a solid suit of his own (or near solid with entries in other suits) and is inviting you to try and find it. This usually means you will lead your shortest suit (on the assumption that both opponents are likely to be balanced). If in doubt, a major suit should be preferred to a minor for reasons discussed earlier.

4 If both you and your partner have bid a suit, then there is a difference of opinion but common sense indicates a solution. Let us say that you bid hearts; your partner bids spades and the opponents finish in 3NT with you on lead, your partner having doubled. I would suggest that the main purpose of the double is to give information that *you do not have already*. Without the double, you would have known about the spades and probably partner would have been expecting you to lead one. The double is there to give you *extra* information, i.e. that he has something in hearts with you. I suggest therefore, that a double asks for the lead of the suit bid by the partner of the doubler.

Remember that the above are only guidelines and common sense must take first priority. Bear that in mind when you try the following exercises. You should produce answers in about fifteen seconds each.

Start your stop-watch. In all cases, you are West, and South deals at love all.

(1)   The auction goes:

W	N	E	S
			1NT
Pass	3NT	Dbl	end

What do you lead from:

(a) ♠ 6
     ♡ K 8 7 5
     ◇ Q 9 8 7 5
     ♣ 10 9 7

(b) ♠ K 5 3
     ♡ 8 5
     ◇ J 8 6 4
     ♣ J 7 5 3

(c) ♠ 8 5
     ♡ Q J 9 7 5
     ◇ 8 5
     ♣ A 7 6 4

(d) ♠ –
     ♡ J 10 9 6 5
     ◇ Q 10 8 6 4 2
     ♣ 8 3

(2)   The auction goes:

W	N	E	S
			1♦
Pass	1♡	1♠	1NT
Pass	3NT	Dbl	end

What do you lead from:

(a) ♠ 6
     ♡ K 8 7 5
     ◇ Q 9 8 7 5
     ♣ 10 9 7

(b) ♠ J 5 3
     ♡ 8 5
     ◇ J 8 6 4
     ♣ J 7 5 3

(c) ♠ K 5
     ♡ Q J 9 7 5
     ◇ 8 5
     ♣ J 9 4 2

(d) ♠ –
     ♡ Q 10 9 6 5
     ◇ J 10 9 8 4 2
     ♣ Q 3

(3)   The auction goes:

W	N	E	S
			1♦
1♡	1♠	Pass	1NT
Pass	3NT	Dbl	end

What do you lead from:

(a) ♠ 6
     ♡ Q J 10 8 7 5
     ◇ A K 6
     ♣ 10 9 7

(b) ♠ K 5 3
     ♡ Q J 8 7 5 2
     ◇ A 8
     ♣ J 7

(c) ♠ 8 5
     ♡ A J 10 9 7 5
     ◇ 8 5
     ♣ A Q 6

(d) ♠ 9 8
     ♡ A K 6 4 3
     ◇ Q 2
     ♣ Q J 10 4

(4)   The auction goes:

W	N	E	S
			Pass
Pass	1♠	Pass	1NT
Pass	3♦	Pass	3NT
Pass	Pass	Dbl	end

What do you lead from:

(a)   ♠ 6
      ♡ K 8 7 5
      ◊ Q 7 5
      ♣ J 10 9 7 4

(b)   ♠ K 5 3
      ♡ 8 7 6 5 4 2
      ◊ 8
      ♣ J 7 5

(c)   ♠ 8 5
      ♡ Q 10 9 7 5 2
      ◊ 8 5
      ♣ K 7 4

(d)   ♠ 2
      ♡ K Q J 10 9
      ◊ 8 6 4 2
      ♣ J 8 3

(5)   The auction goes:

W	N	E	S
			1◊
1♡	2♣	2♠	2NT
Pass	3NT	Dbl	end

What do you lead from:

(a)   ♠ 6
      ♡ Q J 10 8 7 5
      ◊ A K 6
      ♣ 10 9 7

(b)   ♠ K 5 3
      ♡ Q J 8 7 5 2
      ◊ A 8
      ♣ J 7

(c)   ♠ 8 5
      ♡ A J 10 9 7 5
      ◊ 8 5
      ♣ A Q 6

(d)   ♠ 9 8
      ♡ A K 6 4 3
      ◊ Q 2
      ♣ Q J 10 4

Let us work through the answers:

(1)   Here no suits have been bid so partner, who had no chance to bid below the four-level, clearly has a good suit of his own and is inviting you to try and find it. South has limited his hand to 15–17, but North is only limited to the degree that he did not try for a slam; thus he could have up to 15 points. Partner has thus taken something of a risk in doubling, in that there could be a redouble and/or over-tricks. He therefore obviously thinks it is worth taking the risk to increase our chances of setting the contract.

     (a)   Here he is most likely to have spades, therefore we lead the ♠6.

(b) Now hearts are favorite, so we lead the top of a doubleton ♡8.

(c) It seems to be a toss-up between spades and diamonds and it is also noteworthy that we have 7 points, leaving, on the reasonable assumption that opponents have 25, very little for partner. The likely explanation is that North has bid the game on a long running suit rather than on points; that suit is almost certainly a minor (otherwise he would have tried to play in four of a major). So North will probably have a diamond suit, leaving the spades with partner, and we lead the top-of-a-doubleton ♠8.

(d) Partner clearly has spades and we are unfortunately void. In this situation, it is probably best to assume that partner has the maximum point-count consistent with the bidding (here about 12) and treat it as a position where the opponents have crawled up to their contract. They are in for most unpleasant breaks in at least three suits and our aim should be to avoid giving anything away. A diamond lead – our longest suit – carries the risk of giving South a free finesse and a club could well ruin a delicate holding in partner's hand and is thus also best left alone. The safe lead is the top-of-sequence ♡J.

(2) Here partner has bid a suit and we should respect his strong request to lead it. Probably South has only one stop and partner has a certain side entry.

(a) We lead our only spade, ♠6.

(b) We lead low from three to an honor, the ♠3.

(c) We lead top of a doubleton, the ♠K.

(d) Sorry, partner – not today! Again, it is probably best to treat it as a passive position as in (1d) above and lead a solid ◇J.

(3) Here we have bid a suit and partner's double confirms help in it. He probably also has an unpleasant surprise for opponents in one or both of their suits.

(a) Top of a sequence ♡Q.

(b) Fourth-high ♡7 – no need to lead the ♡Q, partner will

have something and indeed leading an honor could well block the suit. Actually from ♡ Q J 10 4 3 2, it is probably correct to lead the ♡4; otherwise, there will be a blockage in this likely layout:

$$♡ \; x \; x$$

♡ Q J 10 4 3 2   ♡ K x (or A x)

$$♡ \; A \; 9 \; 8 \; x$$
$$(or \; ♡ \; K \; 9 \; 8 \; x)$$

(c) Top-of-an-interior-sequence ♡J.
(d) Normal fourth-high ♡4.

(4) In this kind of situation, partner is asking for North's first-bid suit, i.e. spades. Before leading, note that both opponents have limited their hands. North will be just under a two-opener, South about 6–10. Also South failed to give preference to spades when promised at least a five-card suit from North, so he will have a doubleton at most and probably less. On (a), (b) and (c), we have no reason to ignore the request for a spade lead and in accordance with usual guides, lead the ♠6, ♠3, and ♠8 respectively. On (d), it is less clear, but with 7 points in our hand, it is most unlikely that partner is going to turn up with five quick spade tricks against an announced five-card suit in a strong North hand. It is far more probable that he has something like ♠ A Q 10 x x and perhaps a diamond picture. There is no hurry to lead spades and we should prefer our solid heart suit, starting with the ♡K, the top of the sequence.

(5) This time, both partners have bid a suit and, as explained earlier, the double should indicate a heart lead. In the absence of a double, partner would be expecting a spade; there is little point in bidding it otherwise. The answers are thus the same as in (3) above.

The dummy goes down

Once the opening lead has been made, North displays his hand, remembering to place any trumps on the right. At this point, there should be pause for thought. As emphasized in the declarer section, South should form a complete plan of campaign before he calls for a card from the board, and that applies even if the play to the first trick or two is obvious.

At the same time, the player sitting East should be doing the same thing. His first job is to review the bidding and, taking into account the opening lead, try to place as many cards as possible, i.e. do the two-closed-hand exercise. He will then form a plan of campaign himself or, particularly if he has a very poor hand, deem it prudent to try to give his partner information so that the latter, who will be better informed, can take any necessary decisions. In that case, the language of defensive signalling comes into play and we shall spend a lot of time working on these two basic elements of defence.

The best way to illustrate this is to do some simple examples. We can then graduate on to more difficult problems. In my earlier books for tournament players, I coined the phrase 'seven roll-calls'. They are:

1 Distribution round the table of spades.
2 Same for hearts.
3 Same for diamonds.
4 Same for clubs.
5 Same for high-card points.

These we studied intently in the one-closed-hand exercise at the start of *The Expert Beginner*. We are now going to add two more elements.

6 How many tricks are immediately available or easily establish-able by the declarer?
7 Same question for the defenders.

These last two we also studied in the beginners' book by considering how many rounds of each suit were likely to be played, and how many would be won by each side. We learnt that this not only depends on the actual cards held, but also possibly on who leads to each round.

The total of (6) and (7) is critical to the degree of dictating how the play will go. If it is greater than thirteen and, especially at no-trump, it could be considerably so, then a race is on and it will be worth taking desperate measures to get in first. If it is less than thirteen, then both sides will have to work for their tricks and now the priority will be to avoid giving anything away unnecessarily.

So as soon as the dummy goes down, a large number of decisions need to be taken and a few moments thought are appropriate. Let us think our way through this problem:

Hand No. 45
Dealer East
Neither vulnerable

♠ 6 5 2
♡ Q J
◇ Q 9
♣ A Q J 10 8 7

		N		♠ K Q 9 8 7 3
W			E	♡ 7 3
	S			◇ A J 5
				♣ K 6

W	N	E	S
		1♠	1NT
Pass	3NT	end	

After our opening call, South's 1NT showed 15–17 points and North had an obvious raise to game. Partner dutifully leads the ♠10, the board playing low. What can we work out? Let us go through the roll-calls on the information so far:

Spades: We have six and the board three, leaving four unaccounted for. Partner has led the ♠10, which clearly denies the ♠J, so that must be with South, who will also need the ♠A for an adequate stop for his call. That just leaves the ♠4 missing and that could be in either hand at the moment.

Hearts: We and the board have two each, leaving nine unaccounted for. With the no-trump bid from South, he is likely to have between two and four, leaving five to seven with partner.

Diamonds: We have three, the board two, leaving eight unaccounted for. In a minor, South could have between two and five (on rare occasions six), leaving between three and six for partner.

Clubs: We have two and the board six, leaving five unaccounted for. Thus South could have between two and five; partner none to two.

Points: We have 13 and the board 12, totalling 25, leaving 15 unaccounted for. South's bid promised 15–17, so he must have exactly 15 leaving partner with none!

So we can now go further and place all the outstanding honors with South: ♠ A J ♡ A K and ♢ K to make up his 15 points.

Having done that, we can now try to answer roll-call questions (6) and (7).

Spades: All hangs on that ♠4. If South has it, he will make two tricks, leaving us with four; if he hasn't, he will only make one trick, leaving us with five.

Hearts: This time, it depends on how many cards South has. He will make from two to four tricks; clearly we will make none.

Diamonds: They have the ♢K and ♢Q against our ♢A so that should certainly be one each, but further tricks to either side will depend on who has the ♢10.

Clubs: Here there is little to discuss. This will be declarer's principal source of tricks. Our ♣K is well placed, so he will make five tricks and we will make one.

Let us collate what we have so far. Declarer has at least one spade trick, two hearts, five clubs and a diamond, totalling nine and that is assuming that he has the ♡ A K as a doubleton only. It is likely that he has more, in which case he will not need the diamond trick, which would involve losing the lead to our ace. Against that, we have a certain trick in each minor and one of our spade honors, but have no hope of reaching five tricks unless the long spades can be brought in.

So let us look at that spade position in more detail. We have already established that it is either:

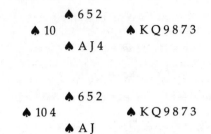

or

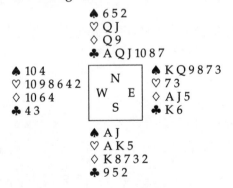

In the first case, South has two stops and therefore is assured at least two spade tricks, two hearts and five clubs, only losing the lead once to the ♣K and without touching diamonds. Therefore, as we would have to lose the lead twice to establish our spades, we have no hope of setting the contract. However, in the second case, South has only one stop and even if he had as many as five hearts, he could not run more than seven tricks without giving us the lead in one of the minors (in practice clubs).

In this type of situation, the expert defender realizes that he must place the cards so that he has some hope and plays for the full deal to be something like:

We thus play the ♠Q on trick one. South can win or duck as he pleases and when we get in with the ♣K, we will cash our five spades and the ♦A to put the contract down three. Note the play of the ♠Q rather than the ♠K at trick one. When leading or playing in second position, we lead the higher of touching honors (here it would be king from king-queen) but in third position, we go as near to the card led as possible (i.e. the queen is nearer to the ten than the king). The play of the queen thus denies the jack, but does not deny the king.

Now let us stop and reflect for a moment. As soon as the dummy went down, we went through our seven roll-calls, decided which suit(s) were critical, formed a line of play based on a particular lie of the cards which was consistent with the bidding so far and played accordingly. Yes, it was a great deal of hard work and teachers and beginners might ask why it was all necessary. Wasn't it simply a matter of 'third man high', and have done with it? Nothing to wait for or finesse against on the board, so what were we thinking about? The ♠Q is automatic!

Is that so? In fact, we only have to juggle a few cards around and we have to think again. This is a hand I regularly give to my advanced class.

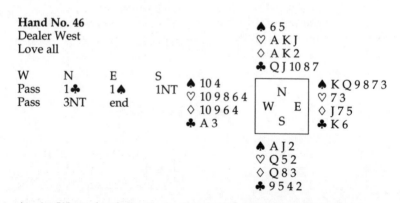

Hand No. 46
Dealer West
Love all

W	N	E	S
Pass	1♣	1♠	1NT
Pass	3NT	end	

North
♠ 6 5
♡ A K J
♢ A K 2
♣ Q J 10 8 7

West
♠ 10 4
♡ 10 9 8 6 4
♢ 10 9 6 4
♣ A 3

East
♠ K Q 9 8 7 3
♡ 7 3
♢ J 7 5
♣ K 6

South
♠ A J 2
♡ Q 5 2
♢ Q 8 3
♣ 9 5 4 2

Again West dutifully leads the ♠10 and the board plays low. Now shall we play an 'automatic ♠Q' and go on to the next hand or work the hand out properly? If you elect to play 'third man high', you have presented declarer with an unmakeable contract and +100 (plus the value of the non-vulnerable game) instead of 50 in your favor – an expensive loss. Surely it must be worthwhile making the effort. Let us go through it all again:

Spades: With our announcement of a good suit (remember we have made an overcall, guaranteeing at least a good five-card suit) South may well have a double stop to bid 1NT. The lead confirms this. Partner has denied the ♠J and the ♠A and the lead must come from a singleton or doubleton. We shall learn later that, from three small cards, we do not normally lead the top card in the absence of the one immediately below it.

Hearts: With five or more cards, South would probably have at least suggested the suit for a possible game. With a singleton or void, it is unlikely that he would have bid no-trump, even with the double spade stop. He is thus likely to have two, three or four.

Diamonds: Here it is less likely that he would have looked for game, which would have to be at the five-level, so he might have between two and five cards in the suit.

Clubs: With five or more clubs, he might have looked for five or six clubs as final contract, especially with first-round control of spades. With a singleton or void club, he might well have looked towards a red-suit game or slam; in any case, there was no hurry to rush into no-trump. That could always come later. It is likely that he has between two and four cards.

Points: The 1NT call promised between 6–10 points. The board has 18 and we have 9. That leaves partner with about 3–7.

Tricks: This time, South will certainly have two spade tricks and he is likely to look to clubs for many of the rest. That leads us to the crucial question of who has the ♣A! The whole hand rests on this and that is what a good player in the East seat should be considering in detail.

In this kind of situation, the way to a solution is play the hand out both ways. First, assume South has the ♣A. In that case, our king is caught in the finesse, South will make five tricks to add to his two spade tricks and, even allowing partner 5 points in the red suits, South will have several more tricks in those suits and will probably finish with it least eleven tricks – hopeless. Therefore, if there is to be any chance, the ♣A will have to be with partner and we can now complete our roll-calls far more accurately *on that assumption*.

South will have nearly all the rest of the points and that will give him both red queens. Thus he has three top tricks in each red suit to go with his two spades, to total eight. Thus we realize that, if he has four cards in either red suit, he will have nine tricks without touching clubs, and again we will have no hope. So we must assume that he has no more than three cards in each and therefore that the full hand is something like that shown above. In that case, South will have to attack clubs and now, as that involves losing the lead twice, the race between the two black suits is on.

The defenders, with the lead, are a move ahead and South is in trouble. If he wins the opening lead and plays a club, West will rise with the ♣A (protecting our entry to the long suit) and play his second spade, knocking out the second stopper. On gaining the lead with the ♣K, we can cash our four established spades to put the contract down two (although South can save a trick by cashing his six red winners to add to the two spade tricks for down one only).

The end of the story – not quite? South might be able to save himself. Let us look at that spade situation more closely:

                    ♠ 6 5
        ♠ 10 4   ♠ K Q 9 8 7 3
                    ♠ A J 2

On the lead of the ♠10, if we play the ♠Q, South is not obliged to win. So he simply ducks and, on winning the second round, he plays a club to partner's ace. But now partner is exhausted of spades and has to shift, leaving us a move behind. The clubs now come in and South makes ten tricks in comfort. But now try the effect of playing low on trick one. Now, if South ducks, we can play the ♠K on the second round and South loses his second stop; so he is forced to take his ♠J. Now, on taking his ♣A, West has his second spade to lead and the contract fails.

This hand is markedly above our current standard but it shows how hopeless these 'beginners' rules' are and how important it is to work out every hand in detail. I would strongly urge you to replay the above hand in all the variations given and satisfy yourself that you understand each line in detail.

I hope I have now satisfied you of the importance of working out each hand and the use of the extension of the one-closed-hand exercise. So let us practice some examples on this. I would like you to draw up a table with the seven roll-calls like this:

	West	North	East	South
Spades				
Hearts				
Diamonds				
Clubs				
Points				

Note the totals must always be 13.

Tricks on top or easily establishable: N-S
                                                              E-W

Any problems, e.g. with entries, in cashing those tricks?
Is there any hope of setting the contract? If so, how do you place the whole deal?

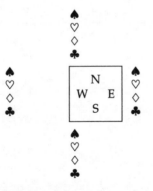

Assuming the deal is as above, how do you propose to set the contract? You should be able to do each example against the stop-watch in under two minutes, but accuracy is more important at the moment.

Problem 1
Hand No. 47
Dealer East
Neither vulnerable

♠ 6 4
♡ A Q J
♢ A 5 4 2
♣ Q J 10 9

W	N	E	S
		Pass	1NT
Pass	3NT	end	

```
        N
   W         E
        S
```

♠ Q J 10 3
♡ 9 7 4 3
♢ K 7
♣ 8 6 4

Partner leads the ♢ J and the board plays low.

Problem 2
Hand No. 48
Dealer South
Neither vulnerable

♠ J 7 6
♡ A Q 10
♢ A 5 4
♣ Q J 10 9

W	N	E	S
			1♣
Pass	3♣	Pass	3NT
end			

```
        N
   W         E
        S
```

♠ Q 4 3
♡ 9 7 4 3
♢ K 7 2
♣ A 8 6

Again, partner leads the ♢ J and the board plays low.

♠ Q 7 6
♡ A Q J
♢ 5 3 2
♣ K Q 10 9

Problem 3
Hand No. 49
Dealer East
E-W vulnerable

W	N	E	S
		Pass	1♣
Pass	3♣	Pass	3NT
end			

```
        N
   W         E
        S
```

♠ 5 4 3
♡ 9 7 4 3
♢ A 7
♣ A 8 6 2

This time, partner leads the ♢ Q and the board plays low.

Problem 4

This is similar to Problem 3 but this time, East has the ◊ K instead of the ◊ A. How do you defend now?

Problem 5				♠ J 6
Hand No. 50				♡ K Q J
Dealer South				◊ Q 5 3
E-W vulnerable				♣ A Q 10 9 8

```
                                        ┌─────────┐  ♠ K Q 10 8
                               N        │    N    │  ♡ 9 7 4
W          N          E          S      │ W     E │  ◊ A 7 2
                                1♣      │    S    │  ♣ K 6 2
Pass       3♣        Pass       3NT     └─────────┘
end
```

W	N	E	S
			1♣
Pass	3♣	Pass	3NT
end			

Partner leads the ◊ J and the board plays low.

Problem 6				♠ Q 6 4
Hand No. 51				♡ A J 10
Dealer East				◊ K 5 3
N-S vulnerable				♣ Q J 10 9

```
                                        ┌─────────┐  ♠ 10 9 8 6
                               N        │    N    │  ♡ 9 7 4 3
W          N          E          S      │ W     E │  ◊ A 7 4
                     Pass       1NT     │    S    │  ♣ 7 6
Pass       3NT       end                └─────────┘
```

W	N	E	S
		Pass	1NT
Pass	3NT	end	

Again, partner leads the ◊ J and the board plays low. How do you defend now?

Problem 7				♠ J 6 3
Hand No. 52				♡ A J 10
Dealer East				◊ K J 5
Both vulnerable				♣ Q J 10 9

```
                                        ┌─────────┐  ♠ K 9 2
                               N        │    N    │  ♡ 9 7 4 3
W          N          E          S      │ W     E │  ◊ A 7 4 2
                     Pass       1NT     │    S    │  ♣ 7 6
Pass       3NT       end                └─────────┘
```

W	N	E	S
		Pass	1NT
Pass	3NT	end	

Partner leads the ♠ 4 to the board's ♠ 3.

Problem 8
Hand No. 53
Dealer East
Neither vulnerable

♠ J 6 3
♡ A 10 5
◇ 8 5
♣ A Q J 10 9

W	N	E	S
		Pass	1NT
Pass	3NT	end	

```
            N        ♠ K 9 2
         W     E     ♡ 9 7 4 3
            S        ◇ A 7 4 2
                     ♣ 7 6
```

Again, West leads the ♠4 to the board's ♠3. How do you defend this time?

Problem 1

South has announced a balanced hand of 15–17 points and we assume that partner has led his longest suit.

Spades: South has denied a five-card major, therefore he will have two, three or four, leaving partner with five, four or three respectively. Partner is unlikely to have five, so probably the unseen hands have four and three (one way or the other).

Hearts: South has two, three or four, leaving partner with four, three or two respectively.

Diamonds: Partner, having led the suit, is likely to have at least four, which would leave South with three; or partner has five and South two.

Clubs: In the minor suit, South could have two, three, four or five, leaving partner with four, three, two or one respectively.

Points: We have 6 and the board 14 to total 20, leaving 20 unaccounted for, of which South has at least 15. Partner will have 3, 4 or 5.

Tricks: On the board alone, we can see three heart tricks (irrespective of who has the ♡K), two club tricks and the ◇A to total six. We know that partner has denied the ◇Q with his lead; therefore that will be a seventh. With partner limited to 5 points, he cannot have both black aces, so South's black ace will be an eighth and a further trick can easily be set up in clubs. It is clear that we must take five tricks now or never. South has two diamond stops once we have taken our king and thus we must look to spades. The ♡K is a dead duck in partner's hand so we must give that to South. Similarly, if partner has the ♣A, South will have both top spades and nine easy tricks so the only hope is to find a favorable spade position and partner with a maximum 5 points:

The deal:

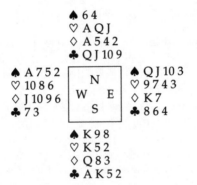

```
              ♠ 6 4
              ♡ A Q J
              ◇ A 5 4 2
              ♣ Q J 10 9

♠ A 7 5 2            ♠ Q J 10 3
♡ 10 8 6      N     ♡ 9 7 4 3
◇ J 10 9 6  W   E   ◇ K 7
♣ 7 3         S     ♣ 8 6 4

              ♠ K 9 8
              ♡ K 5 2
              ◇ Q 8 3
              ♣ A K 5 2
```

Thus, on winning the first trick, we shift to the top-of-a-sequence ♠Q to take the first five tricks. Note that South could have delayed the spade shift by going up with the ◇A on the first trick but it doesn't help him as he only has seven tricks in clubs and hearts to total eight in all. His play was correct in that his contract would only fail if we had the ◇K and West the ♠A. He was thus on a 75 per cent chance. Had he risen with the ◇A, he would have failed in a contract, which was makeable if partner's lead had come from ◇ K J 10 x x.

Problem 2
Repeating our seven roll-calls:

Spades: South has two, three or four, leaving partner with five, four or three respectively. Five is unlikely as partner did not lead the suit.

Hearts: South again has two, three or four, leaving partner with four, three or two respectively.

Diamonds: As this has been led, partner is likely to have at least four, which would leave South with three; the alternative is that partner has five, leaving South with two.

Clubs: Here South could have two, three, four or five, leaving partner with four, three, two or one respectively.

Points: We have 9 and the board 14, leaving 17 unaccounted for, and we have already seen the ♢J from partner, leaving South with the ♢Q among his minimum 12 points.

Tricks: At the moment, the number of tricks available to either side in spades is doubtful but it is certain that, irrespective of the positions of the ♡K and ♡J, South will make at least three heart tricks as any finesse against partner will be working. In diamonds, South will make his ♢A and ♢Q but no more as partner will have the ♢10 and length in the suit. In clubs, South will make at least two tricks on the board and, if he has the ♣K, he will make three.

Thus, with three hearts, two diamonds and two club tricks assured, we can now consider which outstanding honors partner might have to give us a chance, bearing in mind that he cannot have more than 4 points in addition to his ♢J. Clearly a heart honor is of no use, so let us give the ♡K and ♡J to South. That gives him 6 points, so it is clear that out of the ♠A, ♠K and ♣K, South will have two and partner one. If partner has only the ♠K, South will have three club tricks, three hearts, two diamonds and one spade to total nine, so that is ruled out. However, if partner has the ♠A or ♣K, we have a chance. In the first case, declarer has three club tricks, three hearts and two diamonds and whether he takes any spade tricks depends on who has the ♠10. In the second case, South has two clubs, three hearts, two diamonds and at least two spades to total nine, and will have one more if he has the ♠10. Either way, in order to get five tricks, we must establish long cards in diamonds and so we must win the first trick and return partner's suit.

The deal:

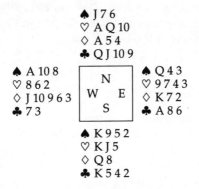

```
                    ♠ J 7 6
                    ♡ A Q 10
                    ◇ A 5 4
                    ♣ Q J 10 9
    ♠ A 10 8        ┌─────────┐      ♠ Q 4 3
    ♡ 8 6 2         │    N    │      ♡ 9 7 4 3
    ◇ J 10 9 6 3    │ W     E │      ◇ K 7 2
    ♣ 7 3           │    S    │      ♣ A 8 6
                    └─────────┘
                    ♠ K 9 5 2
                    ♡ K J 5
                    ◇ Q 8
                    ♣ K 5 4 2
```

With the spade situation above, South cannot make a spade trick without losing three others first and will make his eight tricks and no more. He will knock out the ♣A first and then, when we clear the diamonds, will cash his clubs and play a spade from the board towards his ♠K, hoping the ♠A is in our hand.

Problem 3

Spades: There are seven missing, likely to be divided 4:3 one way or the other.

Hearts: Six missing, will be split 3:3 or 4:2.

Diamonds: Partner is likely to have at least four, having led them, so the missing eight will split 4:4, 5:3 or 6:2, partner having the length.

Clubs: Five missing; South could have five, four, three, or two, leaving partner with none, one, two, or three respectively.

Points: We have 8 and the board 14, leaving 18 unaccounted for. Partner's lead has guaranteed the ◇J, giving him 3 so far. Thus even if we give South a minimum 12 for his bid, the most partner can have is another 3. The ♡K or the ♣J would be well placed for declarer and therefore useless to the defence and so the only realistic hope is that partner has the ♠K, which would be well placed over South's ♠A.

Tricks:　　South will certainly have one diamond (the well-placed $\Diamond$ K), three clubs, after losing the ♣A, at least three hearts and the ♠A to total eight and it will be no problem to give up the ♠K and take more tricks in spades for the contract.

So we must realize that the race is on and we must establish our diamonds first. It will be instructive to rewrite the above collations on hopeful assumptions.

Spades:　　No change at the moment.

Hearts:　　South must be debarred from having more than three; otherwise he will have nine tricks.

Diamonds:　We have only the ♣A and ♠K to take outside this suit and therefore need three tricks. Partner must have started with at least four, and they will have to include $\Diamond$ Q J 9 x or better. If South is as good as $\Diamond$ K 10 9 x, we cannot take three tricks in the suit – you will be well advised to satisfy yourself that this is correct.

Clubs:　　South must be restricted to three tricks in the suit and therefore must be debarred from having all five outstanding clubs.

Points:　　We have already implied that South will have to be minimum in his announced 12–14 point range and that partner will have to have the ♠K if we are to have any chance.

So we can now tabulate the deal as something like this:

```
                    ♠ Q 7 6
                    ♡ A Q J
                    ◇ 5 3 2
                    ♣ K Q 10 9
    ♠ K 10 8      ┌─────────┐      ♠ 5 4 3
    ♡ 8 6 2       │    N    │      ♡ 9 7 4 3
    ◇ Q J 10 9 4  │  W   E  │      ◇ A 7
    ♣ 7 3         │    S    │      ♣ A 8 6 2
                  └─────────┘
                    ♠ A J 9 2
                    ♡ K 10 5
                    ◇ K 8 6
                    ♣ J 5 4
```

Obviously, we must clear the diamonds and hope that South cannot take nine tricks without giving up the ♠K, after which partner will cash the rest of the diamonds to put the contract at least down one. Observe what happens if we play low on the first trick. South can block the suit completely by ducking, after which we have no hope at all, never being able to take more than two diamond tricks, the ♣A and the ♠K. However, he is unlikely to do so for fear of the actual position being:

$$\diamond\ 5\,3\,2$$
$$\diamond\ A\,Q\,J\,10\,x \qquad\qquad \diamond\ 7\,x$$
$$\diamond\ K\,x\,x$$

and now he may never make his diamond trick. So he will probably win, and now an interesting position arises. He will realize that there will be no problem if the spade finesse is right and no chance if partner has both the ♠K and ♣A. The critical case will thus arise if the deal is as above, when partner's spade entry will have to be knocked out first. Accordingly, he will cross to the board in hearts and try the spade finesse. Partner will win with the ♠K and, with our ◇A still blocking the diamond suit, will never get on play again. You should satisfy yourself that South now makes an overtrick. By playing the ◇A on trick one, we simply observe the principle of playing high from the short hand first to avoid blocking the the suit.

Problem 4

Again, we must put on the honor. The diamond position is now:

$$\diamond\ 5\,3\,2$$
$$\diamond\ Q\,J\,10\,9\,4 \qquad\qquad \diamond\ K\,7$$
$$\diamond\ A\,8\,6$$

If we play low, South simply ducks (no danger this time) and, on the second round, he ducks again, leaving us on play with no further diamonds. When partner gets in with the ♠K, he will be able to knock out the ◇A, but he will never get in again to cash his established winners. We will have only taken four tricks, leaving South with nine and his contract.

Problem 5

Let us do our collations:

Spades: Seven missing – with South having failed to bid the suit and partner having failed to lead it, they will probably split 4:3 one way or the other.

Hearts: Same applies as in spades.

Diamonds: Seven missing – likely to be partner's longest suit; so he will have four or five, leaving South with three or two respectively.

Clubs: Five missing; South could have five, four, three, or two, leaving partner with none, one, two or three respectively.

Points: We have 12 and the board 15, leaving 13 unaccounted for. Therefore, even allowing South a minimum 12 leaves only one for partner and that is the $\diamond$ J which he has led. It is therefore clear that he does not have another honor in his hand.

Tricks: South will clearly have the $\spadesuit$ A, at least three (possibly four) hearts and four club tricks out of five after losing to our $\clubsuit$ K. That totals at least eight and with both $\diamond$ K and $\diamond$ Q, he cannot be denied at least one diamond trick for his contract.

It is therefore clear that, if those clubs can be brought in, the contract will be made in comfort and thus that a race is on and we must establish five tricks first. Let us look at those diamonds in close detail. The position will be something like:

$$\diamond \text{ Q 5 3}$$
$$\diamond \text{ J 10 9 x x} \qquad \diamond \text{ A 7 2}$$
$$\diamond \text{ K x}$$

If we go up with the $\diamond$ A, South will make his two honors separately. If we play low, we keep the $\diamond$ A poised over the $\diamond$ Q and now South will only make one trick in that suit. We shall make the $\diamond$ A in any event and therefore, in the context of the diamond suit *considered in isolation*, it is correct to play low. However, as I pointed out in the beginners' book, the correct play in a single suit may not be correct *in the context of the whole hand*.

Let us consider the consequences of playing low. South will win and take the club finesse, losing to our ♣K. Although the diamond position is now in our favor, we cannot profitably attack it from our side. We are therefore obliged to shift (or give the board the ◊Q after all) and that will allow South to take his nine tricks, as explained above.

So let us try winning the diamond instead. That will allow South an extra diamond trick but if we shift to the ♠K, there is a chance that we can take three spade tricks in addition to the ♣K and ◊A. Let us look at those spades in closer detail:

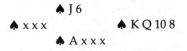

♠ J 6

♠ x x x   ♠ K Q 10 8

♠ A x x x

If South only has three spades, they will be swallowed by our ♠ K Q 10 and we will make the fourth round. If he has four, all rests on the position of the ♠9. If South has it, he will have a second stop and there will be no hope. We must therefore assume that partner has it and that the full deal is something like:

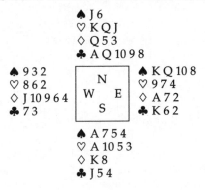

♠ J 6
♡ K Q J
◊ Q 5 3
♣ A Q 10 9 8

♠ 9 3 2
♡ 8 6 2
◊ J 10 9 6 4
♣ 7 3

N
W   E
S

♠ K Q 10 8
♡ 9 7 4
◊ A 7 2
♣ K 6 2

♠ A 7 5 4
♡ A 10 5 3
◊ K 8
♣ J 5 4

Problem 6

Spades: Six missing – will be divided 3:3 or 4:2 either way.

Hearts: Same applies.

Diamonds: Seven missing – partner has led the suit and is therefore likely to have at least four; thus in practice, he will have four or five, leaving South with three or two respectively.

Clubs:	Seven missing – South could have five, four, three or two, leaving partner with two, three, four or five respectively.
Points:	We have 4 and the board 13, leaving 23 unaccounted for, of which South has at least 15. That leaves partner with a maximum of 8 and he has already shown the ◇J, thereby denying the ◇Q.
Tricks:	It is clear that, irrespective of who holds the ♡Q, South will make all the board's hearts and a further trick in his own hand if he started with four. In clubs, he has certainly two tricks; if he has the ♣K or ♣A he will have three; if he has both that will be four. In spades, much depends on who has the ♠J and on how many cards South has. In diamonds, he will have one trick if we play low on this trick, two if we go up with the ◇A.

In this case, there are too many possible combinations to consider individually but we can briefly say this much: first, regarding the two heart honors, if either or both are in partner's hand, they will be of little use under the board's A J 10 so they are best credited to South. That gives him (together with the ◇Q) 7 points. It is likely, therefore, that he will have two of the top outstanding black honors, leaving the other two for partner. Both those two cards will be well placed behind declarer and can be expected to make tricks. Where are the other three to come from? With the ♠Q well placed for declarer, there is little hope in that suit and so we must play the diamonds for maximum benefit – at least three tricks.

The difference between this hand and the last is that, this time, partner has some top cards and will be able to attack the board's diamond position from the right side. So we should play low on this trick and keep the ◇A poised over the ◇K so that it can be caught next round.

The deal:

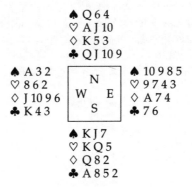

```
              ♠ Q 6 4
              ♡ A J 10
              ◇ K 5 3
              ♣ Q J 10 9
♠ A 3 2                      ♠ 10 9 8 5
♡ 8 6 2          N          ♡ 9 7 4 3
◇ J 10 9 6    W     E       ◇ A 7 4
♣ K 4 3          S          ♣ 7 6
              ♠ K J 7
              ♡ K Q 5
              ◇ Q 8 2
              ♣ A 8 5 2
```

As we shall learn in more detail in a moment, the card we shall actually play to the first trick will be the ◇ 7.

Problem 7

Spades: As we can see the ♠3 and ♠2, we know that partner's ♠4 is his lowest card and therefore that he started with four, leaving South with three.

Hearts: Six missing – will be split 3:3 or 4:2.

Diamonds: Six missing – similar argument applies, except that South could have five and partner one.

Clubs: Seven missing – South could have five, four, three, or two, leaving partner with two, three, four, or five respectively.

Points: We have 7 and the board 13, leaving 20 unaccounted for, of which South will have at least 15, leaving partner with, at most, 5.

Tricks: Partner cannot have both outstanding club honors so South will have at least three tricks, maybe more, in the suit. In diamonds, he will have at least two tricks if he has the ◇ Q and at least one (the finesse against her being right) if partner has it. Further tricks will depend on who has the ◇ 10 and on South's length in the suit. In hearts, South will take at least two tricks, even if he is missing both king and queen, and could take up to four if he has either honor and started with four cards. In spades, it is impossible for partner to have both ♠A and ♠Q (which would total 6 points) but he could have one. Considering the suit in isolation there are several positions we have to consider:

(a)
	♠ J 6 3	
♠ 10 x x x		♠ K 9 2
	♠ A Q x	

(b)
	♠ J 6 3	
♠ Q 10 x x		♠ K 9 2
	♠ A x x	

(c)
	♠ J 6 3	
♠ Q x x x		♠ K 9 2
	♠ A 10 x	

(d)
	♠ J 6 3	
♠ A x x x		♠ K 9 2
	♠ Q 10 x	

First of all, note that, if South has ♠ A Q 10, then he has three tricks, irrespective of our play, and will make the contract easily so we can forget about that one. Now, in (a), South will make three tricks if we rise with the ♠K, but only two if we play the ♠9. In (b), he will make two tricks if we rise with the ♠K, but only one if we play the ♠9. In (c), he will make two tricks, irrespective of our play and in (d), he will make one trick, again irrespective of our play. So we see that there is everything to gain and nothing to lose by playing the ♠9 now.

If partner has the ♠A, we will make three spade tricks and the ◇A, but no more as all four jacks are on the board and partner cannot have another honor card. If partner has no spade honor, then he will have a badly-placed red queen and again there will be little hope. The only hope is that we can take three spade tricks without the ♠A and the ♣K, with the full deal looking like this (opposite):

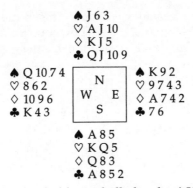

```
                    ♠ J 6 3
                    ♡ A J 10
                    ◇ K J 5
                    ♣ Q J 10 9
♠ Q 10 7 4      ┌───────┐      ♠ K 9 2
♡ 8 6 2         │   N   │      ♡ 9 7 4 3
◇ 10 9 6        │ W   E │      ◇ A 7 4 2
♣ K 4 3         │   S   │      ♣ 7 6
                └───────┘
                    ♠ A 8 5
                    ♡ K Q 5
                    ◇ Q 8 3
                    ♣ A 8 5 2
```

If the ♠9 is allowed to hold, we shall play the ♠K next, following the principle of playing high from the short hand first, to avoid blocking the suit.

Problem 8

The positions in spades remains unaltered but those in the other suits have changed considerably so we must reconsider the whole situation. In clubs, the ♣K is missing and, if it is in partner's hand, it will be badly placed and of no use unless the position is

```
                    ♣ A Q J 10 9
♣ K x x x                        ♣ 7 6
                    ♣ x x
```

In that case, the ♣K cannot be caught and if South wants four tricks in the suit, he will have to concede a trick to West. However, we note that he can take three tricks in the suit *without losing the lead* and that could well be sufficient. In hearts, any honors in partner's hand will be badly placed under the board's tenace and indeed partner will have to have two honors if he is to take any tricks in the suit at all, and, even then, he will only take one.

We still have our 7 points and the board 12, leaving 21 unaccounted for, of which South will have at least 15, leaving partner a maximum of 6. We have already established that any honors in clubs or hearts in partner's hand will be of little or no use, so we had best credit them to South. That gives him the ♣K and ♡ K Q J for 9 points so far, and we can start counting his tricks: five in clubs and three in hearts (and that assumes he only has three hearts – he may have four). This means that, if he has any sort of spade stop, the contract must be made and we must assume that the full deal is something like this:

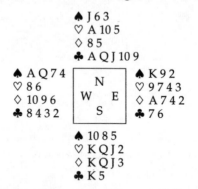

```
                    ♠ J 6 3
                    ♡ A 10 5
                    ◇ 8 5
                    ♣ A Q J 10 9
   ♠ A Q 7 4      ┌─────────┐     ♠ K 9 2
   ♡ 8 6          │    N    │     ♡ 9 7 4 3
   ◇ 10 9 6       │ W     E │     ◇ A 7 4 2
   ♣ 8 4 3 2      │    S    │     ♣ 7 6
                  └─────────┘
                    ♠ 10 8 5
                    ♡ K Q J 2
                    ◇ K Q J 3
                    ♣ K 5
```

Thus, instead of finessing against the board's ♠J (which is what we were effectively doing last time) we must rise with the ♠K and return the suit, hoping to take four tricks plus the ◇A.

Well, it was a lot of hard work but let us review what we have done. We defended a series of 3NT contracts in which the board was fairly strong. We went through each suit and the point-count to find the combination of cards, consistent with the bidding and lead, to give us a chance to take five tricks before the declarer could take nine.

Very often, as East is the first defender to play with two hands on view, he is the one to take the decision on how the defence will be conducted. In the set of problems we have just done, he had the choice of whether to win a trick with the highest card in the suit led or whether to play low, trying to win it cheaply.

However, on many occasions, notably where West has the most of the defenders' forces and either he or South wins the first trick, it will be West's duty to take command. In order to assist him in placing the unseen cards, it will be the duty of East to give as much relevant information as possible. We touched on this very briefly in the beginners' book and now we are going to review what we learnt there and apply it to situations which regularly occur when defending no-trump contracts.

I discussed defensive signalling in considerable depth in my book *Signal Success in Bridge* (published by Victor Gollancz in the Master Bridge Series, October 1989) and the student will do well to study at least the early chapters. For the purpose of this book, we shall confine ourselves to the three basic signals:

1 Attitude: Following with a high card encourages, while following with a low card discourages the suit led by partner.

2 Distribution: Following with high card indicates an even number (always remembering that there is no choice with a singleton), while following with a low card indicates an odd number.

3 Suit preference: When discarding, we shall use *natural* discards for the time being: a high card encourages, a low discourages.

Before we proceed with some examples, a word of advice is appropriate to all aspects of defensive signalling. Its purpose is to *give partner information* rather than to tell him what to play or not to play. An encouragement is not an order; a discouragement is not a ban. Very often, the partner of the signaller knows more about the hand than the signaller himself and is therefore better placed to decide the best line of defence. He should certainly take his partner's information into account but, as always, common sense must take precedence. Let us work our way through a few everyday examples.

Hand No. 54
Dealer East
E-W vulnerable

♠ A K 3
♡ Q 2
◇ J 6
♣ Q J 10 9 6 4

♠ J 10 9 7 4
♡ 8 6 4
◇ 8 4 3
♣ A 3

W	N	E	S
		Pass	1NT
Pass	3NT	end	

You lead the ♠J to the ♠A, partner's ♠2 and South's ♠5. The board's ♣Q is played to partner's ♣2, South's ♣5 and your ♣A. How do you continue?

Partner's ♠2 is clearly a discouraging card, indicating that, if we continue spades, he cannot help. However, before going any further, we must do our seven roll-calls – vital in any situation, as we have just learnt.

Spades: Five missing and South's bidding suggests he has two, three or four, leaving partner with three, two or one respectively – remember that, if he does indeed have a singleton, he is forced to play that card and it is, in terms of defensive signalling, of no meaning whatsoever.

Hearts: Eight missing and again South's bidding marks him with two, three or four, leaving partner with six, five or four respectively.

Diamonds: Eight missing and, as South has bid the suit, he will almost certainly have four or five (possibly six, but then his rebid will usually be 3♦ rather than 2NT), leaving partner with four or three respectively.

Clubs: Five missing – South will probably have two or three leaving partner with three or two respectively.

Points: We have 5 and the board 13, leaving 22 unaccounted for and South has indicated 15–17, leaving partner with 5–7.

Tricks: South clearly has two spade tricks on the board and partner's signal indicates that East does not hold the ♠Q and therefore that South has her. So South has three spade tricks. The ♠Q accounts for 2 of his points, leaving at least 13 unaccounted for. It is therefore obvious that, if that club suit comes in, he will make his contract easily, probably with over-tricks. Therefore the race is on and our first consideration is who has the ♣K. If it is South, we must take five tricks immediately otherwise he is waiting with five tricks in clubs, three spades and at least one red ace. (Partner, with 7 points, cannot have both.) If East has the ♣K, however, we have one trick's grace to set up our three tricks to add to the two top clubs.

Any diamond honors in partner's hand will be badly placed under the opener but a strong heart holding over the board's ♡Q may give us a chance. Continuing spades is out of the question with South having two more stops. We must shift to hearts, hoping that the deal is something like this:

```
              ♠ A K 3
              ♡ Q 2
              ◊ J 6
              ♣ Q J 10 9 6 4
♠ J 10 9 7 4  ┌─────────┐  ♠ 6 2
♡ 8 6 4       │    N    │  ♡ K J 10 7 5
◊ 8 4 3       │  W   E  │  ◊ 9 7 5 2
♣ A 3         │    S    │  ♣ K 2
              └─────────┘
              ♠ Q 8 5
              ♡ A 9 3
              ◊ A K Q 10
              ♣ 8 7 5
```

Note a number of instructive points on this hand:

1 There is nothing to be gained by our holding up the ♣A. South always has the spade entry and as you see, holding up would have led to an unholy crash of honors on the next round. Also note that, had South indeed been worried about entries, he could have won the first spade in hand leaving both the ♠A and ♠K on the board. In fact, he was more concerned about hiding the fact that he had the ♠Q and hoped that the defenders would continue the suit rather than shift to hearts.

2 We credited partner with useful heart honors rather than badly-placed diamond honors. We did this kind of exercise several times in the problems of the last section.

3 The first heart has to come from our side of the table as the ♡Q cannot be profitably attacked from partner's. Thus, if South had indeed won the first spade in hand and played a club, we would have had to rise with the ♣A to make the heart shift.

I make these points because I am keen that you should get into the habit of picking them up at the table. It's amazing what you can find out about the unseen cards by considering the reasons for what has *or has not* happened up to now.

Let us alter the hand slightly and try the exercise again.

Hand No. 55
Dealer South
Neither vulnerable

♠ A K
♡ J 5
◇ J 6 2
♣ Q J 10 9 6 4

♠ J 10 9 7 4
♡ 8 6 4
◇ 8 4 3
♣ A K

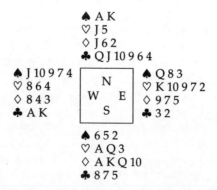

W	N	E	S
			1NT
Pass	3NT	end	

Once again, you lead the ♠J. The board plays the ♠K, partner the ♠8 and South the ♠2. Now comes the ♣5 to your ♣K, the board and East playing low. How do you continue?

This time, partner has shown a positive interest in spades and should have the ♠Q. If we continue the suit, we will establish three more tricks which we can cash when we get in with the ♣A.

The deal:

♠ A K
♡ J 5
◇ J 6 2
♣ Q J 10 9 6 4

♠ J 10 9 7 4   ♠ Q 8 3
♡ 8 6 4   ♡ K 10 9 7 2
◇ 8 4 3   ◇ 9 7 5
♣ A K   ♣ 3 2

♠ 6 5 2
♡ A Q 3
◇ A K Q 10
♣ 8 7 5

Note that South can only take eight tricks outside clubs. In practice, he will hope that our spades are 4–4 so that he loses only two tricks in the suit in addition to the two top clubs. If he tries to sneak a third heart trick by passing the ♡J, partner will cover to ensure that South only takes two tricks in the suit rather than the three available if he fails to do so. Let us juggle the cards around once more.

Hand No. 56
Dealer South
E-W vulnerable

```
                        ♠ A K
                        ♡ J 5
                        ◇ J 6 2
                        ♣ Q J 10 9 6 4

                ♠ Q J 10 7 4    ┌─────────┐
                ♡ 8 6 4         │    N    │
W    N    E    S  ◇ 8 4 3       │ W     E │
              1NT ♣ A K         │    S    │
Pass 3NT end                    └─────────┘
```

You lead the ♠Q to the board's ♠K, partner's ♠2 and South's ♠5. Again, South plays a club and you win. How do you continue?

The fact that partner has discouraged the spades is, on this occasion, purely of academic interest. As long as South cannot run nine tricks in the red suits, we have the contract beaten in our own hand. We simply play a low spade to knock out the ♠A and wait for the next club. The full deal is exactly as in the last example except that the spade layout has changed to:

```
                    ♠ A K
        ♠ Q J 10 7 4      ♠ 8 3 2
                    ♠ 9 6 5
```

This should give you the idea regarding encouragement/discouragement.

We now turn to situations in which declarer is trying to establish a long suit but may be short of entries. In this situation, defenders need to know how long to hold up their stop to avoid the whole suit coming in, while at the same time ensuring that declarer does not steal too many tricks before turning his attention elsewhere. Usually this will mean releasing the stop on the trick which exhausts the hand of the partner of the hand with the long suit. Let us start with a simple example.

Hand No. 57
Dealer North
Both vulnerable

♠ 7 6 4
♡ 8 5 3 2
◇ A
♣ Q J 10 9 6

W	N	E	S
	Pass	Pass	2NT
Pass	3♣	Pass	3♠
Pass	3NT	end	

```
        N        ♠ Q J 9 3
   W        E    ♡ J 10 9 7
        S        ◇ 6 3
                 ♣ A 4 3
```

After two passes, South opens 2NT which, as we learnt in the beginners' book, shows a balanced hand with 20–22 points. North tried a Stayman enquiry of 3♣, attempting to find a 4–4 heart fit, probably advisable, despite the poor hearts, because he has a singleton and possible entry difficulties to the clubs. When South denied a four-card heart suit, North settled for 3NT.

Partner finds the one lead to cause declarer trouble – the ◇ J. The board's ◇ A wins and declarer plays a low club from the board. As South must have at least two clubs for the 2NT opener, you play low and South's ♣K wins, partner following with the ♣2. South continues with the ♣7, partner plays the ♣5 and the board the ♣9. How do you defend and would it make any difference if partner had played the ♣8 on the first round and the ♣2 on the second?

It is clear that, with at least 20 points in the South hand, the contract will be easily made if those clubs can be cashed, so we must ensure that we take our ♣A on the round in which South becomes exhausted. Partner's discarding has indicated that, in the first case, he has an odd number of clubs and, in the second, an even number. However, before taking any decisions, it will do us no harm to do the roll-calls.

Spades: Six missing – on the auction, South has promised four, but it is in order for 2NT to be opened on a five-card major. Thus partner will have two or one respectively.

Hearts: Five missing – South denied a four-card suit with his 3♠ call but must have two or three for the 2NT opener, leaving partner with three or two respectively.

Diamonds: Ten missing – with South having announced a four-
            card spade suit, he is unlikely to have more than four
            diamonds in a 'balanced' hand; so he will have two,
            three or four, leaving partner with eight, seven or six
            respectively. It has to be said that eight-card suits are
            very rare.

Clubs: Five missing. In the first case, where partner showed
            an odd number, that must be three. (Had it been one,
            he would have shown out on the second round; had
            it been five, South would have shown out on the first
            round!) In the second case, it must be two. (Had it
            been four, South could not have played a second
            round.)

So, in the first case, we must win the second round and hope that
South can only gather seven tricks in the non-club suits in a deal
like this:

```
                    ♠ 7 6 4
                    ♡ 8 5 3 2
                    ◇ A
                    ♣ Q J 10 9 6
    ♠ K 10                          ♠ Q J 9 3
    ♡ 6 4           ┌─────────┐     ♡ J 10 9 7
    ◇ J 10 9 8 4 2  │    N    │     ◇ 6 3
    ♣ 8 5 2         │  W   E  │     ♣ A 4 3
                    │    S    │
                    └─────────┘
                    ♠ A 8 5 2
                    ♡ A K Q
                    ◇ K Q 7 5
                    ♣ K 7
```

South has one trick in spades, three in hearts, three in diamonds
and one in clubs, but no more.

In the second case, we shall win the third round and hope that South is slightly weaker:

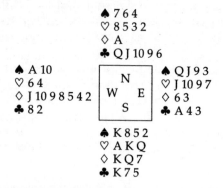

On winning the third club, we return a diamond, South winning. A low spade follows, won by West, who clears the diamonds and, although the ♠A drops 'on air' on the second round of the suit, West is ready to cash his remaining diamonds.

Again a word of warning is appropriate here – the same applies as with encouragement/discouragement. We have just looked at an example where the fate of the contract hinged on the correct handling of the club control. There are hands, however, where what is correct in the context of an individual suit may not be appropriate to the whole hand. That is why we do our seven roll-calls *every time*.

The third type of signalling refers to suit preference. Although, as we shall see later in more advanced studies, suit preferences can be indicated when following suit, we shall, for the time being, confine ourselves to situations where suit preference is given when discarding. Again, a high card shows encouragement, while a low card shows discouragement. In no-trump, it is usually better to discard low from suits not wanted as you will want to keep as many cards as possible in the suit where you hope to make tricks. However, in order to protect cards which may be stoppers in opponents' suits, it may not always be possible to discard from 'unwanted' suits.

Suit preference signals have a number of purposes. The two that we are going to consider are an indication of what partner is expected to lead and guiding partner on which cards to keep when declarer is running his long suit. This second consideration is badly neglected, and yet poor discarding is the cause of countless unmakeable contracts being thrown at declarer. This applies especially to high-level contracts, and therefore mistakes are heavily penalised. Let us work through some examples.

					♠ A K 7
Hand No. 58					♡ Q 6
Dealer South					◇ Q 4
Both vulnerable					♣ J 9 7 6 4 3

W	N	E	S	♠ J 10 9 8	
			1NT	♡ 7 4 2	N
Pass	3NT	end		◇ 9 6 3	W E
				♣ K Q 10	S

You lead the ♠J to the board's ♠K, partner's ♠2 and South's ♠3. South plays a low club, partner discarding the ♡8. South plays low and you win with the ♣10. How do you continue, and would it make any difference if partner had discarded the ◇8 instead?

In the first case, partner is expressing an interest in hearts; in the second, he prefers diamonds. However, let us first do our roll-calls if only to get used to the exercise as a matter of course.

Spades: Six missing – South must have two, three or four for his bid, leaving partner with four, three or two.

Hearts: Eight missing – again South must have two, three, or four, leaving partner with four, five or six.

Diamonds: Same applies, except that South could also have five, leaving partner with three.

Clubs: Four missing and the play so far has revealed South to have four and partner none.

Points: We have 6 and the board 12, leaving 22 unaccounted for, of which South has at least 15, leaving partner with at most 7.

Tricks: South has three top spades and there is clearly no future for us there. After losing two club tricks, he will make four tricks in that suit, to total seven, and will surely have two more in the red suits as he must have at least 8 points in them to join the board's queens.

It is thus clear that, if those clubs come in, the contract cannot be set; thus we must take five tricks first and the race is on. Partner has indicated that hearts will be our source of tricks so we must shift to one now.

The deal:

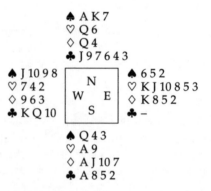

```
                    ♠ A K 7
                    ♡ Q 6
                    ◇ Q 4
                    ♣ J 9 7 6 4 3
        ♠ J 10 9 8    ┌─────────┐   ♠ 6 5 2
        ♡ 7 4 2       │    N    │   ♡ K J 10 8 5 3
        ◇ 9 6 3       │  W   E  │   ◇ K 8 5 2
        ♣ K Q 10      │    S    │   ♣ –
                      └─────────┘
                    ♠ Q 4 3
                    ♡ A 9
                    ◇ A J 10 7
                    ♣ A 8 5 2
```

Where partner discarded the ◇8, we must assume that the positions in the red suits above are exchanged and shift to a diamond instead.

Note the excellent discarding of partner. He could just as easily have asked for a heart by discarding a discouraging ◇2, spades and clubs obviously being out of the question. He could not, however, afford that discard as declarer can now pick up the ◇K and take four tricks in the suit to add to three spades and the aces of clubs and hearts. The ♠5 or ♠6 would have told us little. He could afford a high heart as he has enough tricks in that suit to set the contract.

Alter the unseen hands, however, to give:

```
                    ♠ A K 7
                    ♡ Q 6
                    ◇ Q 4
                    ♣ J 9 7 6 4 3
      ♠ J 10 9 8                    ♠ 6 5 2
      ♡ 7 4 2         N             ♡ K J 10 9
      ◇ 9 6 3     W       E         ◇ K 10 8 7 5 2
      ♣ K Q 10        S             ♣ –
                    ♠ Q 4 3
                    ♡ A 8 5 3
                    ◇ A J
                    ♣ A 8 5 2
```

and now East will discard the ◇2 as he cannot afford a heart. We need three heart tricks to add to our two clubs.

Now let us try an exercise in discarding on a long suit.

Hand No. 59
Dealer East
Both vulnerable

```
                                    ♠ 9 8 7
                                    ♡ K 8 5
                                    ◇ A J
                                    ♣ K J 9 6 4
                                    ♠ J 6 5 2
                                    ♡ J 7 4 2        N
                                    ◇ 10 9 8     W       E
                                    ♣ 8 5            S
```

W	N	E	S
		Pass	2NT
Pass	6NT	end	

You lead the ◇10. South tries the ◇J but partner produces the ◇K and returns the ◇4 (his original fourth highest) and South's ◇Q and the board's ◇A crash to the second trick. South now runs five rounds of clubs, partner following twice and discarding the ♠10 and ♠4 on the third and fourth rounds and a diamond on the fifth. Declarer discards the ♡3 on the fifth round. That is seven tricks – which six cards do you keep?

Let us do our seven roll-calls:

Spades: Partner has clearly abandoned the suit and has given his distribution at the same time. Clearly he started with a doubleton, leaving South holding ♠ A K Q x.

Hearts: Six missing, one has been discarded by South, leaving five. The count will be worked out from those in the other three suits.

Diamonds: This is an 'open book' – partner started with ◊ K x x x x x and South with ◊ Q x, which were played to the first two tricks.

Clubs: This again is an open book: South started with ♣ A Q 10 x and partner with ♣ x x.

Points: We have 2 and the board 12, leaving 26 unaccounted for, of which South promised 20–22, leaving partner with 4–6, and he has already shown the ◊ K.

Tricks: South has already made five clubs and a diamond and cannot be denied three spades and the two top hearts. All therefore hangs on the ♡ Q and partner must now be holding it, this being the original deal:

```
              ♠ 9 8 7
              ♡ K 8 5
              ◊ A J
              ♣ K J 9 6 4
♠ J 6 5 2    ┌───────────┐    ♠ 10 4
♡ J 7 4 2    │     N     │    ♡ Q 9 6
◊ 10 9 8     │  W     E  │    ◊ K 7 5 4 3 2
♣ 8 5        │     S     │    ♣ 7 3
              └───────────┘
              ♠ A K Q 3
              ♡ A 10 3
              ◊ Q 6
              ♣ A Q 10 2
```

Clearly we must keep our spades, the position now being:

```
              ♠ 9 8 7
              ♡ K 8 5
              ◊ –
              ♣ –
♠ J 6 5 2    ┌───────────┐    ♠ –
♡ J 7       │     N     │    ♡ Q 9 6
◊ –          │  W     E  │    ◊ 7 5 3
♣ –          │     S     │    ♣ –
              └───────────┘
              ♠ A K Q 3
              ♡ A 10
              ◊ –
              ♣ –
```

We could have kept the ♡J singleton and the ◇10 with the spades but with the ◇10 having no chance to score, there are positions in which it pays to give partner's heart holding as much support as possible. For example, if the position in that suit came down to:

$$♡ K 8 5$$
$$♡ J \qquad\qquad ♡ Q 9 6$$
$$♡ A 10 3$$

South could make the contract by cashing the ♡K and taking a finesse against partner's ♡Q. But if we hold on to two hearts to keep it to:

$$♡ K 8 5$$
$$♡ J 7 \qquad\qquad ♡ Q 9 6$$
$$♡ A 10 3$$

declarer has no chance.

I therefore want you to get into the habit of discarding cards that can never be of any use and keep potentially helpful cards. Note the importance of partner's spade discards, putting you in the picture as early as possible. Try this game contract:

Hand No. 60
Dealer East
Neither vulnerable

```
                        ♠ K Q 9 8
                        ♡ A 8
                        ◇ A 9 4 3
                        ♣ 9 6 4
                        ♠ 5 2
                        ♡ J 10 7 5       N
                        ◇ K 6 5      W       E
                        ♣ K Q 5 2        S
```

W	N	E	S
		Pass	1♣
Pass	1◇	Pass	1♡
Pass	1♠	Pass	1NT
Pass	3NT	end	

North's 1♠ call was fourth-suit-forcing although South was allowed to support if he had four cards in the suit, this 1NT call suggested a balanced hand of about 12–14 points. You lead the ♣2 and strike gold when partner produces the ♣A and returns the suit. South follows with ♣J 10 8 and on your fourth round, the board discards a diamond, partner the ♡2 and South the ◇2.

You exit with a spade and South, who started with ♠ A J 3, plays four rounds, partner following while declarer discards the ◇ 8 on the fourth round. You have to find two discards from ♡ J 10 7 5 and ◇ K 6 5. What are they and would it have made any difference if South had discarded a heart on the fourth spade? Let us do our roll-calls.

Spades: Open book – South started with ♠ A J x and partner ♠ 10 x x x.

Hearts: Partner has discarded the ♡2, suggesting no interest. The bidding marks South with four cards which he still holds; partner still has two.

Diamonds: Six missing, South has already discarded two.

Clubs: Open book – the other three players had three each.

We know that South started with 3433, so he has one diamond left.

Points: We had 9 and the board 13, leaving 18 unaccounted for of which South had 12–14. He has shown 6 in the black suits, leaving 6–8 in the reds. But he only has one diamond card left. Even if that is the ◇Q, he must have both outstanding heart honors and the full deal must have been:

```
              ♠ K Q 9 8
              ♡ A 8
              ◇ A 9 4 3
              ♣ 9 6 4
  ♠ 5 2                        ♠ 10 7 6 4
  ♡ J 10 7 5      N            ♡ 4 3 2
  ◇ K 6 5      W     E         ◇ J 10 7
  ♣ K Q 5 2       S            ♣ A 7 3
              ♠ A J 3
              ♡ K Q 9 6
              ◇ Q 8 2
              ♣ J 10 8
```

and the position is now (with our hand still to play):

```
              ♠ —
              ♡ A 8
              ◇ A 9 4
              ♣ —
  ♠ —                      ♠ —
  ♡ J 10 7 5    ┌─────┐    ♡ 4 3
  ◇ K 6         │  N  │    ◇ J 10 7
  ♣ —         W │     │ E  ♣ —
                │  S  │
                └─────┘
              ♠ —
              ♡ K Q 9 6
              ◇ Q
              ♣ —
```

Clearly we must hang on to the hearts, even if it means blanking the ◇K. Partner will look after the diamonds after we have covered the ◇Q. Had South discarded a heart on the last spade, we can abandon our heart stop and hang on to two diamonds. What we are doing is referred to as *keeping parity*, an important principle in discarding. The basic guide is that, if it is clear that a certain number of rounds of a particular suit are going to be played, keep the required number of cards. This can easily apply even if they are losers. Try this example.

Hand No. 61
Dealer East
N-S vulnerable

```
              ♠ K J 10
              ♡ K Q 6
              ◇ Q 9 8
              ♣ K Q 9 4
                          ┌─────┐  ♠ 7 6 4
                          │  N  │  ♡ 4 2
                        W │     │ E  ◇ 10 7 6 5 3
                          │  S  │  ♣ 10 6 2
                          └─────┘
```

W	N	E	S
		Pass	2NT
Pass	5NT	Pass	7NT
end			

As we learnt in the beginners' book, after South showed 20–22, North's 5NT was forcing and quantitative. South is expected to bid 6NT with a minimum, or 7NT with a maximum. He also has the option to bid a four-card suit at the six-level with a view to a 4–4 fit, while keeping the option of 6NT open.

Partner leads the ♡10. Now with a hand like East's, it is very easy to lose interest in the proceedings but, with a vulnerable grand slam at stake (worth $220 + 1500 + 700$ rubber bonus, against 100 your way if you set it) it is well worthwhile making an extra special effort to work out the hand. The board wins the first trick and South reels off four rounds of clubs (having started with ♣ A J 7 3 himself) and two further rounds of hearts (having started with ♡ A J 5 himself). Partner discards two hearts on the third and fourth round of clubs and follows to all the hearts. What are your two discards?

It appears not to matter because nothing in your hand has any chance of making a trick, but this is the very type of position where defenders continually let their partners down. Let us do our roll-calls as usual:

Spades: Seven missing – likely to be divided 4:3, one way or the other.

Hearts: Open book – partner started with five low cards and declarer as stated above.

Diamonds: Five missing – we already know that South started with three hearts and four clubs and he must have at least two spades. So he has four, three or two diamonds, leaving partner with one, two or three.

Clubs: Open book as stated above.

Points: We have none and the board has 16, leaving 24 unaccounted for. South's bidding promises 21–22, leaving partner with 2–3. If partner has a king, that can only be in diamonds (the others are on the board). In that case, the finesse is wrong and declarer has no chance, irrespective of our defence. If he has only a queen, that would be the ♠Q (again the others are all on the board). This is the position we have to consider and we now have to place the ◇J. If South has it, we shall have to assume that he is 3334 otherwise, if he is 2344, he has thirteen tricks (two spades, three hearts, four diamonds, four clubs). If he doesn't, then with 21 points only, he should bid 6♣ with a 2344 shape, after which 7♣ is made comfortably. The critical case, therefore, arises when he is 3334 with the ◇J and the deal is:

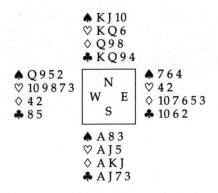

```
              ♠ K J 10
              ♡ K Q 6
              ◇ Q 9 8
              ♣ K Q 9 4
♠ Q 9 5 2               ♠ 7 6 4
♡ 10 9 8 7 3    N      ♡ 4 2
◇ 4 2        W   E     ◇ 10 7 6 5 3
♣ 8 5           S      ♣ 10 6 2
              ♠ A 8 3
              ♡ A J 5
              ◇ A K J
              ♣ A J 7 3
```

So we have had three rounds of hearts and four rounds of clubs and there are three rounds of diamonds and three of spades still to come with the contract hanging on whether South can guess the position of the ♠Q. For that reason, it is unwise for us to discard spades early giving the impression that we have nothing in the suit. It is more sensible to discard diamonds, leaving South to guess who is guarding the ♠Q.

It has all been very hard work, but I hope I have satisfied you of two things. First, if only you are prepared to do your roll-calls (and note how accurate you can be late in the play) you can make defence a much easier task. Second, playing by general rules is hopeless if you want to reach even a modest standard.

Try the following examples against the stop-watch, aiming for under two minutes, but noting that accuracy is our prime concern.

Problem 1
Hand No. 62
Dealer East
Neither vulnerable

```
                        ♠ 6 5
                        ♡ 7 3
                        ◇ Q J 10 9 3
                        ♣ A K 6 2
                        ♠ J 10 9 8 3
                        ♡ A Q 6 5      N
                        ◇ A         W      E
                        ♣ 8 5 3        S
```

W	N	E	S
		Pass	1NT
Pass	3NT	end	

You lead the ♠J to the board's ♠5, partner's ♠2 and South's ♠K. The ◇K goes to the ◇A, the board's ◇3 and partner's ◇2. How do you continue?

Problem 2
Hand No. 63
Dealer South
E-W vulnerable

♠ K 6 5
♡ K J 2
◇ K 3 2
♣ A Q 6 2

W	N	E	S
			1NT
Pass	3NT	end	

```
        N          ♠ A J 9 2
   W         E     ♡ A 10 4
        S          ◇ 10 9 8 5
                   ♣ 7 3
```

Partner leads the ♠7 and the board plays low. How do you defend?

Problem 3
Hand No. 64
Dealer South
E-W vulnerable

♠ 5
♡ K 10 4 2
◇ A Q J 8 5
♣ A 6 4

W	N	E	S
			1♣
Pass	1◇	Pass	1NT
Pass	3NT	end	

```
        N          ♠ K 8 6 3
   W         E     ♡ J 8 6 5
        S          ◇ K 3
                   ♣ Q 8 7
```

Partner leads the ♠4 to the ♠5, your ♠K and South's ♠A. He passes the ◇10 to your ◇K and you return your original fourth-highest spade, the ♠3. This goes to South's ♠9 and partner's ♠10, the board discarding the ♣4. Partner now leads the ♠Q, the board discarding a low heart. How do you defend?

Problem 4
Hand No. 65
Dealer North
E-W vulnerable

♠ Q 7
♡ A Q J 10
◇ 5 3
♣ K J 10 5 4

```
                   ♠ J 10 9 2
                   ♡ 4 3 2          N
                   ◇ A Q 10 7 6   W     E
                   ♣ A             S
```

W	N	E	S
	1♣	Pass	1◇
Pass	1♡	Pass	3NT
end			

You lead the ♠J to the ♠Q, partner's ♠3 and South's ♠8. The ♣4 now goes to partner's ♣5, South's ♣Q and your ♣A. How do you continue?

Problem 5
Hand No. 66
Dealer West
N-S vulnerable

♠ 7 5 4
♡ 8 2
◊ 7 6 3
♣ A J 10 9 6

W	N	E	S
Pass	Pass	Pass	2NT
Pass	3NT	end	

```
              ♠ 6 3
        N     ♡ J 10 9 7 5
   W       E  ◊ J 9 2
        S     ♣ K 8 4
```

Partner leads the ♠Q to the ♠4, your ♠3 and South's ♠K. On South's ♣Q, partner plays the ♣2 and the board plays low. How do you defend, and would it make any difference if partner played the ♣7 instead?

Problem 6
Hand No. 67
Dealer South
N-S vulnerable

♠ A 9 7
♡ K Q 8
◊ J 7 6
♣ J 10 9 6

W	N	E	S
			1NT
2♡	3NT	end	

```
        ♠ 5 4
        ♡ J 10 9 7 6 5      N
        ◊ A 5 4        W       E
        ♣ A Q              S
```

You lead the ♡J to the board's ♡Q and partner discards the ♠8, South following with the ♡2. On the board's ♣J, partner plays the ♣2, South the ♣5 and your ♣Q wins. How do you continue?

Problem 7
Hand No. 68
Dealer South
N-S vulnerable

♠ A 9
♡ K Q 8
◊ 7 6 4 3
♣ J 10 9 6

W	N	E	S
			1NT
2♡	3NT	end	

```
        ♠ 7 5 4
        ♡ J 10 9 6 5 3      N
        ◊ A 5         W       E
        ♣ A Q              S
```

You lead the ♡J to the board's ♡Q and partner discards the ♠8, South following with the ♡2. On the board's ♣J, partner plays the ♣2, South the ♣5 and your ♣Q wins. How do you continue?

Problem 8
Hand No. 69
Dealer East
Both vulnerable

♠ Q 6 2
♡ J 4
◇ K Q 10 7 3
♣ Q J 8

```
                              N          ♠ A 7 3
                         W         E     ♡ 10 8 7 2
                              S          ◇ 8 4 2
                                         ♣ K 4 3
```

W	N	E	S
		Pass	1NT
Pass	3NT	end	

Partner leads the ♠5 and the board plays the ♠6. How do you defend?

Solutions

Problem 1

Spades: Six missing – likely to split 3:3 or 4:2 one way or the other.

Hearts: Seven missing – South can have two, three or four, leaving partner with five, four or three respectively.

Diamonds: Seven missing – South can have two, three, four or five, leaving partner with five, four three or two respectively.

Clubs: Six missing – South can have two, three, four or five, leaving partner with four, three, two or one respectively.

Points: We have 11 and the board 10, leaving 19 unaccounted for, of which South has promised 15-17, leaving partner with 2-4.

Tricks: Partner's lack of interest in spades marks South with the ♠A and ♠Q and he has shown the ♠K and ◇K. That is 12 points and we can see that there are four diamond tricks waiting to add to the three top spades and two top clubs, totalling nine. That means we must take four more tricks now or never. Giving partner honors in clubs is no good and our only hope is in hearts. He will need at least the ♡K and we must hope for a deal something like the following:

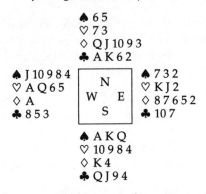

```
                    ♠ 6 5
                    ♡ 7 3
                    ◇ Q J 10 9 3
                    ♣ A K 6 2
   ♠ J 10 9 8 4                    ♠ 7 3 2
   ♡ A Q 6 5      ┌─────┐          ♡ K J 2
   ◇ A           │  N  │          ◇ 8 7 6 5 2
   ♣ 8 5 3       │W   E│          ♣ 10 7
                  │  S  │
                  └─────┘
                    ♠ A K Q
                    ♡ 10 9 8 4
                    ◇ K 4
                    ♣ Q J 9 4
```

If partner has four or more hearts, it does not matter which heart
we play but, where he has only three, we must be careful not to
block the suit by observing the guide of playing high from the
short hand first. Thus we must start with a low heart.

Problem 2

Spades: Six missing – partner, having led them, is likely to
           have four, leaving South with two.

Hearts: Seven missing – likely to split 4:3 one way or the
           other.

Diamonds: Six missing – South can have two, three, four or five,
           leaving partner with four, three, two or one
           respectively.

Clubs: Seven missing – South can have two, three, four or
           five, leaving partner with five, four, three or two
           respectively.

Points: We have 9 and the board 13, leaving 18 unaccounted
           for, of which South has 15–17, leaving partner with
           1–3.

Tricks: Much will depend on how little partner has. The ♣K
           and ♡Q would both be badly placed under the
           board so they are best credited to South, giving him
           at least two heart tricks and three clubs. With partner
           limited to 3 points, South must have the ◇A, giving
           him at least two diamond tricks to total seven so far
           and it is clear that we are not going to come near to
           five tricks unless partner has the ♠Q. In fact, if we

use the rule of eleven, we can work out his exact holding. 11 − 7 = 4, and we can see the ♠A, ♠K, ♠J and ♠9. In other words, South cannot beat the ♠7.

The deal:

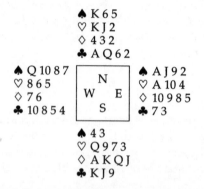

```
                    ♠ K 6 5
                    ♡ K J 2
                    ◇ 4 3 2
                    ♣ A Q 6 2
      ♠ Q 10 8 7                      ♠ A J 9 2
      ♡ 8 6 5          N              ♡ A 10 4
      ◇ 7 6        W       E          ◇ 10 9 8 5
      ♣ 10 8 5 4       S              ♣ 7 3
                    ♠ 4 3
                    ♡ Q 9 7 3
                    ◇ A K Q J
                    ♣ K J 9
```

Thus all we need do is to play low to this trick, allowing the ♠7 to hold, after which a further spade will assure us of four tricks in the suit to add to the ♡A. No, don't worry that partner will think our ♠2 is a discouraging card. He will notice that his ♠7 has won the trick and ask himself why!

Problem 3

Spades: Open book: South failed to produce a four-card major over the 1◇ call so he must have two or three. Partner led the ♠4 and we have the ♠3, so the only card lower than the ♠4 outstanding is the ♠2. Therefore partner cannot have more than five, leaving South with three.

Hearts: Five missing – again South, having denied a four-card major, must have two or three, leaving partner with three or two respectively.

Diamonds: Six missing – South can have two, three, four or five, leaving partner with four, three, two or one respectively.

Clubs: Seven missing – South can have three, four or five, leaving partner with four, three or two respectively.

Points: We have 9 and the board 14, leaving 17 unaccounted for, of which South has 12–14, leaving partner with 3–5.

Tricks: South has already taken the ♠A and clearly has four diamond tricks to come. Partner has already shown the ♠Q and cannot have more than 3 more points. If they are represented by the ♣K, South will have the ♡A and ♡Q to give three heart tricks and the ♣A to total nine. And, if South has the ♣K, he has ace and king in both hearts and clubs to add to the other five tricks, again totalling nine.

So it is clear that we must take five tricks now or never and that can only be achieved with four spades in addition to the ◊K. The ♠Q will drop South's remaining spade and note that must be the ♠J. Were it not, partner would have started with ♠ Q J 10 x x and would have led the ♠Q. If we play low to this trick, our ♠8 will remain the highest outstanding spade and will win the next round, while partner still has his fifth spade. We will never be able to get partner in again and South will escape with the loss of only three spades and the ◊K.

The deal:

```
                    ♠ 5
                    ♡ K 10 4 2
                    ◊ A Q J 8 5
                    ♣ A 6 4
♠ Q 10 7 4 2    ┌─────────┐    ♠ K 8 6 3
♡ Q 3          │    N    │    ♡ J 8 6 5
◊ 7 6 2        │  W   E  │    ◊ K 3
♣ J 10 3       │    S    │    ♣ Q 8 7
                └─────────┘
                    ♠ A J 9
                    ♡ A 9 7
                    ◊ 10 9 4
                    ♣ K 9 5 2
```

Accordingly, we must throw the ♠8 under the ♠Q now so that the ♠7 on the next round will beat our ♠6, *leaving partner on lead*. He can now cash the ♠2 for the setting trick.

Problem 4

Spades: Seven missing – the likely distributions are slightly
            debatable here but it is clear from partner's dis-
            couragement that South has both ♠A and ♠K, plus
            the ♠8 he has shown. That is three and it is most
            unlikely that he has five or more on this auction. If he
            has four, then he might well have bid them in case
            his partner started with 4414, in which case 4♠ is
            likely to be a better contract than 3NT. Many players,
            however, prefer to bid 3NT direct in these situations.
            Thus all we can say at the moment is that South has
            three or four, leaving partner with four or three
            respectively.

Hearts: Six missing – South failed to support his partner so
            he will not have as many as four. A void is most
            unlikely on this auction, so he will have three, two or
            one, leaving partner with three, four or five
            respectively.

Diamonds: Six missing – South, having bid them, will have at
            least four and could have five or six, leaving partner
            with two, one or a void.

Clubs: Seven missing: South has already shown one and
            could have up to four; with five or more, it is likely
            that he would have investigated a possible club slam;
            partner is thus left with six, five, four or three.

Points: We have 11 and the board 13, leaving 16 unac-
            counted for, and as South has insisted on game, he
            should have at least 13, leaving partner with 3 at the
            most, and he could be down to nothing.

Tricks: With the ♣A knocked out, South has four club tricks
            waiting and the spade play at trick one gives him
            three tricks in that suit. The ♡A on the board brings
            the total up to eight and if South has the ♡K, he has
            plenty more and in that event, we must set the
            contract now or never. Alternatively, if partner has
            the ♡K, South will have to knock it out to establish
            the rest of his hearts. Now he can push a diamond
            through South (now marked with at least ◇ K J x x)

and we can take two diamond tricks but no more. Our total will comprise those two diamonds, the ♣A and ♡K – not enough. Thus we will have to give the ♡K to South and the ◊K to partner and assume that the deal is something like this:

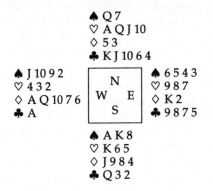

Now the lead of a low diamond to partner's ◊K and a return of the suit will net five tricks and set the contract by two tricks.

Allow me a couple of comments on this hand. First, notice the auction. The vast majority of players would bid 3NT direct over 1♣ on this hand and indeed there is much to be said for it. However, give partner a holding like ♡ Q x and we shall want the hand played from his side, and if he is desperately short of hearts, a suit game may be preferable. Second, and far more important, this hand is another illustration of the hopelessness of playing to general rules. Beginners are taught not to lead away from holdings like A Q, least of all round to suits bid under them. Here, by the use of roll-calls, we discovered that this was the only hope of setting the contract.

Problem 5

Spades: Eight missing – partner, having led them, is likely to have at least four while South, having opened 2NT, will have at least two. Thus South has two, three or four, leaving partner with six, five or four respectively.

Hearts: Six missing – South can have two, three, four or five, leaving partner with four, three, two or one respectively.

Diamonds: Seven missing – South can have two, three, four or five, leaving partner with five, four, three, or two respectively.

Clubs: Five missing – partner's low card indicates an odd number, which could be one or three, leaving South with four or two respectively.

Points: We have 5 and the board 5, leaving 30 unaccounted for, of which South has promised 20–22, leaving partner with 8–10. We already know that they include the ♠ Q J, leaving 5–7 still outstanding.

Tricks: We do not know exact details at the moment but we do know that South has at least 15 points outside his announced ♠K and ♣Q and thus it is fairly certain that, if that club suit comes in for four tricks, the contract will be made in some comfort. We must therefore assume that partner's odd number of clubs is actually three and cut the club suit out by ducking. South may go up with the ♣A next time to ensure two tricks in the suit but is, in practice, likely to repeat the finesse and be held to one trick only.

The deal:
```
                    ♠ 7 5 4
                    ♡ 8 2
                    ◇ 7 6 3
                    ♣ A J 10 9 6
    ♠ Q J 10 9 2                      ♠ 6 3
    ♡ 4 3           ┌─────────┐       ♡ J 10 9 7 5
    ◇ K Q 5         │    N    │       ◇ J 9 2
    ♣ 7 5 2      W  │       E │       ♣ K 8 4
                    │    S    │
                    └─────────┘
                    ♠ A K 8
                    ♡ A K Q 6
                    ◇ A 10 8 4
                    ♣ Q 3
```

Here, despite the maximum point-count, South has only six tricks outside clubs and cannot make the contract even if he guesses correctly to rise with the ♣A on the second round. In practice, he will go down two.

If partner, however, indicates an even club holding, then it is a
different story. This can only be a doubleton as South must have
at least two. That leaves South with three and we must now
accept that the suit cannot be stopped. In this situation, we have
to play for miracles and try to set the contract immediately. There
is nothing to be gained by ducking the first club because, if South
wants to bring in the suit, he can always duck the second round.
Indeed, it could be fatal to do so when the full deal turns out to
be:

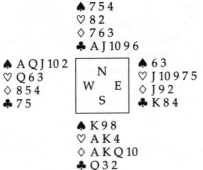

```
                  ♠ 7 5 4
                  ♡ 8 2
                  ◇ 7 6 3
                  ♣ A J 10 9 6
  ♠ A Q J 10 2   ┌─────────┐   ♠ 6 3
  ♡ Q 6 3        │    N    │   ♡ J 10 9 7 5
  ◇ 8 5 4        │  W   E  │   ◇ J 9 2
  ♣ 7 5          │    S    │   ♣ K 8 4
                 └─────────┘
                  ♠ K 9 8
                  ♡ A K 4
                  ◇ A K Q 10
                  ♣ Q 3 2
```

It will now cost South nothing to test the diamonds before
attempting a second round of clubs and, when they break
favorably, he can run home for nine top tricks by rising with the
♣A on the second round of the suit.

Problem 6

Partner's discard is a strong encouragement for us to shift to
spades but before doing so, it will pay to do our seven roll-calls
as usual, if only to satisfy ourselves that such a defence will be
effective.

Spades: Eight missing – South will have two, three or four,
            leaving partner with six, five or four respectively.

Hearts: Open book – partner has shown out, leaving South
            with ♡ A 4 3 2.

Diamonds: Seven missing – South can have two, three, four or
            five leaving partner with six, five, four or three
            respectively.

Clubs: Same applies.

Points: We have 11 and the board 11, leaving 18 unac-
             counted for, of which South will have 15–17, leaving
             partner with 1–3 and what little he has is likely to be
             in spades. Considering this point in more detail, even
             if we give him a maximum 3 points, that would have
             to be the ♠Q and ♠J, leaving South with the ♠K.
             Thus South has two stops in the suit and we can
             never take more than one trick in it. Add our two
             club tricks and the ◇A gives only four in total – not
             enough.

Tricks: We have already done most of the calculation. South
             has at least two spade tricks, three hearts and, as we
             have credited him with the ◇K Q and ♣K, two
             diamonds and two clubs to total nine. However, in
             order to establish these tricks, he will have to lose the
             lead twice more and that gives us time to establish
             our heart suit. We can see that the ♡8 is dropping on
             the third round so a continuation of hearts will set
             the contract – actually by two tricks.

The deal:

                              ♠ A 9 7
                              ♡ K Q 8
                              ◇ J 7 6
                              ♣ J 10 9 6

        ♠ 5 4   ♠ Q J 10 8 6 2
        ♡ J 10 9 7 6 5   ┌─────────┐   ♡ –
        ◇ A 5 4   │   N   │   ◇ 10 9 8 2
        ♣ A Q   │ W   E │   ♣ 4 3 2
                            │   S   │
                             └─────────┘
                              ♠ K 3
                              ♡ A 4 3 2
                              ◇ K Q 3
                              ♣ K 8 7 5

Problem 7

This is remarkably similar to the previous problem but just the
exchanging of a few small cards has altered the picture completely. In particular, the ♡7 has been given to South, who now
has a fourth stop in the suit, ruling out its establishment.
However, the ♠7 is now in our hand and, with the board's
holding weakened, the spades have a chance if the full deal is:

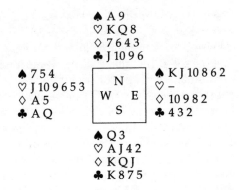

♠ A 9
♥ K Q 8
♦ 7 6 4 3
♣ J 10 9 6

♠ 7 5 4
♥ J 10 9 6 5 3
♦ A 5
♣ A Q

♠ K J 10 8 6 2
♥ –
♦ 10 9 8 2
♣ 4 3 2

♠ Q 3
♥ A J 4 2
♦ K Q J
♣ K 8 7 5

Thus, on this occasion, we must respect partner's signal and shift to a spade – the reward, this time, being a three-trick set.

Problem 8

Spades: Seven missing – partner, having led them, will have at least four, confirmed by the fact that South did not bid them. However, South will have at least two, possibly three, leaving partner with five or four respectively.

Hearts: Seven missing – South will have two or three, leaving partner with five or four respectively.

Diamonds: Five missing – South could have two, three or four, leaving partner with three, two or one respectively.

Clubs: Seven missing – South having bid 1NT, will have two, three, four or five, leaving partner with five, four, three or two respectively.

Points: We have 7 and the board 11, leaving 22 unaccounted for, of which South has promised 15–17 with his rebid. That leaves partner with 5–7.

Tricks: Much depends on the positions of the two minor aces. Partner, restricted to 7 points, cannot have both. If South has both, then, with our ♣K badly placed and the diamonds breaking favorably, the contract will be easily made as we cannot prevent at least one spade stopper. We shall thus have to work on two alternative assumptions. First, let us give South the

◇ A and partner the ♣A. That leaves at most 3 more points for partner. If he has the ♠K, South has five diamond tricks, one spade and three top hearts for nine tricks. If it is the ♡K, then South will have five diamonds, two spades and two hearts unless his hearts are exactly ♡ A Q doubleton, in which case a heart shift will beat him. However, that implies that partner started with ♡ K x x x x, which he surely would have led in preference to a poor spade suit.

So that looks hopeless and we must consider the possibility of partner holding the ◇ A and South the ♣A. Now our ♣K can be caught, but South will have to get to the board to take the finesse and that may give us a chance to set up five tricks before he can get both the clubs and diamonds going. Those five tricks will have to be the ◇ A and four spades, implying that partner started with a five-card suit including the ♠K. Let us reconstruct the deal:

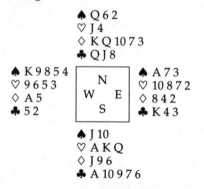

Thus, if we clear the spades and get in with the ◇ A, we can cash five tricks. There is, however, a problem in how to clear the spades. We could play ♠A, ♠K, and another round and the long hand has the diamond entry. Alternatively, we could win the first round and duck the second. Or we could duck the first round. All three methods work in the context of the spade suit considered in isolation but only one is correct in the context of the whole hand. We spent a considerable time in the beginners' book discussing the importance of not only which side won a trick but which individual player, and this is an excellent illustration. Because of the precarious position of our ♣K, we must insist that North be kept off play, at least as long as possible, and that, if a spade trick must be lost (and that cannot be avoided) it will be lost to South. To ensure this, we play our ♠7 on the board's ♠6, forcing South to overtake. Now if South tries to reach the board in diamonds (there is obviously no other way), partner will rise with the ◇A (he can see that there is nothing to be gained by ducking) and then continue with a low spade to our ♠A, after which we can cash three more to set the contract.

In the next chapter we are going to turn to trump contracts. These will obviously require a broader dicussion as there are many more techniques involved. Whereas, with a no-trump contract, it is usually a question of a straight race with a limited number of obstacles, the appearance of a trump suit usually proves an insurmountable obstacle and the defenders have to resort to other methods of taking their tricks including, of course, the use of their own trumps.

One thing, however, remains unchanged – the need to recon-struct the unseen hands and anticipate our own and enemy plans well in advance. Once the bidding is over, we should have some idea of how declarer intends to set up his tricks and ensure that we avoid enjoying ours. With the trump suit available as stoppers, he may be able to:

1 Discard losers on high cards in other suits before or after trumps are pulled.

2 Arrange to ruff them (usually on the board) before or after trumps are pulled.

3 Set up a long side-suit (usually on the board), if necessary ruffing losers in that suit (in hand) and subsequently discard his losers on it. (2 and 3 can be done the other way round, by reversing the dummy.)

4 Ruff losers in both hands (crossruff), usually without pulling trumps but sometimes after pulling all or a limited number of rounds of trumps.

SECTION 4:

Defence against Trump Contracts

When considering no-trump contracts, it was emphasized that, on the vast majority of occasions (although there are exceptions), the play will usually involve a race between the declarer and defenders to see who can set up their long suit(s) first.

With trumps around, it is more likely that the defenders will be able to take tricks in suits in which they are *short*. Long suits are likely to give little joy as declarer will run out early and be able to ruff any subsequent rounds. Thus the defenders will achieve little unless, as we shall see later, they can cause declarer to run embarrassingly short of trumps, after which he may lose control of the hand.

Let us first consider the opening lead. Before selecting it, we have to ask ourselves a number of questions:

1 Was the final contract reached confidently or did they obviously 'stretch' to get there? As discussed earlier, in the former case, desperate measures may be justified (at the worst, they will cost unnecessary but cheap overtricks). In the latter case, passive defence is called for, the emphasis being on avoiding giving anything away unnecessarily, leaving declarer to do all the work for himself.

2 What is the likely trump situation? Will declarer have plenty available, or is it a minimum 4–3 or 5–2 fit? How are trumps breaking for him? If they are breaking evenly, again desperate measures may be justified and vice versa; this point has to be weighed up against the considerations in 1 above.

3 How is declarer likely to set about making his tricks? The various possibilities were set out a couple of paragraphs back.
4 What is the situation in the various side-suits? Again similar thoughts to those set out in 1 above apply.

To answer these questions, it is obviously necessary to understand fully the opponents' bidding in detail. For this first exercise, we are not even going to look at our cards at all but simply listen to the auction. What I should like you to do is to consider the following sequences by North and South (you will be sitting West and your partnership will be silent throughout) and state how much you know about the opposing hands in terms of strength and distribution, and whether you consider that the final contract was reached confidently or at a stretch. For example:

(a) N	S	(b) N	S	(c) N	S
1◇	1♡	1NT	3♠		1♡
2♣	2♡	4♠	Pass	2♡	4♡
Pass				Pass	

In (a), North has shown at least five diamonds and four clubs and has not proceeded over 2♡. South has shown at least five hearts, probably six, and probably not much more than his minimum 6 points. North has stopped, either because he fears a misfit and/or because he is minimum for his opening call. 3154 is a typical shape and he will probably have 12–16 points.

In (b), North is limited to 15–17 points and a balanced hand as we defined in the beginners' book. Over 3♠ (game forcing), he had three options:

1 Rebid 3NT (implying a doubleton spade or a flat minimum hand).
2 Raise to 4♠, as he did, promising a three- or four-card support and a likely (but not certain) ruffing value in a side-suit doubleton.
3 Bid a side-suit at the four-level (suggesting the ace in that suit), indicating a good spade fit and a probable maximum with a view to a slam invitation (note that it costs nothing to do this

below game). South did not proceed beyond game so he will have at least 10 points but not enough to consider a slam opposite a partner who showed no more than tolerance.

In (c), North has limited his hand and is likely to have scattered values outside his three-card or longer trump support. South must be markedly stronger than his original opening call but not strong enough to consider a slam opposite a partner who is limited to about 9 points. He could, however, have a fair amount to spare for the game.

Get the idea? Now start your stop-watch and see if you can discuss each example in under thirty seconds, completing the whole exercise in well under five minutes.

(1)	N	S	(2)	N	S	(3)	N	S
		1NT			1♣			1♠
	2♣	2♡		2♣	2NT		3♢	3♠
	3♡	4♡		3♣	Pass		4NT	5♢
	Pass						5♠	Pass

(4)	N	S	(5)	N	S	(6)	N	S
		2♡*		Pass	1♠			1♠
	4♡	Pass		3♢	3♠		2♢	2♠
				Pass			4♠	Pass

*Strong

(7)	N	S	(8)	N	S	(9)	N	S
	1♠	2♢			1♢			1NT
	2♠	2NT		1♠	3♢		2♣	2♡
	3♢	Pass		3♡	4♢		Pass	
				Pass				

(10)	N	S
		1♠
	2♢	3♢
	4♠	Pass

The number of possible bidding sequences runs into millions, so we could go on for centuries but all that is necessary at this stage is to develop the habit of judging what the weather is like and the appropriate measures to be taken. Let us work through the answers:

(1)   This is an excellent illustration of a stretch or, as some

writers describe it, an *eventual contract*. South has limited his hand to 15–17 points, balanced, and has promised a four-card heart suit. North has also limited his hand with the invitational but non-forcing 3♡, so he will also have at least a four-card suit and about 8 points. South's acceptance marks him with a good 16–17 points, and notice that he had the option to bid 3NT over 3♡ and would surely have done so had he been 3433 (remember North could always correct to 4♡). The inference is that South has a doubleton in a side-suit.

(2)   South has limited his hand to 18–19 points, balanced, and probably has at least modest cover in the other three suits (he could have made forcing suit bids at the two-level to encourage his partner to show stops for no-trump had he wanted to). North is clearly minimum for his 2♣ raise (the original range being about 6–10 points, or less with very good distribution) and has signed off in 3♣, clearly indicating a preference for a suit contract. He almost certainly has plenty of ruffing values.

(3)   Here the opponents were heading for a slam but stopped short, presumably because they found that two aces were missing. They will certainly have plenty of strength and desperate measures will be justified to try to set 5♠. It might be a very different matter if they had actually bid the slam, when the diamond and trump situation will be particularly relevant, North having promised a big diamond suit and some spade support.

(4)   South has shown a strong two-opener in hearts – 18 or more points and probably six good hearts – and his partner has raised him to game, simultaneously denying an ace. South has elected not to bid further so he is unlikely to hold more than two aces himself. However, in terms of general strength, it is likely that the partnership has at least enough for the game and probably more.

(5)   In this case, North has shown a hand at the top of the Pass (0–11) range with a diamond suit and at least three spades. South has indicated a minimum opening call and was obviously not impressed by the diamond suit opposite.

Presumably he is short of the suit and may well have low honor cards in hearts and clubs which will be of little value opposite his partner's implied shortages.

(6)   Here North has shown a diamond suit and then given a delayed game raise after his partner has confirmed at least a five-card spade suit but no extra strength above that promised by his opening call. He is therefore limited to about 14 points, but North may well have been slam-minded and could have a fair amount to spare. Desperate measures will probably be in order to try to set this game unless there is good reason to believe that both diamonds and trumps are lying very unfavorably for declarer.

(7)   Here both North and South have limited their hands, South with his 2NT call and North with his 3♢ call, both of which were non-forcing. North has rejected the game try and preferred to play in diamonds. It is noteworthy that he did not support his partner the first time and there are two possible explanations.

South probably preferred to rebid his spades to show a six-card or longer suit, 4♠ being the favorite goal contract. Alternatively, South could have a 5134 shape with a predominance of 'quick' as opposed to 'slow' tricks and consider that 3♢ has a better chance than 2NT, even if North only has four diamonds.

(8)   Here South has limited his hand to about 15 points and a six-card or longer diamond suit, the 3♢ bid certainly being forward-going but not forcing. North's 3♡ call is not necessarily a suit. 4♡, at the moment, is not in the running for goal contract because South denied a four-card heart suit with his 3♢ call. Had he had one, he would have bid 2♡ on a hand which is obviously strong enough to reverse. Thus North is showing no more than a feature (typically a stop) with a view to 3NT and South's failure to bid 3NT shows that he lacks a good club stop (note that North has strongly indicated fear of clubs in that he did not bid 3NT directly). At the time he bid 3♡, 5♢ and 4♠ were also candidate game contracts and the partnership still had the option to stop in 4♢, as indeed they did.

(9) Here South is strictly limited to 15–17 and has promised a four-card heart suit (he could have four spades as well). North could well be very weak as he has preferred a suit contract to 1NT, even if it meant raising the level of bidding. A hand shaped 4450 is ideal for Stayman, even without a single point, as responder is happy to pass any reply. There is no guarantee, by the way, that North has four hearts. He could bid the same way with 4351, prepared to play in a 4–3 fit with a singleton outside, knowing that any ruffing of clubs will be done advantageously in the short hand.

(10) Here the opponents have found a double fit. Both South and North are unlimited except to the degree that they did not, despite the secondary fit, investigate a slam.

Thus, from the auctions alone, we already know a fair amount about the two enemy hands by considering not only what they bid but – very often more illuminating – *what they did not bid*.

In each case, we consider how the declarer is going to set about the contract and how well his plan is going to work in the light of what we can see in our own hand and place in partner's. His bidding may well help in this respect but – as is very often forgotten – so may his *failure to bid*.

In a trump contract, our first thought is whether to lead a trump or not. There are a number of standard situations in which a trump lead is likely to be hot favorite but note that there are always exceptions so these must be considered *guides* rather than *commands*. Let us set them out, giving good reasons for each so that they are clearly understood.

1 You make a take-out double (usually of a one-level contract) and partner passes, converting it into a penalty double. Remember here that partner's pass is a *strong call* indicating a long and solid trump holding (note that it should be solid because it is badly placed under the call). It is most distressing to hear people say (and it still happens frequently) 'Well, I had to pass because I did not have enough points to bid.' Poor teaching and/or absorption is indicated. The partner of the take-out doubler is required to bid his longest suit and does not promise any points at all. This is simply an extension of the

basic principle that, when a partner makes a forcing call *he* (i.e. the forcer) is responsible for partner's reply and must therefore have the points and/or distribution to cover it. The defenders' aim is to pull declarer's poor trumps before he can use them for ruffing (the only way they will score tricks with such a bad split around). Thus leading a side suit merely helps declarer.

2 Opponents bid two suits and end up in a third. This is a typical example:

N	S
	1♡
1♠	2♢
Pass	

Here North's refusal to return to 2♡ opposite an announced five-card heart suit indicates a considerable dislike and that could well be a singleton or void. Similarly, South's failure to support spades and his announcement of at least nine red cards suggests a similar attitude towards spades. It may well be that the declarer will play on crossruff lines as he will be unable to set up long tricks in either major.

3 Opponents bid three suits and end up playing in the fourth. This implies that they have some strength in all four suits and yet they stayed away from no-trump. This clearly indicates singletons or voids in the other three suits and an intention to crossruff.

4 Opponents find a fit in their trump suit and have also mentioned a side suit in which you are very strong or have reason to believe that partner is very strong. Now declarer will not be able to enjoy tricks in his side suit, on which he intended to discard his losers, and will have to look to ruffing those losers instead.

5 The declarer has bid a suit and been supported; he has then suggested no-trump but has been corrected to his original suit. Here the dummy hand thinks that a larger number of tricks (remembering that removal from no-trump involves raising the level of bidding) can be obtained in a trump contract. That view can only be justified because he intends to use his trumps for ruffing.

6 You have reached a high-level contract and the opponents have sacrificed. In fact, in most situations where you and your partner have comfortably the balance of the points, the opponents will only have their trumps to look to as sources of tricks and you should ensure that they do not make them separately.

7 Opponents have used a take-out double or two-suited conventional bid and it is clear that they will make full use of the shortages for ruffing.

8 Opponents have bid an eventual contract and you have broken holdings in all side suits and it is clear that a trump lead is least likely to give anything away.

Certainly in the first seven of the above situations, it is worth leading a trump even if it has to be from an embarrassing holding like Q x x. The trick given up will usually be returned, as often as not with interest.

If we decide not to lead a trump, then we must consider other aims. These include:

1 Building up our own side-suit tricks before declarer discards his losers; this is likely to be applicable when it is clear that declarer is going to be able to cash a long suit and a race is on in a similar manner to no-trump.

2 Organizing one or more ruffs for our side before declarer pulls trumps. This applies when we have a shortage in a suit (doubleton or less) and it is clear that we can take the tricks immediately or have sufficient trump control to stop the pulling of trumps in time.

3 Attacking declarer's entries to his long suit, and that includes forcing the board to ruff where it is clear that the board's trumps will constitute the entries to the long suit. This applies when it is clear that the board has few, if any, entries to that suit.

4 Attacking declarer's long suit so that he runs out prematurely before trumps are pulled. This applies when the suit is solid and there are no outside entries.

5 Forcing declarer to ruff our long suit so that he runs out of trumps, or at least reaches a stage where he is shorter than we

are. This applies when the hand on lead has length in trumps, or when it is clear that his partner is long.

It is time to do some illustrative examples. For each of the ten auctions we have just looked at, I am going to give you two hands and ask you to choose your opening lead. In each case, you should state your reasons and how good the prospects are, bearing in mind the comments we made before we looked at our cards. You should complete each example in under thirty seconds so that the whole exercise should take comfortably under ten minutes.

(1) (a) ♠ Q 10 8 6   (b) ♠ Q 10 5 3
          ♡ 6   ♡ 10 9 8
          ◇ J 10 9   ◇ K 8 6 4
          ♣ K 8 6 5 3   ♣ J 6

(2) (a) ♠ K Q J 7   (b) ♠ Q 8 6
          ♡ 7 5   ♡ Q J 10
          ◇ J 8 6   ◇ 8 7 5
          ♣ Q 7 5 3   ♣ 6 5 4 2

(3) (a) ♠ 8 6   (b) ♠ J 8
          ♡ K 7 5 3 2   ♡ J 9 8 6 4
          ◇ Q 7 5   ◇ 7 5
          ♣ 7 6 4   ♣ Q 9 7 5

(4) (a) ♠ Q J 10 7   (b) ♠ 9 8 7
          ♡ K 8   ♡ Q 8 6
          ◇ 9 7 6 4   ◇ K 7 6 4
          ♣ 8 6 4   ♣ K 8 5

(5) (a) ♠ 9 6   (b) ♠ 8 7 5
          ♡ K 8 6 4   ♡ Q 7
          ◇ A Q 7   ◇ K Q 10 9 7
          ♣ J 7 5 3   ♣ K 8 6

(6) (a) ♠ 10 8 6   (b) ♠ 8 6 4
          ♡ 6   ♡ 10 8 7 4
          ◇ Q 8 6 4   ◇ 7 5 3 2
          ♣ J 7 5 3 2   ♣ A K

(7) (a) ♠ K 10 8 6   (b) ♠ 7
          ♡ 8 6 4   ♡ K Q J 6
          ◇ Q 7 5   ◇ 7 5 4
          ♣ Q 8 6   ♣ Q 8 6 5 4

(8) (a) ♠ Q 8 7   (b) ♠ Q 7 5 4
          ♡ J 8 6   ♡ K Q J 10
          ◇ 8 6   ◇ 9
          ♣ A J 8 7 5   ♣ K J 7 5

(9) (a) ♠ K Q J 7   (b) ♠ A Q 6 4
          ♡ Q 7 6   ♡ 6 4 2
          ◇ 10 7 6   ◇ K J 4
          ♣ J 6 4   ♣ Q 10 5

(10) (a) ♠ 8 6   (b) ♠ Q 8 7
          ♡ K Q 10 7   ♡ K J 9 5
          ◇ A 7 5 3 2   ◇ 10 7 5
          ♣ Q 2   ♣ J 8 6

Let us work through the answers:

(1) Here opponents have stretched and, on hand (a) in partic-
     ular, an unpleasant surprise awaits them in a likely 4–1
     trump split. Passive defence is called for and the leads least
     likely to give anything away are the solid ◇ J on (a) and the
     solid ♡ 10 on (b).

(2) Here North has preferred a trump contract to a no-trump
     contract and has clearly bid on ruffing potential, which
     should be removed as quickly as possible. A low trump
     lead is appropriate on both hands. The major-suit tricks are
     unlikely to run away unless they are ruffed.

(3) On (a) the ◇ Q is perfectly placed for declarer and prospects
     are very poor. The best chance is probably to find partner
     with the ♡ A (well on the cards as the opponents have
     announced that there are aces missing). With luck it may be
     doubleton and our third trick may be a ruff if the enemy
     hearts break 3–3. On (b), the club suit offers the best chance
     of setting up tricks. Partner may be able to use his two aces
     to set up our ♣ Q. The fourth-high ♣ 5 is appropriate.

(4) On (a), a trump trick is certain and we have no reason to
     lead anything but the solid ♠ Q. On (b), the position is less
     clear but with a likely trump trick (which the opponents
     may well not expect to lose), passive defence is probably
     appropriate with two kings well placed behind the strong
     call, North having made it clear that there is no ace behind
     them. A passive spade is appropriate and prospects are
     bright.

(5) On (a), the diamond position is disastrous and the trumps appear to be breaking well for declarer. Desperate measures are called for and any defensive tricks are most likely to come from hearts. The fourth-high ♡4 is appropriate. On (b), South may well have a singleton diamond and North shortages in the other suits which suggests a crossruff. A trump lead is called for.

(6) Here desperate measures are called for and, with partner marked with most of the defenders' combined strength, there is every chance that he will have an early entry. Particularly if that is in trump, the situation will be ideal to try for a ruff, perhaps two. Thus on (a), the singleton heart stands out and the suit would probably be the best lead even with a doubleton. Although the hand in (b) is markedly stronger, leaving partner with less this time, the best chance is probably to play for a club ruff. We thus cash our honors in the 'wrong' order, king then ace, to show partner the doubleton.

(7) This is similar to 2 and a trump lead is called for in both cases. We can see that in (a) we can stop the spades and in (b), it is likely that partner is strong in the suit. A low diamond is appropriate on both hands.

(8) The opponents have made it clear that they are weak in clubs and that suit should be led on both hands – the ♣A on (a) and the ♣5 on (b). Much depends on how many club tricks we can take.

(9) On (a) there is little reason to ignore the solid spade lead. On (b) it is best not to lead from those tenace holdings round to a 1NT opener. It may well be that North is very weak and a trump lead is appropriate.

(10) On (a), it is clear that partner is void (or, at most, singleton in diamonds) and the ◇A followed by another is obvious. On (b) the diamonds are well behaved for declarer and there is no guarantee that the ♠Q will score. Desperate measures are called for and our best hope lies in hearts – we should lead the ♡5.

Having made the opening lead, we are now going to cross over to the East seat and consider our action once the board has been revealed. We shall again be doing our seven roll-calls as with the no-trump contracts, but taking the ruffing into account, which may dramatically alter the number of winners and losers available to each side.

Defensive signalling is even more important in trump contracts than in no-trump contracts and we shall extend our knowledge of the suit-preference signal to cover situations where ruffing is relevant.

When following to the opening lead, you may well play a high card in an attempt to win a trick. If, however, it is clear that partner or the board is going to win, you can play a low card and now the option to signal is available. We have so far learnt three types:

1 Encouragement/discouragement of the suit led.
2 Distribution, odd or even, of the suit led.
3 Suit-preference, where a shift is likely to be in order.

How are we to know which is relevant to a particular occasion? Before taking any sort of decision, we do our seven roll-calls and then ask the crucial question: 'What does partner need to know?'

Let us start with half-a-dozen simple examples where the choice should be fairly obvious. Start your stop-watch and try and complete a full analysis of the hand in under thirty seconds for each example, so that the whole test will be completed in under three minutes.

Hand No. 70
Dealer East
Both vulnerable

```
                              ♠ J 9 8
                              ♡ A 8 4
                              ◇ K Q J 10
                              ♣ J 6 2
                                        ♠ 6 3
                              N         ♡ K 9 5 3
                           W     E      ◇ 9 8 7 2
                              S         ♣ Q 9 7
```

W	N	E	S
		Pass	1♠
Pass	2◇	Pass	2♠
Pass	4♠	end	

Partner leads the ♡Q to the board's ♡A. How do you defend?

From now on, instead of doing the seven roll-calls in detail, I shall merely pick out the salient points of the hand and explain how they guide us to the correct defence. It will, however, be a useful exercise for you to do the roll-calls yourself in the way we did them in the last chapter, if only to satisfy yourself that they are consistent with the solution I give.

Here partner has promised the ♡J so that, once the ♡A is knocked out, we shall be able to cash up to two heart tricks provided South can follow. Diamonds are clearly declarer's suit and we have little to offer in clubs. We know that partner does not have both ♣A and ♣K as he did not lead them. We shall have to hope for two heart tricks, possibly a trump (any honor in partner's hand should be well placed behind the call) and one further trick in one of the minors.

Our first duty is to inform partner that we have the ♡K and that we want him to continue the suit when he next wins a trick. We do so by playing a high card to encourage, here the ♡9.

The deal:

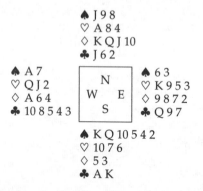

```
                    ♠ J 9 8
                    ♡ A 8 4
                    ◇ K Q J 10
                    ♣ J 6 2
     ♠ A 7                          ♠ 6 3
     ♡ Q J 2          N             ♡ K 9 5 3
     ◇ A 6 4        W   E           ◇ 9 8 7 2
     ♣ 10 8 5 4 3     S             ♣ Q 9 7
                    ♠ K Q 10 5 4 2
                    ♡ 10 7 6
                    ◇ 5 3
                    ♣ A K
```

Faced with four losers, South will attack diamonds first, hoping to discard at least one heart loser, as he does not have time to pull trumps. However, partner will win and continue hearts and the defenders get there first.

Let us, however, alter the deal slightly:

Hand No. 71
Dealer East
Both vulnerable

		♠ J 9 8
		♡ 10 8 4
		◊ K Q J 10
		♣ A J 6

W	N	E	S
		Pass	1♠
Pass	2◊	Pass	2♠
Pass	4♠	end	

```
                    N        ♠ 763
                 W     E     ♡ 9752
                    S        ◊ 98
                             ♣ K Q 10 7
```

Again, partner leads the ♡Q and the board plays the ♡4. How do you defend this time?

It is clear that South has both ♡A and ♡K and, even if he has a third one, it will not pay for partner to play a second round with the ♡10 on the board. Again diamonds are South's suit and our only hope of tricks lies in clubs. Our message to partner must be that we cannot help in hearts and we should tell him so by playing the two.

The deal:

```
                    ♠ J 9 8
                    ♡ 10 8 4
                    ◊ K Q J 10
                    ♣ A J 2
        ♠ A                       ♠ 763
        ♡ Q J 6 3        N        ♡ 9752
        ◊ A 7 6 4 2   W     E     ◊ 98
        ♣ 9 8 5          S        ♣ K Q 10 7
                    ♠ K Q 10 5 4 2
                    ♡ A K
                    ◊ 5 3
                    ♣ 6 4 3
```

Threatened by club losers, South is likely to go for the diamonds immediately with a view to discarding clubs on the third and fourth rounds. Fortunately for the defenders, however, our diamonds are splitting 5–2 and we can ruff on the third round. On taking his ◊A, partner, warned of hearts by our discouragement, will have little alternative but to shift to clubs and we shall take two club tricks and the two aces to set the contract.

We now turn to count or distributional signals. These have a wide application and many pairs, including a large number of the top echelon, like to play them in all situations, believing that, more often than not, it pays to help partner to count the whole hand. As in no-trump, a distributional signal is appropriate to tell partner how long to hold up an ace in declarer's long suit but, in trump contracts, it is also used on trick one in positions where the defenders are planning a ruff.

On the opening lead, we distinguish between a doubleton and a trebleton as follows: with a doubleton, we play high-low, i.e. *echo* or *peter*. So with ♡ 8 5, we play the ♡8 and then the ♡5. With a trebleton, there are various styles, but we shall learn what is commonly known as MUD (Middle, Up, Down). Thus with ♡ 9 7 2, we lead the ♡7 and follow with the ♡9 (so that partner knows that we do not have a doubleton on the second round) and then the ♡2. When following to partner's lead, we play:

1 High-low to show an *even* number of cards (it will usually be obvious to partner whether it is two, four or six from the bidding and the twenty-six cards he can see).
2 The lowest card to show an *odd* number (three or five).

The mnemonic for remembering this is that the words 'peter' and 'even' both contain the letter 'e' twice and that the words 'normal' and 'odd' both contain the letter 'o' once.

Hand No. 72
Dealer East
Both vulnerable

♠ J 9 8 4
♡ Q J 6 3
♢ K 10
♣ Q 8 2

```
                              N         ♠ A 6 3
                          W       E     ♡ 9 2
                              S         ♢ Q J 9 8
                                        ♣ 10 7 4 3
```

W	N	E	S
		Pass	1NT
Pass	2♣	Pass	2♠
Pass	3♠	Pass	4♠
Pass	end		

After South's 1NT opener and North's Stayman inquiry, a spade fit was found and North invited game with a non-forcing 3♠. South's acceptance showed a good 16–17 points. Partner leads the ♡A and the board plays low. How do you defend?

The lead is likely to come from ♡ A K and others and, as we shall run out after the second round, a third will enable us to take a ruff. Partner knows that South, having opened 1NT, will have to follow at least two rounds and will be able to judge whether a ruff is on from his own holding. We must indicate an even number of hearts in our hand by playing the ♡9 followed by the ♡2.

The deal:

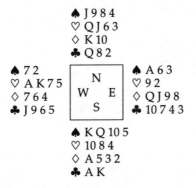

♠ J 9 8 4
♡ Q J 6 3
◇ K 10
♣ Q 8 2

♠ 7 2   ♠ A 6 3
♡ A K 7 5   ♡ 9 2
◇ 7 6 4   ◇ Q J 9 8
♣ J 9 6 5   ♣ 10 7 4 3

♠ K Q 10 5
♡ 10 8 4
◇ A 5 3 2
♣ A K

We thus take two top hearts, the ruff and the ♠A to set the contract. Note that, if partner has five hearts, he will know that South will also have run out after the second round and will then probably shift, knowing that our trumps will be overruffed.

The peter to show an even number is also given in this type of situation:

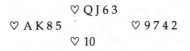

♡ Q J 6 3
♡ A K 8 5   ♡ 9 7 4 2
♡ 10

Where South's bidding shows a more distributional hand, a peter by East warns West that the position may be as above and that the ♡K will be ruffed, setting up the ♡Q and ♡J for declarer. It is up to West to judge whether the peter shows two or four cards. It will usually be clear, from the auction and sight of the board, which applies.

But now let us alter the hand to:

Hand No. 73
Dealer East
Both vulnerable

♠ J 9 8 4
♡ Q J 6 3
◇ Q J
♣ A 8 2

		N	
W			E
		S	

♠ A 6 3
♡ 9 4 2
◇ J 10 9 8
♣ K 10 3

W	N	E	S
		Pass	1NT
Pass	2♣	Pass	2♠
Pass	4♠	end	

Again, partner leads the ♡A and the board plays low. How do you defend this time?

Here, are we able to follow three times and thus a continuation of hearts will only help declarer to set up the suit for discards. This time, we indicate an odd number by playing the lowest card, here the ♡2.

The deal:

♠ J 9 8 4
♡ Q J 6 3
◇ Q J
♣ A 8 2

♠ 7 2
♡ A K 7 5
◇ 7 6 4
♣ 9 6 5 4

	N	
W		E
	S	

♠ A 6 3
♡ 9 4 2
◇ 10 9 8 5
♣ K 10 3

♠ K Q 10 5
♡ 10 8
◇ A K 3 2
♣ Q J 7

Partner will realize that the ♡2 cannot be a singleton because that would leave South with four, which he would have bid in response to the Stayman enquiry. So it will be clear to him that there is no future in hearts. The solid holding in diamonds is also unattractive – our ◇A, if we have it, will not run away and there are clearly no other tricks there for us. The only hope, therefore, rests in clubs and you should satisfy yourself that only a club shift at this point sets the contract. If West plays anything else,

South will pull trumps, losing to our ♠A and the club suit cannot profitably be attacked from our side of the table. Later, South will play on hearts and, by the time the ♣A is knocked out, he will have two winning hearts on the board on which to discard his losing clubs.

We now turn to the third type of signal, suit-preference. When defending no-trump contracts, we learnt that by *discarding* a high or low card from a specific suit, we could, respectively, encourage or discourage that suit. We are now going to learn how to signal suit-preference when *leading* or *following suit*. Suit-preference will apply, third in priority, when encouragement/discouragement and distribution are obviously irrelevant to the defence.

Suit-preference has a very wide scope but the two situations on which we are going to concentrate are:

1 Guiding partner as to your entry when you are in a position to give him a ruff.
2 Guiding him as to which suit you want him to shift to if he has originally attacked a suit in which there is clearly no hope for the defenders.

Assuming that it is obvious that there are two suits from which to choose, a *high* card indicates preference for the *higher-ranking* suit, while a *low* card indicates the *lower-ranking* suit. Here are some examples:

Hand No. 74
Dealer West
E-W vulnerable

♠	A K J
♡	J 8 6 5
◇	K 10 5
♣	K 10 5

```
              N        ♠ J 6
          W       E    ♡ A 10 7 4 2
              S        ◇ 7 4
                       ♣ A 7 4 3
```

W	N	E	S
Pass	1NT	Pass	4♠
end			

Partner leads the ♡Q. With the ♡J visible on the board, this is clearly a singleton; at least, if it isn't, there is little hope. So you win with the ♡A.

What do you return and would it make any difference if your minor-suit holdings were reversed?

South has promised a little under opening strength and a six-card or longer spade suit and any minor-suit honors in partner's hand will be poorly placed under the K 10 tenaces on the board. It is clear, therefore, that our only realistic hope is to take our two aces plus two heart ruffs in partner's hand. So we must return a heart for partner to ruff. But what happens then? How will partner know that he has to return a club rather than a diamond to get us back on lead before trumps are pulled? That is where the suit-preference signal comes in. With the hand above, we prefer clubs, the *lower-ranking* of the outstanding suits and therefore we return our *lowest* heart, here the ♡2.

Reverse our minor-suit holdings, i.e. imagine our hand was ♠ 8 6 ♡ A 10 7 4 2 ◇ A 7 4 3 ♣ 7 4, and now we would ask for a diamond, the *higher-ranking* of the minor suits and thus return our highest heart, here the ♡10.

The deal:

```
                    ♠ A K J
                    ♡ J 8 6 5
                    ◇ K 10 5
                    ♣ K 10 5
      ♠ 7 2                        ♠ 8 6
      ♡ Q          ┌─────┐         ♡ A 10 7 4 2
      ◇ J 9 8 6 2  │  N  │         ◇ 7 4        (A 7 4 3)
      ♣ J 9 8 6 2  │ W E │         ♣ A 7 4 3    (7 4)
                   │  S  │
                   └─────┘
                    ♠ Q 10 9 5 4 3
                    ♡ K 9 3
                    ◇ A Q 3        (Q)
                    ♣ Q            (A Q 3)
```

Notice that, without the suit-preference signal, West would have no better a guide than the toss of a coin. Having grasped the idea, you should have no difficulty with this next example:

				♠ J 7 3 2
Hand No. 75				♡ J 8 6 5
Dealer West				◇ A
Both vulnerable				♣ J 8 6 5

W	N	E	S	
				♠ 5 4
				♡ 10 7 4
Pass	Pass	Pass	1♠	◇ 9 7 5 4 3
Pass	2♠	Pass	4♠	♣ K Q 10
end				

Partner leads the ◇Q to the board's ◇A. How do you defend and would it make any difference if your club and heart holdings were exchanged?

With a singleton ◇A and plenty of trumps on the board, it is clear that there is no hope for the defenders in that suit and therefore encouragement/discouragement and distribution in it are irrelevant to them. What is important is that partner is guided as to how to shift when he (hopefully) gets in with a trump.

With the hand shown, we shall want to attack clubs, the *lower-ranking* of the two candidate suits, clubs and hearts, and we show that by playing our *lowest* diamond, here the ◇3. Reverse the club and heart holdings and now we should want the *higher-ranking* of the two candidate suits and would indicate that with our highest diamond, here the ◇9.

The deal:

```
                    ♠ J 7 3 2
                    ♡ J 8 6 5
                    ◇ A
                    ♣ J 8 6 5
    ♠ A Q          ┌─────────┐        ♠ 5 4
    ♡ 9 3 2        │    N    │        ♡ 10 7 4   (K Q 10)
    ◇ Q J 10 8 6   │ W     E │        ◇ 9 7 5 4 3
    ♣ 9 3 2        │    S    │        ♣ K Q 10   (10 7 4)
                   └─────────┘
                    ♠ K 10 9 8 6
                    ♡ A K Q   (A 7 4)
                    ◇ K 2
                    ♣ A 7 4   (A K Q)
```

Note a number of points about this hand:

1 Once again, without the suit preference signal, West has no clue as to how to shift when he wins his first trump trick.

2 North-South have lamentable duplication of values or, as some people like to say, *overkill* in diamonds, and a discard on the ◇K achieves nothing.

3 South cannot profitably take a discard of a loser on the thirteenth heart until trumps have been pulled but, if West fails to find the appropriate shift in time, i.e. on taking his first trump trick, the discard on the ♡J represents the difference between failure and success.

You are encouraged to play the hand out for yourself to ensure that you understand these points.

Having explained the three basic signals given by East to West on the opening lead, we must now do some exercises on interpretation of them against the stop-watch. Remember the order of priority:

1 Encouragement/discouragement of the suit led.
2 Distribution (odd or even) of the suit led.
3 Suit-preference where the necessity of a shift is obvious.

In the examples that follow, however, they do not appear in any particular order. Decide what is relevant in each case in under two minutes.

Problem 1
Hand No. 76
Dealer East
Both vulnerable

				♠ 4 3
				♡ J 10 4
				◇ Q J 10 6
				♣ Q 10 6 3

♠ K 2
♡ Q 7 2
◇ A K 8 2
♣ 9 8 5 4

W	N	E	S
		Pass	1♠
Pass	1NT	Pass	3♡
Pass	3NT	Pass	4♡
end			

```
      N
   W     E
      S
```

You lead the ◇A to the ◇6, partner's ◇7 and South's ◇4. How do you continue?

Problem 2
Hand No. 77
Dealer West
Neither vulnerable

				♠ 9 6 4
				♡ A K Q 3
				◇ K 6 5
				♣ K 6 5

♠ A 10 7 3
♡ 5
◇ J 10 8 2
♣ J 10 8 2

W	N	E	S
Pass	1NT	2♠	3♡
3♠	4♡	end	

```
      N
   W     E
      S
```

You lead the ♠A to the ♠4, partner's ♠K and South's ♠5. How do you continue and would it make any difference if partner had played the ♠2?

Problem 3
Hand No. 78
Dealer West
Both vulnerable

♠ A K Q J
♡ J 8
♦ Q 9 6 5 4
♣ J 9

W	N	E	S	♠ 9 6	
1♦	Pass	Pass	1♡	♡ 6 2	N
Pass	2♦	Pass	3♡	♦ A K 10 8 2	W E
Pass	4♡	end		♣ A Q 8 5	S

First, a word about the auction – North's 2♦ call is what is called an *unassuming cue-bid* about which we shall learn more in the bidding section. With West having bid the suit, North has no interest in playing there, particularly as game would involve playing at the five-level. As a general rule, bidding the opponents' suit asks partner to describe his hand further (at this stage 3NT, 4♡ and 4♠ are all candidate goal contracts) and is forcing, at least to 'suit agreement'. This means that either both partners bid the same suit or game in any denomination is reached. Thus, had South bid 2♡, that would have been forcing and his 3♡ call (which cost a round of bidding) sent the definite message of a strong hand within the overcall range and a solid suit of at least six cards.

You lead the ♦A to the ♦4, partner's ♦3 and South's ♦7. How do you continue?

Problem 4
Hand No. 79
Dealer South
Both vulnerable

♠ J 10 7 2
♡ 8 4 3
♦ K Q J 10
♣ A 2

W	N	E	S	♠ 9	
			1♠	♡ K J 6 2	N
				♦ A 9 5	W E
Pass	2♦	Pass	3♠	♣ J 10 9 6 4	S
Pass	4♠	end			

You lead the ♣J to the board's ♣A, partner's ♣3 and South's ♣5. South plays a round of trumps to his ♠A, all following, and then leads the ♦6. How do you defend?

Problem 5
Hand No. 80
Dealer North
E-W vulnerable

♠ A Q 10
♡ J 8 4
◇ Q J 9 5
♣ J 8 4

♠ 9 7 3
♡ Q 10 9
◇ A K 8 6
♣ Q 10 9

				N	
W	N	E	S	W E	
	Pass	Pass	1♠	S	
Pass	2NT	Pass	3♡		
Pass	3♠	Pass	4♠		
end					

You lead the ◇A to the ◇5, partner's ◇2 and South's ◇4. How do you continue?

Problem 6
Hand No. 81
Dealer East
E-W vulnerable

♠ K 8 5
♡ K 10 8 4 3 2
◇ 7
♣ K 8 5

♠ J 10 6 3
♡ 5
◇ A K 10 6
♣ J 10 6 3

				N	
W	N	E	S	W E	
		Pass	1♡	S	
Pass	4♡	end			

You lead the ◇A to the ◇7, partner's ◇Q and South's ◇8. How do you continue and would it make any difference if partner had played the ◇2?

Problem 7
Hand No. 82
Dealer South
Both vulnerable

♠ J 4
♡ A 5 4
◇ K Q 9 6 4
♣ Q 10 4

♠ 9 8 6 3
♡ J 10 7
◇ A
♣ 9 8 6 5 2

				N	
W	N	E	S	W E	
			1◇	S	
Pass	3◇	Pass	5◇		
end					

You lead the ♡J to the board's ♡A, partner playing the ♡8 and South the ♡2. South now plays a low diamond to your ◇A, East following with the ◇7. How do you continue?

♠ 8 5 4
♡ K Q 10 8
◊ 10 9 5
♣ K 5 4

Problem 8
Hand No. 83
Dealer West
Both vulnerable

				♠ 2	
				♡ 7 4	N
W	N	E	S	◊ 8 6 4 3 2	W E
Pass	Pass	1♠	2♡	♣ Q J 10 9 3	S
Pass	3♡	Pass	4♡		
end					

You lead the ♠2 to the ♠4, partner's ♠A and South's ♠9. Partner returns the ♠10 to South's ♠J and you ruff. How do you continue and would it make any difference if partner had returned the ♠3?

Solutions

Problem 1

With the ◊5, ◊4, and ◊3 missing, partner has clearly played a high card. The top four diamonds are on view and therefore the question of encouragement or discouragement is clear – partner cannot help and, with South having announced a distributional hand, partner has deemed it appropriate to give the count as there is a danger that, if our ◊K is ruffed, the ◊ Q J on the board will be set up for discards. The question now is whether partner has shown a doubleton or four. As usual, our seven roll-calls will keep us on the right track. Let us do them in detail:

Spades: Nine missing – South has shown at least five, leaving partner with four or fewer.

Hearts: Seven missing – again South has shown at least five; the spades will be at least as long as the hearts, possibly longer: 5:5 or 6:5 are favorites. Partner is thus left with two or fewer.

Diamonds: Five missing – partner, having promised an even number, has two or four, leaving South with three or one.

Clubs: Five missing – we have established that South has at least ten major cards and one diamond. That would leave two or fewer clubs. If he started with three diamonds, he will be void of clubs.

Points: We have 12 and the board 6, leaving 22 unaccounted for. South forced to game when his partner promised no more than 6 and a possible misfit. He should have about 17 minimum, leaving partner with 5 points at most.

Tricks: We can see that South has to lose one trick in each major and thus may have up to four tricks in each. In the case where his shape is 5530, he will also lose the two top diamonds, irrespective of our defence. Also giving him that shape implies that all the missing clubs are with partner, including the ♣ A K J – 8 points, which would leave South with 14 points at most, impossible on the auction. Thus we must assume that his shape is 5512 and consider the clubs in closer detail. If partner has the ♣A, South must lose a trick in each suit, come what may, so we must give South the ♣A. Now, if he has the ♣J as well, the finesse against partner's assumed ♣K is right for him and there is no defence if we lead one now (we cannot touch either major without giving away our trick in it).

Thus a critical case arises when the deal is something like this:

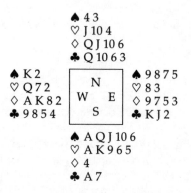

```
                    ♠ 4 3
                    ♡ J 10 4
                    ◇ Q J 10 6
                    ♣ Q 10 6 3
    ♠ K 2                           ♠ 9 8 7 5
    ♡ Q 7 2          N              ♡ 8 3
    ◇ A K 8 2     W     E           ◇ 9 7 5 3
    ♣ 9 8 5 4        S              ♣ K J 2
                    ♠ A Q J 10 6
                    ♡ A K 9 6 5
                    ◇ 4
                    ♣ A 7
```

Now only a club shift sets the contract. If we try to cash the ◇ K,

South ruffs and ensures an entry to the table by playing the ♡A and then a low heart. Now either the ♡J or ♡10 must be a winner, after which the losing club can be discarded on the ◊Q, leaving South with four tricks in each major and one in each of the minors.

Problem 2

The play of an unnecessarily high card like that is usually made to arouse partner's attention. Roll-calling the spade suit, we mark partner with at least five for his overcall and it is lucky that our ♠A hasn't been ruffed. That leaves South with a singleton and therefore we have no more tricks available in that suit. So where do we turn? Partner, having heard our supporting call, has clearly also realized that a spade continuation will serve no purpose and has tried to clarify which of the other suits offers the best chance. A high card indicates the higher-ranking of the two minors, so we must shift to the ◊J, hoping to take three tricks in the suit. Had partner played the ♠2, we should have preferred a club.

The deal:

```
                    ♠ 9 6 4
                    ♡ A K Q 3
                    ◊ K 6 5
                    ♣ K 6 5
   ♠ A 10 7 3                    ♠ K Q J 8 2
   ♡ 5          ┌─────────┐      ♡ 6
   ◊ J 10 8 2   │    N    │      ◊ A Q 7      (9 7 4 3)
   ♣ J 10 8 2   │  W   E  │      ♣ 9 7 4 3    (A Q 7)
                │    S    │
                └─────────┘
                    ♠ 5
                    ♡ J 10 9 8 7 4 2
                    ◊ 9 4 3      (A Q)
                    ♣ A Q        (9 4 3)
```

Note that, if we do not find the correct shift in time, South has ten tricks in seven trumps and three in the 'wrong' minor, one of his losers being discarded on the appropriate king. Once again, I have made the visible minor-suit holdings identical so that, without the suit-preference signal, we would have been on the toss of a coin and thus the contract would be made, on average, half the time.

Problem 3

Let us do our roll-calls on the information so far:

Spades: Seven missing – South, who was invited to bid the suit, is unlikely to have more than three, leaving partner with at least four.

Hearts: Nine missing – South promised six and is unlikely to have any more – with a longer suit, he may well have bid 4♡ at his first opportunity; partner is left with at least three.

Diamonds: Three missing – as both East and South have followed to the first round, it is a question of who has the outstanding card, the ◊J. With the ◊A and ◊K clearly in our hand and the ◊Q on the board, encouragement/discouragement is irrelevant and count is crucial. With a doubleton, East should play the ◊J, i.e. the higher card, so clearly that must be credited to South, leaving partner with the singleton.

Clubs: Seven missing – we know that South has eight red cards and, at most, three spades, leaving him with two, three, four or five clubs and partner with five, four, three or two respectively.

Points: We have 13 and the board 14, leaving 13 unaccounted for. We already know that South has the three top hearts and ◊J, leaving only the ♣K unaccounted for and, in view of the strength of his bidding, he is likely to have that as well, leaving partner with zero or, as is often said, a 'bust'. The extreme case of this, by the way, is the 'Yarborough' (named after an Earl of that name) – a hand containing nothing above a nine. The Earl used to offer odds of 1000:1 against punters dealing one at random, winning in the long term as the actual odds against it are nearly twice as heavy.

Tricks: We have two in diamonds and the ♣A, but where is the fourth to come from? Clearly there is no hope in either major so we need a second trick in clubs. There would be no problem if partner had the ♣K but, as declarer almost certainly has it, we can only be successful if the lead comes from partner's hand, as in this deal:

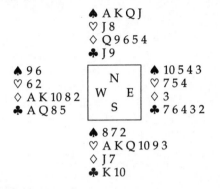

```
                    ♠ A K Q J
                    ♡ J 8
                    ◊ Q 9 6 5 4
                    ♣ J 9
    ♠ 9 6                           ♠ 10 5 4 3
    ♡ 6 2          N                ♡ 7 5 4
    ◊ A K 10 8 2  W   E             ◊ 3
    ♣ A Q 8 5       S               ♣ 7 6 4 3 2
                    ♠ 8 7 2
                    ♡ A K Q 10 9 3
                    ◊ J 7
                    ♣ K 10
```

The only way to get partner in is by a diamond ruff, so we must forego our ◊K and make sure that *he* wins the second diamond trick by leading a *low* one at trick two. Partner is forced to ruff and will return a club to set the contract. If we lead the ◊K, partner may well discard, thinking that we might have four and South three and that he is expected to ruff the third round.

It is instructive to note that 3NT, played by South, cannot be set, but it is not easy to reach and, even in the best of circles, hands where 3NT and four of a major are candidate contracts, the wrong choice is very often made.

Problem 4

South has shown at least a six-card spade suit and it is clear that there are no tricks for us in that suit. In clubs, partner has discouraged, marking at least the ♣K with South, if not the ♣Q as well. Thus, with a doubleton on the table, there is no hope in that suit. In diamonds, we have one trick and it is a question of whether we should take it immediately. If we hold up, partner will give us a count on the first round and we shall take the trick on the last of South's diamonds in an attempt to cut him off from his winners on the board. If he is allowed to make them, he will have at least eleven tricks: six spades, three diamonds and two clubs, not to mention the possibility of the ♣Q or a club ruff on the board.

However, holding up the diamond is not relevant here as South has plenty of entries on the board in trumps and indeed, by holding up, we might well forfeit our diamond trick should the ◇6 be a singleton.

As we learnt in the beginners' book, that also means that South will make one diamond trick rather than three, but there is now no way that we can take more than three tricks. Any tricks outside the ◇A will have to come from hearts and we must look at that suit in more detail. There is clearly no hope if South has the ♡A, so we must credit it to partner and assume that South can follow the suit at least three times.

The critical case arises when South has ♡ Q x x and the full deal is something like this:

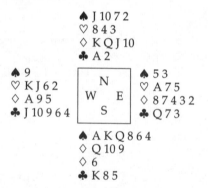

```
              ♠ J 10 7 2
              ♡ 8 4 3
              ◇ K Q J 10
              ♣ A 2
♠ 9                            ♠ 5 3
♡ K J 6 2      N               ♡ A 7 5
◇ A 9 5     W     E            ◇ 8 7 4 3 2
♣ J 10 9 6 4    S              ♣ Q 7 3
              ♠ A K Q 8 6 4
              ◇ Q 10 9
              ◇ 6
              ♣ K 8 5
```

The only defence now is to rise with the ◇A and shift to the ♡2. Note a number of points about this hand:

1 South went straight up with the ♣A on trick one in a desperate attempt to hide the fact that he had the ♣K, hoping the defence would persist with the suit. The implication was that he did not need the ace as an entry to the diamonds.

2 He only played one round of trumps. On the second round, one defender was certain to show out and if it was East, he could throw a high heart to help us.

3 On the ◇A, East should throw his ◇8. With the diamonds set up, encouragement/discouragement and distribution in the

suit are irrelevant and suit-preference (here in clubs or hearts) comes into play. The high card would suggest the higher-ranking suit. Admittedly, he had already discouraged clubs, but suppose he had started with ♣ K 3. Now he does want a continuation but cannot say so.

This is all getting a little advanced, but it illustrates two points well. First, signalling is not completely reliable (the appropriate cards may not be available); and second, for that reason, the opportunity for a second confirmatory or contradictory signal should always be taken.

Problem 5
You have made an unfortunate lead but there may still be time to recover. Let us do our roll-calls on the information we have so far:

Spades: Seven missing – South has promised at least five with his bidding, leaving partner with two or fewer.

Hearts: Seven missing – South promised four with his bidding. With five, he would probably have bid 4 ♡ over 3 ♠ in case North had given false preference with 3 ♠; partner is left with three.

Diamonds: Five missing – with the ♢ A K clearly advertised in your hand, encouragement/discouragement is irrelevant and count is crucial as a ruff could have been on. Partner indicated an odd number and that surely must be three. If it were five, South would be void, and if it were a singleton, that would leave South with four and therefore a void of clubs, which, as we shall see in a moment, is impossible.

Clubs: Seven missing – South has at least nine cards in the majors and two diamonds, leaving him with at most, two clubs, partner having the remaining five or more.

Points: We have 11 and the board also 11, leaving 18 unaccounted for. With South having gone to game, he will have at least 14, leaving partner with 4 or less. Thus he cannot have both ♣ A K and the void of clubs in the South hand is ruled out.

Tricks: There is little we can do now to prevent two dia-
               mond tricks and with partner restricted to one high
               card at best, we must establish our four tricks before
               South is able to discard losers on those diamonds.
               We have two top diamonds and will need to find
               partner with an honor in hearts or clubs – but which?
               The visible holdings are identical but there is, in fact,
               only one hope. In order to take two tricks in the suit,
               South, credited with at least one stop, will have to be
               able to follow at least three times. Our roll-calls have
               established that this is only possible in hearts as
               South will have no more than two clubs. Thus the
               deal we must hope for will have to look like this:

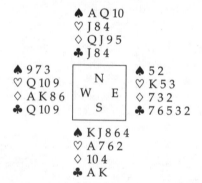

```
                         ♠ A Q 10
                         ♡ J 8 4
                         ◇ Q J 9 5
                         ♣ J 8 4
        ♠ 9 7 3                          ♠ 5 2
        ♡ Q 10 9       N                 ♡ K 5 3
        ◇ A K 8 6    W     E             ◇ 7 3 2
        ♣ Q 10 9       S                 ♣ 7 6 5 3 2
                         ♠ K J 8 6 4
                         ♡ A 7 6 2
                         ◇ 10 4
                         ♣ A K
```

Now a heart shift (and we lead the top of internal sequence – the
♡ 10) will knock out the ♡ A before South can knock out our ◇ K
and we shall take four tricks first. It will be an instructive exercise
to give partner a well-placed ♠ K and satisfy yourself that, as we
cannot attack hearts from our side of the table in this layout:

```
                         ♡ J 8 4
        ♡ Q 10 9                         ♡ 5 3 2
                         ♡ A K 7 6
```

we shall not be able to set up our heart trick before South's two
low hearts are discarded on the diamonds. Hopefully, you did
not take partner's ◇ 2 on trick one as a suit-preference signal for
clubs. In this type of situation, count is the prime consideration

and a high card would have indicated an even number of
diamonds rather than a wish for a heart shift.

Problem 6
With a singleton diamond and plenty of trumps on the board,
there is clearly no further trick available in diamonds and we
must turn our attention to the black suits. The position is
identical and only partner can tell us which he prefers. The high
card under our ace asks for the higher-ranking suit (spades) the
lower for the lower-ranking clubs.

The deal:

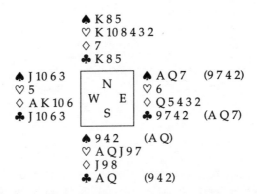

```
                    ♠ K 8 5
                    ♡ K 10 8 4 3 2
                    ◇ 7
                    ♣ K 8 5
    ♠ J 10 6 3                      ♠ A Q 7    (9 7 4 2)
    ♡ 5              ┌─────────┐    ♡ 6
    ◇ A K 10 6       │ N       │    ◇ Q 5 4 3 2
    ♣ J 10 6 3       │W     E  │    ♣ 9 7 4 2   (A Q 7)
                     │    S    │
                     └─────────┘
                    ♠ 9 4 2    (A Q)
                    ♡ A Q J 9 7
                    ◇ J 9 8
                    ♣ A Q     (9 4 2)
```

Note that it costs East nothing to throw the ◇ Q on the first trick –
the ◇ 5 would be very unclear. Also, if we fail to find the spade
shift immediately, South will discard one of his spade losers on
the ♣ K (or vice versa in the second case).

Problem 7
South is bound to have long diamonds, otherwise he would have
looked for 3NT, and we will need at least 15 points to justify his
bidding. Partner has played an encouraging card to your heart
lead and we have no reason to ignore him. We simply continue
with the ♡ 10 (higher from current holding of a doubleton) and
hope that South, despite having his points in the black suits, will
be able to follow twice more.

The deal:

```
                        ♠ J 4
                        ♡ A 5 4
                        ◇ K Q 9 6 4
                        ♣ Q 10 4
        ♠ 9 8 6 3                      ♠ Q 10 7 5 2
        ♡ J 10 7          N            ♡ K Q 8 3
        ◇ A           W       E        ◇ 7
        ♣ 9 8 6 5 2       S            ♣ J 7 3
                        ♠ A K
                        ♡ 9 6 2
                        ◇ J 10 8 5 3 2
                        ♣ A K
```

You note that you found the only lead to set the contract. On any other lead, South would have been able to keep the ♡A on the board and after pulling trumps and cashing the two top clubs in his hand, cross to the board in hearts or diamonds to discard a losing heart on the ♣Q, restricting his losses to two tricks only.

Problem 8
We have taken two tricks and, if we can get partner in again (our third), another spade ruff will set the contract. That club position looks very tempting but partner has returned a high spade, indicating preference for the higher-ranking of the two minor suits, diamonds. If we fail to respect his wishes, we are likely to lose the second spade ruff and present declarer with the contract when the deal is something like this:

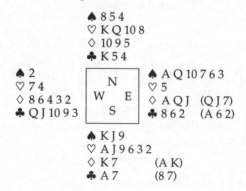

```
                        ♠ 8 5 4
                        ♡ K Q 10 8
                        ◇ 10 9 5
                        ♣ K 5 4
        ♠ 2                            ♠ A Q 10 7 6 3
        ♡ 7 4             N            ♡ 5
        ◇ 8 6 4 3 2   W       E        ◇ A Q J   (Q J 7)
        ♣ Q J 10 9 3     S            ♣ 8 6 2   (A 6 2)
                        ♠ K J 9
                        ♡ A J 9 6 3 2
                        ◇ K 7       (A K)
                        ♣ A 7       (8 7)
```

South will win the club, pull the remaining trumps and play a diamond from the board towards his ◊ K, conceding the ◊ A as the third trick. Only an immediate diamond return enables us to take our second spade ruff. Should partner return a low spade, we must assume that his entry is in clubs and now is the appropriate time to lead one.

You are strongly advised to go through these examples over and over again until you are completely familiar with the three principal types of signalling and are able to recognize situations in which each applies, almost at a glance. The importance of second nature in this respect can hardly be overemphasized because we are now going to proceed to more complex defensive problems. In these, it will be necessary to put the information gleaned from these signals – and there could be several passing between defenders in the course of play of one hand – into use to complete accurate roll-calls in order to be able to play 'seeing' all four hands or, in the familiar jargon, 'double dummy'.

The first problem we are going to tackle is how to prevent South from using a long suit on the board. As mentioned earlier, there are a number of approaches.

The first arises when the board has no outside entries to the long suit. In that case, the aim will be to run South out of the suit before trumps are pulled. This is a typical example:

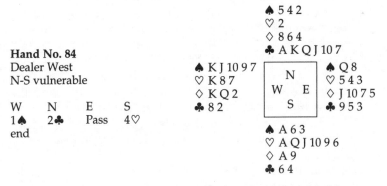

Hand No. 84
Dealer West
N-S vulnerable

W	N	E	S
1♠	2♣	Pass	4♡
end			

♠ 5 4 2
♡ 2
◊ 8 6 4
♣ A K Q J 10 7

♠ K J 10 9 7   ♠ Q 8
♡ K 8 7   ♡ 5 4 3
◊ K Q 2   ◊ J 10 7 5
♣ 8 2   ♣ 9 5 3

N / W E / S

♠ A 6 3
♡ A Q J 10 9 6
◊ A 9
♣ 6 4

To come in at the two-level at adverse vulnerability, North must, above all, have a good long suit of clubs. It seems likely that West will be unable to set up enough tricks in spades and diamonds before trumps are pulled and the clubs cashed. He thus resorts to disrupting declarer's plans by destroying communications in the club suit.

On the lead of the ♣8, the board wins and East considers which card to play. As the defence is trying to run South out of clubs, the relevant information is count, so East plays the ♣3 to show an odd number. When South is able to follow, this must surely be three. Were it a singleton, South would be left with four, in which case they are cold for at least a small slam in clubs and, as the suit cannot be cut out anyway, there is little need to worry.

Now South certainly cannot spare a club entry to take a trump finesse (which is marked wrong on the bidding anyway) so he plays the ♡A and ♡Q, losing to West's ♡K. Now a second round of clubs cuts off South's last link with the board while West's third trump remains at large. South now has nine tricks (five trumps, two clubs and the other two aces) but no more.

Notice a number of other points about this hand:

1 Had East shown an even number, play must take a different course:

   a If it is a doubleton, then South has three and the suit cannot be cut out and West must try to cash what tricks he can in spades and diamonds before South claims the rest.

   b If it is four, then South has a singleton and the damage has been completed. In practice, South will take a discard on a second round of clubs and indeed will take a second discard on a third round, hoping that the defender who has to ruff started with ♡ K x and that the ♡K will then drop under the ♡A. As South is discarding a loser, he will, at the worst, break even, i.e. trade one loser for another.

2 A spade lead will ensure three tricks for the defence (two spades and the trump) but no more. There is no time to set up the diamond as well.

3 North-South have bid the wrong contract – 3NT cannot be beaten. However, this is not easy for South to judge.

Again, the importance of understanding these comments on

hands is emphasized. It all contributes to the understanding and 'feel' for the game.

In situations where South has a long suit on the board which is not solid and especially where it has to be set up by ruffing (implying that South *must* run out first), then the defenders must attack the board's entry. Where the entry is in trumps and South obviously intends to complete the pulling of trumps on the board, then the defence must be to shorten the board's trumps by forcing it to ruff.

Let us look at an example:

Hand No. 85
Dealer East
N-S vulnerable

```
                                    ♠ Q 2
                                    ♡ Q 10 8
                                    ◇ Q 7 3
                                    ♣ A K 5 3 2
                        ♠ A K J 10 6  ┌─────┐  ♠ 9 8 3
W    N    E    S        ♡ 7 5 3       │  N  │  ♡ 6 2
          Pass  1♡      ◇ 9 2      W  │     │ E  ◇ A J 10 5 4
1♠   2♣   Pass  2♡      ♣ Q 10 6     │  S  │  ♣ 9 8 7
Pass 4♡   end                        └─────┘
                                    ♠ 7 5 4
                                    ♡ A K J 9 4
                                    ◇ K 8 6
                                    ♣ J 4
```

West leads the ♠A and when the North hand goes down, he sees that both clubs and trumps are likely to be breaking well for declarer. South's plan will therefore be to ruff the clubs high and pull trumps, making sure he wins the third round on the board so that he can cash the remaining clubs. To avoid this, West cashes the ♠K and plays a third spade at trick three, forcing the board to ruff. The club suit can still be established but the long cards cannot be cashed *after* trumps have been pulled. Thus South can make only five trump tricks, the spade ruff on the board, one diamond and the two top clubs to total nine, while the defenders will make the two top spades and two diamond tricks.

Again, notice the following points:

1 If West fails to force the board, South plays three rounds of clubs, ruffing the third and then three rounds of trumps, ending on the board, to enjoy the two long clubs. What

effectively has happened is that South has given up the extra trump trick (by virtue of the spade ruff on the board), but has taken two club tricks in return, thus making five trump tricks, four clubs and one diamond.

2 South can insist that the club suit comes in by refusing to ruff the third spade with the intention of ruffing the fourth round in hand. However, having taken three spade tricks, West shifts to diamonds to complete four tricks before South takes ten. It is therefore instructive to note that, if we give the ◇ A and ◇ J to declarer in exchange for the ◇ K and ◇ Q (thus the total point-count on each side is unaltered), this line of play ensures the contract and there is now no defence – an excellent illustration of the importance of quick tricks in trump contracts and how the point-count tends to undervalue the ace and overvalue the lower honors when a trump contract is being considered.

3 If West has four or more clubs, it is clear that South, with only one entry to the board, cannot bring in the club suit and will therefore have to resort to ruffing his losers on the board. West will therefore shift to a trump at trick *two* and, when he gets in with the second top spade, will persist with a further trump. Thus, if South started with four spades, he will only get one ruff rather than the two he needs.

The third variation arises when the board has an entry in a side suit. This must be attacked prematurely. Let us alter the last hand slightly:

Hand No. 86
Dealer East
N-S vulnerable

           ♠ Q 2
           ♡ 9 4 3
           ◇ A J 7
           ♣ A K 5 3 2

W	N	E	S
		Pass	1♡
1♠	2♣	2♠	Pass
Pass	3♠	Pass	4♡
end			

West hand: ♠ A K 10 9 6 ♡ 10 7 5 ◇ 9 5 ♣ Q 10 6

East hand: ♠ 8 5 4 3 ♡ 2 ◇ K Q 10 4 2 ♣ 9 8 7

South hand: ♠ J 7 ♡ A K Q J 8 6 ◇ 8 6 3 ♣ J 4

Let us first consider the auction. Many players would be tempted to bid 3♡ on the South hand on the second round, but this promises a stronger hand and could well encourage a misguided North into the slam zone with disastrous results. When the call comes round to North, he has a problem. With a hand easily worth an opening call (even discounting the worthless ♠Q) he must insist on game but 4♡, 3NT and 5♣ are all possibilities. As mentioned earlier, the way to find out more about partner's hand is the unassuming cue-bid and now South is happy to repeat his hearts.

West cashes the two top spades and when East peters to show an even number (encouragement/discouragement being obvious) and South drops the ♠J, the spade position is an open book. Again, West sees that the club suit is breaking well for declarer but, because his trump is higher than the board's highest, South cannot finish the pulling of trumps on the board. Now the entry is the ◊A and this must be attacked prematurely. West thus shifts to the ◊9 and South has no answer. If he wins, the clubs never come in and East waits for his two diamond tricks. If he refuses, the defence simply persists with diamonds until he does win.

You should have grasped the idea by now and I should like you to do two more examples against the stop-watch, completing them in a total of under five minutes. Do your seven roll-calls, decide how South is going to make his tricks and how you propose to stop him.

Problem 1
Hand No. 87
Dealer West
Both vulnerable

♠ 3
♡ 9 4 3
◊ K 8 7 3
♣ A K 8 5 3

W	N	E	S
1♠	2♣	2♠	4♡
Pass	4NT	Pass	5♡
Pass	6♡	end	

♠ A K Q 10 9
♡ 10 7
◊ J 5
♣ Q J 10 5

```
        N
   W         E
        S
```

Here, South bid 4♡ on his own and has shown a very good heart suit. With plenty of second-round controls, North chooses an appropriate moment for a Blackwood enquiry before bidding the slam. Your ♠A holds the first trick, partner playing the ♠J and South the ♠6.

How do you continue?

Problem 2				♠ J 3
Hand No. 88				♡ 6 5
Dealer North				◇ A K 4
Neither vulnerable				♣ A J 9 8 6 5

♠ A K 10 9 8 5
♡ 8 3
◇ Q 9
♣ K Q 4

W	N	E	S
	1♣	Pass	1♡
1♠	2♣	Pass	4NT
Pass	5♡	Pass	6♡
end			

```
        N
    W       E
        S
```

Again, you lead the ♠A to the ♠3, partner's ♠6 and South's ♠Q. How do you continue?

Solutions

Problem 1

Let us first roll-call the hand as far as possible:

Spades: Seven missing – partner must have at least three to have supported us but with six or more, he might have pre-empted to 4♠, even with a very low point-count. He probably has three, four or five, leaving South with four, three or two respectively.

Hearts: Eight missing – South's jump to game indicates at least a six-card suit and he could have all eight, leaving partner with two, one or none.

Diamonds: Seven missing – we know little at the moment except that South must have the ◇A on his bidding and that partner's ♠J indicates that, with a singleton spade on the table, he considered encouragement/discouragement and distribution of spades irrelevant and was trying to indicate a strong diamond holding. That should be at least ◇ Q 10 x x. So South will have the ◇A singleton, doubleton or trebleton.

Clubs:	Four missing – again we know little but all four in the South hand is ruled out; with a void, partner would have played a low spade, trying to get a ruff and South would probably have supported the clubs anyway. With a ruff threatened, 6♣ would be a far safer contract than 6♡.
Points:	We have 13 and the board 10, leaving 17 unaccounted for. Clearly South has the top hearts and the ◇A, leaving partner with, at best, the ♠J and ◇Q and perhaps a useless ♡J. So he has bid on a very low point-count, which suggests he has long spades – four or, more probably, five.
Tricks:	South will certainly have six top hearts in his own hand and the aces and kings of both minors to total ten. Limiting partner to five spades gives South at least two and we cannot prevent a ruff on the board to give eleven.

We can now work out the whole hand because we know that, if South has three or more spades, two ruffs on the board will give him twelve tricks, so he must be credited with only two spades. If he has seven hearts or more, again he has twelve tricks so he must be limited to six. In clubs, if he has three, our holding is solid and now South has no way of discarding his loser so we must credit him with two or one (although we have ruled out one by limiting him to three diamonds). Thus the critical layout is this:

```
                    ♠ 3
                    ♡ 9 4 3
                    ◇ K 8 7 3
                    ♣ A K 8 5 3
  ♠ A K Q 10 9   ┌─────────┐   ♠ J 8 5 4 2
  ♡ 10 7         │    N    │   ♡ 5 2
  ◇ J 5          │ W     E │   ◇ Q 10 9 2
  ♣ Q J 10 4     │    S    │   ♣ 9 6
                 └─────────┘
                    ♠ 7 6
                    ♡ A K Q J 8 6
                    ◇ A 6 4
                    ♣ 7 2
```

Now, the only way South can reach his twelfth trick is by setting up the long club. He will need to ruff them twice in hand and then return again to the board after pulling trumps to cash the winner. All this will require two side entries. Let us understand why. The procedure will be to cash the two top clubs and ruff a third; then use the first side entry to return to the board to ruff the fourth and thus establish the fifth. After pulling trumps from hand, he will then use his second side entry to reach the winning club.

He has one certain entry in the ◇K and as he has the ◇A in hand, we cannot dislodge it now, i.e. a diamond shift would be won in hand. The other entry must come from a spade ruff and that we *can* dislodge prematurely by playing a spade immediately.

As this hand is rather difficult, I am going to clarify it by playing it out together with you twice: first, on the assumption that we shift to a diamond at trick two; and second, with the correct defence. Lay out the cards as above and we shall do it together.

    (i) ♠A won by West.
   (ii) ◇J won by South's ◇A.
  (iii) ♣A won by North.
  (iv) ♣K won by North.
   (v) ♣3 ruffed by South as East discards a spade (no point in ruffing).
  (vi) ♠7 ruffed by North.
 (vii) ♣5 ruffed by South, East discarding another spade.
(viii) ♡A all following.
  (ix) ♡K all following – trumps are now cleared.
   (x) ◇4 to ◇K won by North.
  (xi) ♣8, South discards his last diamond, leaving him with two trumps for the last two tricks and success.

Now let us try again with the correct defence:

   (i) ♠A won by West.
  (ii) ♠K ruffed by North.
 (iii) ♣A won by North.

   (iv) ♣K won by North.

   (v) ♣3 ruffed by South.

  (vi) ◊4 to ◊K won by North.

 (vii) ♣5 ruffed by South.

(viii) ♡A all following.

  (ix) ♡K all following – trumps are now cleared.

   (x) Now what? The ♣8 is high on the board but South cannot get there to cash it. All he can do is cash the ◊A and the two trumps and concede the last diamond to East.

Finally, note that, if South actually has one club only, it makes not the slightest difference to the two variations above.

It is only by playing these hands out that you really appreciate what play and defence are about and I strongly urge you to do this throughout the book until it all becomes second nature.

Problem 2

Again, it appears that South will be trying to set up those long clubs, but let us play safe and do our roll-calls first.

Spades: Five missing – the board can follow twice, and with the possibility of cashing two winners, partner is expected to give count. His ♠6 confirms an even number (surely four) and South's ♠Q is an obvious singleton – a second-round control confirmed by his use of Blackwood.

Hearts: Nine missing – South has bid the slam on his own and will have at least a solid six-card suit, probably longer, leaving three or fewer for partner.

Diamonds: Eight missing – at the moment we know little.

Clubs: Four missing – again we know little at the moment, but we can see that we have to consider the position where South has exactly one. With two or more, our ♣ K Q are solid against the ♣A and there is no way that South can avoid the loser. With a void, South would not have used Blackwood as the number of aces is not critical.

Points: We have 14 and the board 13, leaving 13 unaccounted for – South has already shown the ♠Q and implied the top hearts, leaving the $\diamond$ J as the only useful card partner can possibly hold.

Tricks: Assuming South has a singleton club as agreed earlier, he will either need to have seven hearts and at least $\diamond$ J 8 x x, or eight hearts and at least $\diamond$ J x x to complete twelve tricks. Just to clarify this, in the first case, the diamond layout will be

$$\diamond \text{ A K 4}$$
$$\diamond \text{ Q 9} \qquad \diamond \text{ 10 6 3 2}$$
$$\diamond \text{ J 8 7 5}$$

and after our $\diamond$ Q drops on the second round, South will have a marked finesse against partner's $\diamond$ 10. In the second case, the layout will be

$$\diamond \text{ A K 4}$$
$$\diamond \text{ Q 9} \qquad \diamond \text{ 10 8 7 3 2}$$
$$\diamond \text{ J 6 5}$$

and with our $\diamond$ Q dropping, he will have three top tricks.

In these cases, there is nothing we can do. We thus have to hope that partner has the $\diamond$ J and, in that case, South will have to set up the long clubs. We can see that the suit is breaking 3–3, i.e. favorably for him. The only way to stop him is to realize that he will need an entry to ruff the suit high and another to cash the winners. With our $\heartsuit$ 8 being higher than the board's highest trump, trumps are ruled out and we must therefore shift to a diamond, removing an entry prematurely.

The deal:

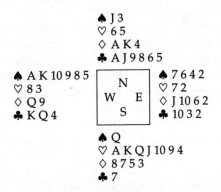

```
              ♠ J 3
              ♡ 6 5
              ◇ A K 4
              ♣ A J 9 8 6 5
♠ A K 10 9 8 5              ♠ 7 6 4 2
♡ 8 3           N          ♡ 7 2
◇ Q 9       W     E        ◇ J 10 6 2
♣ K Q 4         S          ♣ 10 3 2
              ♠ Q
              ♡ A K Q J 10 9 4
              ◇ 8 7 5 3
              ♣ 7
```

Try playing the hand out for yourself in two ways as we did above: first, assuming that West fails to shift to a diamond, and second, assuming that he does shift correctly, and you will see the difference.

When defenders are unable to attack entries to a long suit, there is another ploy available: holding up control of the suit. Try this example:

Hand No. 89
Dealer East
N-S vulnerable

```
              ♠ Q 6 4
              ♡ A 7 5
              ◇ K Q 9 7 3
              ♣ 9 8
                           ♠ K 8 7
              N            ♡ 9 6 2
           W     E         ◇ A 10 8
              S            ♣ K 10 6 4
```

W	N	E	S
		Pass	1♡
Pass	2◇	Pass	2NT
Pass	3♡	Pass	4♡
Pass			
end			

Partner leads the ♠J to the board's ♠4. You encourage with the ♠8 and South wins with the ♠A. At trick two, South plays the ◇5 to partner's ◇2 and the board's ◇Q. How do you defend?

Let us do our roll-calls:

Spades: Seven missing – South has suggested a balanced hand so a singleton or void is ruled out; he will have two, three or four, leaving partner with five, four or three respectively.

Hearts: Seven missing – South has indicated exactly five,
             leaving partner with two.

Diamonds: Five missing – partner's low card has indicated an
             odd number; a singleton is ruled out for two reasons.
             Partner surely would have led it and South, holding
             four, would surely be pulling trumps rather than risk
             running into a ruff. Thus partner must have three,
             leaving South with two.

Clubs: Seven missing – South will have two, three or four,
             leaving partner with five, four or three respectively.

Points: We have 10 and the board 11, leaving 19 unac-
             counted for, of which South has promised 15, leaving
             partner with 4, including the ♠J already played.

Tricks: South has one spade for certain but the rest is very
             unclear at the moment. What is certain, however, is
             that he has preferred to play on his side suit rather
             than pull trumps, which implies that he will need to
             establish long-suit cards in the suit and he is intend-
             ing to use the ♡A as entry. We cannot attack that
             entry unless partner has the ♡K. In that case, South
             will have ♣ A Q J and two finesses against our ♣K
             will give him three club tricks, five hearts, the spade
             and a diamond for ten tricks – no good. A better
             chance is to accept that the ♡A cannot be dislodged
             and credit partner with the ♣Q. That might give us a
             chance for a club trick (which will have to be won by
             partner), two spades and the ◇A. However, in the
             meantime, South is threatening to take five heart
             tricks, three diamonds and the two black aces. Let us
             look at the diamond position closely:

                         ◇ K Q 9 7 3
             ◇ J 6 2   ◇ A 10 8
                         ◇ 5 4

If we win the first diamond and shift to clubs
(remembering that spades cannot be profitably
attacked from our side), South will win, play a
second diamond to the ◇K and ruff a third round in

hand. Now three rounds of trumps ending on the board will enable him to cash the two remaining diamonds for ten tricks.

But now try the effect of refusing the first diamond and winning the second round. Now shift to a low club and South is in trouble.

The deal:

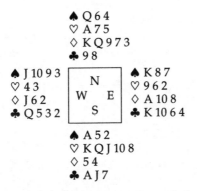

```
              ♠ Q 6 4
              ♡ A 7 5
              ◇ K Q 9 7 3
              ♣ 9 8
♠ J 10 9 3   ┌─────────┐   ♠ K 8 7
♡ 4 3        │    N    │   ♡ 9 6 2
◇ J 6 2      │ W     E │   ◇ A 10 8
♣ Q 5 3 2    │    S    │   ♣ K 10 6 4
             └─────────┘
              ♠ A 5 2
              ♡ K Q J 10 8
              ◇ 5 4
              ♣ A J 7
```

If he ducks, partner gets in immediately and the ♠10 ensures four tricks for the defence, as explained above. If he wins, he cannot get to the board to set up the diamonds without using the ♡A prematurely, after which he can never return to the board to cash the established winners. His only other possible entry (without touching the ♡A) is a club ruff, but he would have to lose a trick first to exhaust the board. West wins and the ♠10 sets the contract as before.

We are now going to look at ruffing in more detail and consider positions where a defender has length in trumps. We saw earlier that one way in which he can take trump tricks is to lead his short suit, most commonly a singleton but occasionally a doubleton. Hopefully, his partner will be able to win immediately or take an early trick before trumps are pulled, after which he can return the original suit for a ruff.

We also learnt that this return could contain a message indicating whether the higher- or lower-ranking of the remaining suits should be returned after the ruff. This would hopefully put partner back on play for a possible second ruff.

An alternative line of defence is to go to the other extreme and lead a long suit, hoping to force declarer to ruff. This might cause difficulty in situations when declarer's trumps are longer than the board's and the North-South partnership have few trumps to spare.

This a typical example:

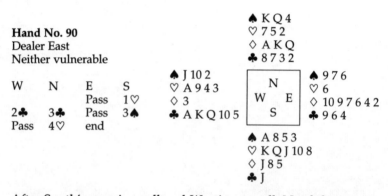

Hand No. 90
Dealer East
Neither vulnerable

♠ K Q 4
♡ 7 5 2
◇ A K Q
♣ 8 7 3 2

♠ J 10 2
♡ A 9 4 3
◇ 3
♣ A K Q 10 5

♠ 9 7 6
♡ 6
◇ 10 9 7 6 4 2
♣ 9 6 4

♠ A 8 5 3
♡ K Q J 10 8
◇ J 8 5
♣ J

W	N	E	S
		Pass	1♡
2♣	3♣	Pass	3♠
Pass	4♡	end	

After South's opening call and West's overcall, North has something of a problem. With 14 points opposite an opening call, he must insist on game but does not, at the moment, know which contract is best.

As indicated earlier, the unassuming cue-bid asks partner to describe his hand further. When South shows his spades, North must settle for 4♡.

West, on lead, realizes that, with 14 points in his own hand and his opponents in game, East will have next to nothing. That implies that a diamond ruff is a non-starter – East will never get in to lead one. West, with long trumps, therefore decides to try and shorten South's trumps by leading top clubs. South ruffs the second round but then what is he to do?

Suppose he tries to pull trumps. West wins the first round and plays a third round of clubs. If South ruffs again, his trumps become shorter than West's. He can pull two more trumps only, but then West is left with the last trump and two more winning clubs waiting and South finishes two tricks short. South might try turning the tables on West by playing on diamonds but now West will take his ruffs after all, finishing with four trump tricks and the first club.

The situation is more complex if North also runs out of clubs early and now South may have a better chance. Suppose we alter the above deal slightly, as follows:

Hand No. 91
Dealer East
Neither vulnerable

♠ K Q 4
♡ 7 5 2
◇ A K Q 2
♣ 8 7 3

♠ J 10 2
♡ A 9 4 3
◇ 3
♣ A K Q 10 5

♠ 9 7 6
♡ 6
◇ 10 9 7 6 4
♣ 9 6 4 2

♠ A 8 5 3
♡ K Q J 10 8
◇ J 8 5
♣ J

W	N	E	S
		Pass	1♡
2♣	3♣	Pass	3♠
Pass	4♡	end	

Again, West leads two top clubs and South ruffs. Now, South plays a trump and West wins to play a third club. This time, South simply refuses to ruff and makes the contract because any further club can be ruffed *on the board* while South's holding remains intact. Now South can pull trumps and claim the rest.

West must therefore defend more carefully. Winning the first round of trumps was fatal. Seeing that the board may be able to look after future club forces, he must refuse to take his ♡ A until the third round, so that North's trumps are exhausted. He can then continue the club force as before. But that is not the end of the story. Once East shows out on the second round of trumps, South realizes that to continue pulling trumps is fatal and turns the tables on West by shifting to diamonds. West must ruff but can take no more than the ♡ A for three tricks in total.

Returning to Hand 90, we can see that South can hold his losses to down one by abandoning trumps after the second round and playing on diamonds. West will be forced to ruff and South will refuse to ruff the fourth round of clubs so that North can ruff the fifth round. South can return to hand with the ♠ A to pull West's last trump and claim the remainder, having lost two trumps and two clubs only. If West refuses to ruff the diamonds, preferring to discard spades, South plays on spades until West does ruff. Notice also that West must take the first or second round of trumps otherwise South can shift to diamonds, conceding only two trumps and a club.

You are strongly urged to play over all the variations on these two hands to satisfy yourself that you understand them. Then you can try the next problem for yourself.

Hand No. 92
Dealer South
E-W vulnerable

♠ 8 7 2
♡ K 3 2
◇ A 10 5
♣ 7 6 4 2

```
                                          N        ♠ Q J 10 5
W        N        E        S           ┌──────┐    ♡ 4
                           1♡        W │      │ E  ◇ K 8 3 2
Pass     2♡       Pass     4♡          │  S   │    ♣ J 10 8 5
end                                    └──────┘
```

Partner leads the ♣A followed by the ♣K. South ruffs the second round, plays a trump to the board's ♡K and a second trump to his own ♡A. You discard a low diamond. Now South leads the ◇Q to partner's ◇7, the board's ◇5 and your ◇K. How do you continue?

South's bidding suggests at least a five-card trump suit and if he had six or more, he would have no reason to refrain from completing the pulling of trumps. What has clearly happened is that he has only five, leaving partner with four, and the enforced club ruff has reduced him to parity. This implies that, if he does complete the pulling of trumps and then loses the diamond finesse, you will be able to cash all the clubs to complete four tricks. He has therefore decided to test the diamonds before losing trump control. We now have a chance to go wrong. It looks tempting to lead that solid spade holding through South, but that will give him the contract. A points roll-call will confirm this. We have 7 and the board 7, leaving 26 unaccounted for and partner has already shown the three top clubs. South must have pretty well the rest of the points to justify his bidding and so it is clear that the deal looks something like this:

The deal:

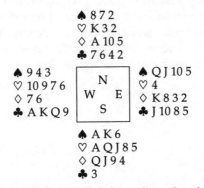

```
                    ♠ 8 7 2
                    ♡ K 3 2
                    ◇ A 10 5
                    ♣ 7 6 4 2
   ♠ 9 4 3                        ♠ Q J 10 5
   ♡ 10 9 7 6         N           ♡ 4
   ◇ 7 6          W       E       ◇ K 8 3 2
   ♣ A K Q 9          S           ♣ J 10 8 5
                    ♠ A K 6
                    ♡ A Q J 8 5
                    ◇ Q J 9 4
                    ♣ 3
```

We must lead a third round of clubs to force South again, leaving him with one trump against partner's two. If he pulls one more trump, partner will be left with the last trump and a club winner. If he doesn't, preferring to continue diamonds, partner will ruff and lead his last club, forcing South for a third time. Partner will be left with the last trump and the defenders will take two trump tricks, the diamond and the first club.

Sometimes it is necessary to force more than once to achieve parity.

Hand No. 93
Dealer West
Both vulnerable

```
                                    ♠ 7 4 3
                                    ♡ 7 6 5 2
                                    ◇ K Q 9
                                    ♣ Q 10 2
W      N      E      S
1♡     Pass   Pass   Dbl      ♠ A 8 2
2♡     Pass   Pass   2♠       ♡ A K 9 8 4 3        N
Pass   3♠     Pass   4♠       ◇ 4 2            W       E
end                           ♣ A 6                S
```

In the first place, South showed a three-suited hand, offering any of the non-heart suits to his partner. On the second round, he showed that his spades were longer than the minors. With 4144 and this strength, he would have doubled again – still for take-out as his partner has not bid. You lead out the two top hearts, partner following with the ♡J and ♡10 to confirm the doubleton, and South with the ♡Q and the ♠9. He continues with the ♠K and you take your ♠A, partner following. How do you continue?

Let us roll-call the hand in detail this time:

Spades: Seven missing – South is likely to have five, leaving partner with two.

Hearts: Three missing – open book, South had one and partner two.

Diamonds: Eight missing – South has promised at least three with the take-out double. He will probably have three or four, leaving partner with five or four respectively.

Clubs: Same applies.

So South's shape should be 5143, 5134 or (less likely) 6133.

Points: We have 15 and the board 7, leaving 18 unaccounted for, and partner has already shown the ♡J. With South having bid so strongly, partner is most unlikely to have any more.

Tricks: Giving South only five spades leaves him with four spade tricks and six tricks out of seven in the minors (losing the ♣A) to total ten, so we are already in difficulties having no more than our three aces at the moment. We can be certain, therefore, that if South does indeed have six spades, we have no chance whatsoever. If, however, he only has five, there is a chance. We have already reduced his holding by one with the first heart ruff and another one now will further reduce him to parity and he still has the ♣A to lose before he can set up his ten tricks. Let us play the hand out looking at the full deal.

The deal:

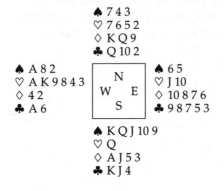

```
              ♠ 7 4 3
              ♡ 7 6 5 2
              ◇ K Q 9
              ♣ Q 10 2
♠ A 8 2                        ♠ 6 5
♡ A K 9 8 4 3      N           ♡ J 10
◇ 4 2          W       E       ◇ 10 8 7 6
♣ A 6              S           ♣ 9 8 7 5 3
              ♠ K Q J 10 9
              ♡ Q
              ◇ A J 5 3
              ♣ K J 4
```

   (i) ♡A won by West.

  (ii) ♡K ruffed by South.

 (iii) ♠K won by West's ♠A.

 (iv) ♡9 ruffed by South. Notice at this point that, if the ♡9 and ♡7 were exchanged, it would make no difference. East simply ruffs with his remaining (otherwise useless) trump and South has to overruff.

  (v) ♠Q won by South.

 (vi) ♠J won by South, completing the pulling of trumps but all trumps are now out.

 (vii) ◇3 to ◇K won by North.

(viii) ◇Q won by North. Note the play of the high honors from the short hand first.

 (ix) ◇9 to ◇A won by South, West discards a losing club.

  (x) ◇J won by South.

 (xi) A club won by West, who cashes the remaining hearts for down two.

South can, in fact, hold his losses to down one by abandoning trumps and playing on the minors himself, or by refusing to ruff the fourth round of hearts. The board's ♠7 controls the fifth round. It will be a useful exercise to replay the hand out for yourself following those lines of play. Trump control is a very big subject and familiarity with this simple position will stand you in good stead for more complicated positions which will follow in advanced books.

There are also positions where it will pay to force the board to ruff and thus shorten its holding. This is likely to occur when South is threatening to take a finesse against an honor in the East hand. Try this example:

Hand No. 94
Dealer West
Neither vulnerable

♠ 8 4
♡ 4 2
◇ K J 10 3 2
♣ A K Q J

W	N	E	S
Pass	1◇	2♠	3♡
Pass	4♣	Pass	4♡
end			

```
        N
  W           E
        S
```

♠ A K Q 3 2
♡ K 7 5
◇ A 9 4
♣ 4 3

West leads the ♠7 to the ♠4, your ♠Q and South's ♠5. On your ♠A, South follows with the ♠10 and West confirms his trebleton by playing the ♠9. How do you continue? Let us roll-call the hand:

Spades: Open book – West started with three and South three.

Hearts: Eight missing – with South having come in at the three-level and repeating the suit rather than show interest in either of North's minors, he will surely have at least a good six-card suit and could well have more, leaving partner with two or fewer.

Diamonds: Five missing – we know little at the moment but South, having failed to show interest in his partner's announced five-card or longer suit, will certainly have fewer than four, leaving partner with two, three, four or five.

Clubs: Seven missing – similar thoughts apply to diamonds, bearing in mind that North has only promised four this time.

Points: We have 16 and the board 14, leaving 10 unaccounted for. It is most unlikely that partner has any at all. Even if he has the ◇Q, it is badly placed under the board's holding.

Tricks: South has four clubs on view and plenty of hearts and diamonds if necessary – it is a question of

whether we can take four. We have already taken
two in spades and must hope that the ◊A is not
ruffed, i.e. that South can follow at least once. All
appears to rest on the ♡K which, as we can see, is
badly placed under an enormous suit in the South
hand. To catch it, however, South will have to take
two finesses, i.e. lead twice from the board. He has
no problems with entries as the board has all those
high clubs. But if we can remove one of those trumps
from the board prematurely, South will not be able to
catch our ♡K.

The best defence is therefore to cash the ◊A (just
in case South can discard a diamond loser on the
clubs) and then play a third spade. We are then
covered if the deal should prove to be something like
this:

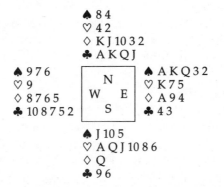

♠ 8 4
♡ 4 2
◊ K J 10 3 2
♣ A K Q J

♠ 9 7 6
♡ 9
◊ 8 7 6 5
♣ 10 8 7 5 2

N
W   E
S

♠ A K Q 3 2
♡ K 7 5
◊ A 9 4
♣ 4 3

♠ J 10 5
♡ A Q J 10 8 6
◊ Q
♣ 9 6

Satisfy yourself that no other line of defence works. If we force
the board at once, South will take the one trump finesse he has
been allowed, cash the ♡A and then play three top clubs. We can
ruff the third, but that will be with the ♡K, which we were going
to score anyway. South simply discards his ◊Q and the rest of
his hand is trumps.

We learnt earlier that, with the advantage of the opening lead,
defenders can often set a contract by arranging ruffs before
trumps are pulled. In the examples shown, these ruffs were
winners, but we are now going to demonstrate that they can be

worthwhile even if the enemy is able to overruff. Consider this example:

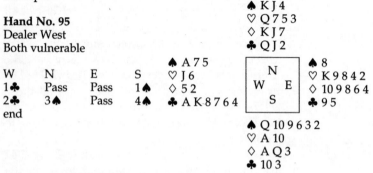

Hand No. 95
Dealer West
Both vulnerable

W	N	E	S
1♣	Pass	Pass	1♠
2♣	3♠	Pass	4♠
end			

♠ KJ4
♡ Q753
◊ KJ7
♣ QJ2

♠ A75
♡ J6
◊ 52
♣ AK8764

♠ 8
♡ K9842
◊ 109864
♣ 95

♠ Q109632
♡ A10
◊ AQ3
♣ 103

West leads out the two top clubs and when all follow, the club situation is an open book. West now realizes that, if he shifts to another suit, trumps will be pulled and the ♣Q on the board will win a trick later on.

Observe the effect, however, of playing a third club now. East is now able to ruff the ♣Q and although South can overruff, the contract cannot now be made. Let us clarify this point by playing the hand out both ways.

  (i) ♣A won by West.
 (ii) ♣K won by West.
(iii) Say West shifts to a diamond. Note that it is dangerous for him to attack hearts. The heart position round the table is such that whichever side touches it will lose one more trick than otherwise. South wins.
 (iv) A spade won by West's ♠A.
  (v) Another diamond won by North (whether North or South wins the diamond tricks does not matter).
 (vi) ♠K won by North.
(vii) ♠J won by North, clearing the trumps.
(viii) ♣Q won by North, South discarding the ♡10.

That leaves South with three trumps, the ♡A and a winning diamond and he claims the rest.

Now let us defend the hand correctly:

  (i)   ♣A won by West.

 (ii)   ♣K won by West.

(iii)   Another club to North's ♣Q, ruffed by East and overruffed by South.

(iv)   A trump won by West's ♠A.

 (v)   A diamond won by North or South.

(vi)   A trump won by North or South.

(vii)   One more trump won by North or South to clear the trumps.

South is now left with two winning trumps, two winning diamonds and the ace and ten of hearts. There is nothing he can do now to avoid a heart loser as he, rather than the defenders, will have to attack the suit. Note the importance of East's being able to use a *losing* trump. Let us alter the spade position from

```
              ♠ K J 4
   ♠ A 7 5              ♠ 8
              ♠ Q 10 9 6 3 2
```

to

```
              ♠ K J 4
   ♠ 8 7 5              ♠ A
              ♠ Q 10 9 6 3 2
```

and now there is no defence. East would have to ruff the ♣Q with the ♠A, which is a winning defensive trick anyway, and South could happily discard his ♡10. What has effectively happened is that the defenders' two tricks in hearts and trumps have been coalesced into one. The position is similar to that which would have arisen in Hand 79 had we failed to cash the ♢A. Nothing is more important than acquiring the habit of recognizing these similar situations. The chances of a given deal cropping up twice may well be negligible, but deals requiring similar handling occur daily.

Having grasped the idea, you should have no difficulty in defending this next hand (overleaf):

248   *The Expert Improver*

Hand No. 96

Dealer East

E-W vulnerable

♠ A Q 8 4
♡ K 5 4 2
◇ 10 7 4
♣ 9 6

W	N	E	S
		Pass	1NT
Pass	2♣	Pass	2♡
Pass	4♡	end	

N

W E

S

♠ J 9
♡ A 6
◇ 9 6 3 2
♣ A J 7 3 2

West leads the ◇K to the ◇4, ◇2 and South's ◇A. South cashes the ♠K, partner following with the ♠2, and then leads the ♠5 to the board's ♠A. Now follows the ♠Q. How do you defend?

First let us roll-call the hand on the information we have so far:

Spades: Seven missing – with a long suit on the board, South advertizing all the big honors and the suit being attacked before trumps are pulled, partner is expected to give count. It is obvious that South is playing spades early in a desperate attempt to discard losers (obviously in diamonds), before giving up the lead to our ace of trumps. There would be no point in playing spades for any other reason. Clearly he started with a doubleton spade confirmed by partner's signalling an odd number, in this case five.

Hearts: Seven missing – South guaranteed four and will, on rare occasions have five, leaving partner with three or two respectively.

Diamonds: Six missing and South will have at least two for his 1NT call. If he had four, the one discard on the spade, for which he is hoping, will achieve nothing, so he must have two or three, leaving partner with four or three respectively.

Clubs: Six missing – South can have two, three or four, leaving partner with four, three or two respectively.

Points: We have 10 and the board 9, leaving 21 unaccounted for and South has promised 15–17, leaving partner with 4–6 respectively. In the light of the play so far, we can be more specific. Partner has led the ◇K, surely promising the ◇Q for 5 points so far. Thus the best we can hope for is another jack. We have the two black jacks and, on the information to date, partner is more likely to have the ◇J, if indeed he has a jack at all.

Tricks: South will probably make at least three heart tricks out of four, or four out of five, and he has both ♣K and ♣Q and they are well placed behind our ♣A, two club tricks unless they are a doubleton. He has already taken two spades and a diamond and any extra clubs can be ruffed on the board. In defence, we have our two aces and the only hope for two more rests in diamonds. South is threatening to discard one immediately on the ♠Q and we must prevent this by ruffing. But it is no good ruffing with the ♡A as South will discard his diamond loser anyway. We must force South to ruff his own trick by ruffing with the ♡6 so that he has to overruff. Nothing now can prevent our taking two diamonds and two aces.

The deal:

```
                    ♠ A Q 8 4
                    ♡ K 5 4 2
                    ◇ 10 7 4
                    ♣ 9 6
     ♠ 10 7 6 3 2   ┌─────────┐   ♠ J 9
     ♡ 9 7          │    N    │   ♡ A 6
     ◇ K Q J        │ W     E │   ◇ 9 6 3 2
     ♣ 10 8 2       │    S    │   ♣ A J 7 4 3
                    └─────────┘
                    ♠ K 5
                    ♡ Q J 10 8 3
                    ◇ A 8 5
                    ♣ K Q 5
```

South was unlucky to find the spades splitting 5–2, but still would have been successful had our ♡A been a singleton.

We are going to conclude this trump contract defence section with some miscellaneous examples which I should like you to do against the stop-watch, aiming for under two minutes each.

Problem 1
Hand No. 97
Dealer North
N-S vulnerable

♠ 7 6 5
♡ J 3 2
◇ K Q J 4 2
♣ K 3

♠ A K J 10 4
♡ 9 7
◇ 9 8 5
♣ J 8 7

W	N	E	S
	Pass	Pass	1♡
1♠	2◇	Pass	3♡
Pass	4♡	end	

```
      N
   W     E
      S
```

You lead the top two spades, partner following with the ♠2 and ♠8 and South with the ♠3 and ♠Q. How do you continue?

Problem 2
Hand No. 98
Dealer West
E-W vulnerable

♠ 10
♡ A J 9 7 4
◇ K J 7 2
♣ A J 8

♠ Q 9 8 7 6 2
♡ K 10 8
◇ 5
♣ K 9 6

W	N	E	S
Pass	1♡	Pass	2◇
Pass	3◇	Pass	4◇
Pass	5◇	end	

```
      N
   W     E
      S
```

Partner leads the ♣5 to the board's ♣8. How do you defend?

Problem 3
Hand No. 99
Dealer North
E-W vulnerable

♠ A 7
♡ 8 6 5 4 3
◇ Q J 9
♣ K 4 2

♠ K J 6
♡ 7 2
◇ K 10 5 2
♣ J 10 7 3

W	N	E	S
	Pass	1♣	1♠
2♣	Pass	Pass	2♡
3♣	4♡	end	

```
      N
   W     E
      S
```

You lead the ♣J to the ♣2, ♣8 and ♣9. You continue with the ♣3 to the ♣4, ♣Q and South's ♡9. South cashes the ♡A, partner dropping the ♡Q. Now a spade to the board's ♠A is followed by a second round to South's ♠Q and your ♠K, partner following with the ♠2 and ♠4. How do you continue?

Problem 4
Hand No. 100
Dealer West
Both vulnerable

♠ Q 10 4
♡ A 8 6 3
◇ K 7 4
♣ K 5 4

				♠ 9 5
W	N	E	S	♡ K 10 7 5 2
Pass	1♣	Pass	1♠	◇ A 10 9
Pass	1NT	Pass	4♠	♣ Q J 3
end				

Partner leads the ◇ 2 to the board's ◇ 4. How do you defend?

Problem 5
Hand No. 101
Dealer East
E-W vulnerable

♠ J 6
♡ K J 7 4 2
◇ J 7
♣ A K 5 4

W	N	E	S		
		Pass	1♡	♠ 8 5	
Pass	2♣	Pass	2♡	♡ A Q	
Pass	4♡	Pass	4NT	◇ K Q 10	
Pass	5◇	Pass	6♡	♣ 10 8 7 6 3 2	
end					

After South's opening call, North gave a delayed game raise, showing his strong clubs first. Remember that, when bidding 2♣, North has no intention of playing in clubs. He knows that 4♡ is favorite as goal contract, but partner could have up to 19 points and a slam could be on, so it is better to give what is likely to be useful information first. Then, after the 4♡ call, partner is better placed to decide whether to go further.

On the auction, it is probable that the ♡K is with South, and you are tempted to double. Before doing so, however, it is wise to consider the odds involved. Opponents are non-vulnerable so, assuming you take the contract down one, your gain is $(100 - 50) = 50$. If they make the contract, your loss is 180 (for 6♡) + 50 (for the insult) = 230. You must, therefore, be confident of about 4:1 on to make the double sensible. To be fair, with your strong diamond holding, a two-trick set is a serious possibility and now the double gains $(300 - 100) = 200$. Even now, the odds needed are better than even money. In all this, we have not considered the possibility of a redouble, and now the loss is $3 \times 180 + 50 = 590$, against $(200 - 50) = 150$ gained for a one-trick defeat, or $(600 - 100) = 500$ gained for a two-trick set. Bearing in mind that they will not redouble unless they are very confident of success, the two-trick set must be deemed highly unlikely. All things considered, a double cannot be worth it and the sight of the ♡K on the board confirms your wisdom.

You lead the ◇K to the ◇7, ◇2 and South's ◇A. South follows with three top spades. All follow to the first two rounds, but how do you defend on the third?

Problem 6
Hand No. 102
Dealer South
Neither vulnerable

♠ 6			
♡ Q J 5 4			
◇ A K Q 10 9			
♣ A 10 6			

W	N	E	S
			1♣
Pass	1◇	1♠	2♣
2♠	4NT	Pass	5◇
Pass	6♣	end	

```
            N
      ♠ 6            ♠ A K Q 8 5 3
      ♡ Q J 5 4      ♡ 7 3
      ◇ A K Q 10 9   ◇ 8
  W   ♣ A 10 6   E   ♣ Q 7 4 2
            S
```

Partner leads the ♠2 to the ♠6, your ♠Q and South's ♠4. How do you continue?

Problem 7
Hand No. 103
Dealer West
Neither vulnerable

♠ 6 5 3			
♡ Q 9			
◇ A J 5			
♣ K Q 6 5 3			

W	N	E	S
Pass	1♣	Pass	1♡
Pass	1NT	Pass	4♡
end			

```
      ♠ 10 9 8 4        N
      ♡ 7 4
      ◇ K 10 9     W        E
      ♣ A J 9 4        S
```

You lead the ♠10. Partner takes his ♠K and ♠A and returns a third round. South wins, having started with ♠ Q J 7. He now pulls trumps in three rounds, finding partner with ♡ 6 3 2, while you discard a spade on the third round. Now comes the ♣8. How do you defend?

Problem 8
Hand No. 104
Dealer West
Both vulnerable

♠ A Q J 9
♡ 7 2
◇ K J 10
♣ A Q 10 5

W	N	E	S
Pass	1♣	Pass	1♠
Pass	3♠	Pass	4♠
end			

```
        N          ♠ 8 5 3
                   ♡ A 9 8 5 4
   W         E     ◇ A
        S          ♣ 8 7 4 2
```

Partner leads the ♡K and the board plays the ♡2. How do you defend?

Solutions

Problem 1

Spades: The play to the first two tricks has revealed the position exactly – partner showed an odd number and South the doubleton queen.

Hearts: Eight missing – in principle, South ought to have six for his rebid but, in view of our overcall, there are hands on which he may have to rebid 3♡ on a good five-card suit – typically 2533 or similar shapes with no spade stop. On such hands, he would have rebid 2NT in the absence of our overcall. Remember that, with North having passed originally, the 2◇ call is non-forcing.

Diamonds: Five missing – at present, we know little except that South failed to support his partner – thus four or more in his hand are unlikely.

Clubs: Eight missing – again, we know little but South failed to bid 3♣; therefore he will not have as many as five. So partner will have four or more.

Points: We have 9 and the board 10, leaving 21 unaccounted for, and South is likely to have at least 14, probably more as they include a devalued ♠Q. Partner is left with 7 at the most.

Tricks: South is likely to have six trump tricks and the diamonds are breaking evenly so they will produce at least another four. South will be able to discard any further losers on those diamonds, so there is no time to lose. There are clearly no more tricks available to us in spades and we must immediately shift to the only other likely source, clubs. We hope that the deal will look something like this:

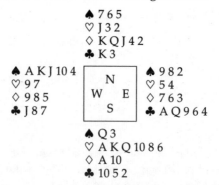

```
                    ♠ 7 6 5
                    ♡ J 3 2
                    ◊ K Q J 4 2
                    ♣ K 3
♠ A K J 10 4                        ♠ 9 8 2
♡ 9 7              N                ♡ 5 4
◊ 9 8 5        W       E            ◊ 7 6 3
♣ J 8 7           S                ♣ A Q 9 6 4
                    ♠ Q 3
                    ♡ A K Q 10 8 6
                    ◊ A 10
                    ♣ 10 5 2
```

We can now take four tricks before South takes ten. Were you tempted to lead a third spade to force declarer? In itself, this can hardly give anything away, but you should not adopt forcing tactics without good reason. Here there was no hope of damaging declarer by shortening his trumps, even if he only started with five of them. Our hand can never regain the lead and thus the force cannot be repeated.

Problem 2

Spades: Six missing – at the moment, we know little except that South did not bid them and partner did not lead them; South is therefore unlikely to have more than four, leaving partner with at least two.

Hearts: Five missing – South preferred 5◊ to 4♡ as final contract and is therefore unlikely to have more than a doubleton heart, leaving partner with at least three.

Diamonds: Eight missing – South's bidding suggests at least five. It will be a useful exercise to prove this. South has denied three hearts and if he only had four diamonds (his first call guaranteed no more), that would leave at least seven cards in the black suits, i.e at least four in one of them. Over 1♡, he would have bid a four-card suit in either spades or clubs in front of a four-card diamond suit on the principle of bidding four-card suits in ascending order to give the partnership as much bidding space as possible.

I have included this discussion because I want you to get into the habit of picking up these inferences. I must warn you that you will have to be prepared to look silly periodically when opponents have bid or played incorrectly – it happens to me time and again! Nevertheless, I am carrying on regardless. The overall gain outweighs the loss severalfold.

Clubs: Seven missing – at present, we know little but South must have at least a doubleton. With a singleton, he would have gone up with the ♣A and saved himself a loser. So partner will have five or fewer.

Points: We have 8 and the board 14, leaving 18 unaccounted for and South, having bid two-over-one, should have at least 9 unless his diamonds are very long. Thus the best we can hope for from partner is about 7.

Tricks: South will have at least four in diamonds and possibly up to two spade ruffs. The hearts are breaking favorably so there could be another four there, assuming South has the queen to add to the ♣A. It is thus a question of whether we can take three tricks first. In situations like this, we must make reasonably optimistic assumptions, bearing in mind that they must be consistent with the auction and play so far and the roll-calls above. We have already confirmed that South has at least a doubleton club, giving us one trick there. In hearts, if he has a singleton or void, there is no hope for our ♡K so we must credit him with a doubleton. Remember we have already deemed it unlikely that he has as many as three. That will give us a heart trick and we shall have to hope that partner has either the diamond or spade ace. Note that, with a singleton on the table, the ♠K is of no use to the defence and is therefore best credited to South. With the strong diamond tenace on the board, a similar argument applies to the ◇Q.

On that basis, the aces of diamonds and spades could be split between West and South. There remains the question of the ♣Q. Let us take a look at that lead in more detail. When leading a long suit against a trump contract, the guide of leading fourth-highest and the associated rule of eleven still apply. $11 - 5 = 6$ and we can see six cards higher than the five in our hand and the board's. That means that South must be credited with two very low clubs and the full deal will have to look something like this:

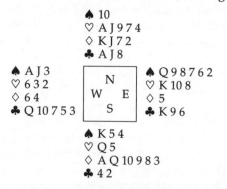

```
                  ♠ 10
                  ♡ A J 9 7 4
                  ◇ K J 7 2
                  ♣ A J 8
  ♠ A J 3                        ♠ Q 9 8 7 6 2
  ♡ 6 3 2          N             ♡ K 10 8
  ◇ 6 4         W     E          ◇ 5
  ♣ Q 10 7 5 3     S             ♣ K 9 6
                  ♠ K 5 4
                  ♡ Q 5
                  ◇ A Q 10 9 8 3
                  ♣ 4 2
```

We can see that we must play the ♣9 to this trick. Rising with the ♣K gives South the opportunity to take a finesse against partner's ♣Q and then discard his losing heart on the ♣A. He will then lose the ♠A but no more. When the ♣9 holds, we can safely return any card except, of course, a heart.

Problem 3

Spades: Eight missing – South's bidding has indicated at least five and partner's indication of an odd number confirms that it is five exactly, leaving partner with three.

Hearts: Six missing – again, South has suggested at least five, confirmed by partner's ♡Q, which is obviously a singleton.

Diamonds   Six missing – the distribution is an open book as we shall see when we consider the clubs.

Clubs: Open book – South started with a singleton, leaving partner with five and thus we can confirm that, with five spades, five hearts and one club, South has exactly two diamonds, leaving partner with four.

Points: We have 8 and the board 10, leaving 22 unaccounted for and partner's opening call indicated at least 12 (and that would be minimal, particularly when we consider that he has no more than 5 clubs and his points include a stiff ♡Q). South is already marked with the ♠Q and ♡ A K J so the whole hand is an open book:

```
              ♠ A 7
              ♡ 8 6 5 4 3
              ◇ Q J 9
              ♣ K 4 2
  ♠ K J 6                      ♠ 5 4 2
  ♡ 7 2          N             ♡ Q
  ◇ K 10 5 2   W   E           ◇ A 7 6 4
  ♣ J 10 7 3     S             ♣ A Q 8 6 5
              ♠ Q 10 9 8 3
              ♡ A K J 10 9
              ◇ 8 3
              ♣ 9
```

Tricks: South is threatening to ruff out the spades and discard two of the board's diamonds on the two established spades. That would give him five top hearts, the ♠A, the two long spades and, after giving up a diamond trick, a diamond ruff on the board for ten in total.

There is therefore no time to lose. Counting our own tricks, we have the ♣A and the ♠K already in the bag and we must cash our two diamonds before one of them runs away.

Notice South's play in the trump suit. He had to play one round because, had our hand shown out, he would have needed to use the ♠A as an entry to take the marked finesse against partner's protected ♡Q. However, once he had been informed that the trumps were breaking favorably, there was no rush for the second round. This would have given partner a chance to discard a high diamond to make our life much easier. Fortunately roll-calling led us to the correct defence, but players brought up on 'Never lead away from a king!' would have presented South with an unmakeable contract.

Problem 4

Spades: Eight missing – South's bidding promises at least six and he could have more; partner thus has two or fewer.

Hearts: Four missing – at the moment, we know little, but a singleton in partner's hand is unlikely as he would surely have led it.

Diamonds: Seven missing – partner's ♢2 will come from three or four to an honor, leaving South with four or three respectively.

Clubs: Seven missing – again, we know little, but South is unlikely to have more than four. With a 6:5 or more eccentric two-suiter, he might well have bid both suits, jumping first to 3♠ with the intention of bidding 4♣ over 3NT, a slam being a strong possibility.

Points: We have 10 and the board 12, leaving 18 unaccounted for. With his partner having promised no more than 12 and a doubleton spade, South has insisted on game. With only six spades, he ought to have a minimum of about 11 points; he could have fewer if his spades are longer. Thus the best we can hope for from partner is about 7.

Tricks: There are various possibilities but we know that
           South has at least nine cards in spades and dia-
           monds, leaving four for the other two suits. Partner's
           lead of a low card rather than an honor suggests that
           he does not have both queen and jack in either red
           suit. With such a holding, he is more likely to have
           led the queen. It is therefore likely that South will
           have at least one honor in each of these suits. We
           may go further and say that it is almost certain that
           he has exactly one honor in each. If he had both heart
           honors, partner would have been left with nothing
           but low cards, which would have made a much safer
           opening lead than a low card from a diamond honor,
           both opponents having shown reasonable hands.

           This implies that he has at least one diamond trick,
           however we play to the first trick, and the ♣K must
           score, irrespective of the position of the ♣A. We
           have given partner at least 2 points in the red suits so
           that he is unlikely to have more than a black ace
           outside. That will leave South with five spade tricks
           and another club, or six spade tricks, to total eight
           and the ♡A gives a ninth.

It thus appears that the diamond suit is critical and we must look
at the layout in more detail. If it is

$$\diamond \, K\,7\,4$$
$$\diamond \, Q\,x\,x\,x \qquad \qquad \diamond \, A\,10\,9$$
$$\diamond \, J\,x\,x$$

we can win two tricks in the suit by winning immediately and
returning the suit or by ducking and waiting for a second round
from partner.

But if it is

$$\diamond \, K\,7\,4$$
$$\diamond \, J\,x\,x\,x \qquad \qquad \diamond \, A\,10\,9$$
$$\diamond \, Q\,x\,x$$

then we can only win two tricks by ducking now and waiting for a second round from partner. We hope to add those to the ♡K and a black ace or, where South is 6133, two club tricks.

The deal:

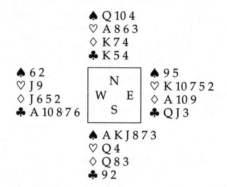

```
                      ♠ Q 10 4
                      ♡ A 8 6 3
                      ◇ K 7 4
                      ♣ K 5 4
      ♠ 6 2                          ♠ 9 5
      ♡ J 9           N              ♡ K 10 7 5 2
      ◇ J 6 5 2    W     E           ◇ A 10 9
      ♣ A 10 8 7 6     S             ♣ Q J 3
                      ♠ A K J 8 7 3
                      ♡ Q 4
                      ◇ Q 8 3
                      ♣ 9 2
```

Note that the low diamond on trick one can never cost. Given that South has at least three diamonds, even if he were unkind enough to turn up with a singleton ♣A, he could take one diamond discard on the ♣K but would still have one diamond left and our ◇A will never run away.

Problem 5

Spades: Nine missing – South has already shown three and East two, but apart from that, we only know that South's spades will be shorter than his hearts.

Hearts: Six missing – South rebid the suit and will have at least five. His advance to the slam zone indicates that he has all six, leaving partner void. Thus South cannot have more than five spades at the moment.

Diamonds: Eight missing – on the opening lead, it should be clear to partner that we have the ◇Q and South the ◇A. Thus encouragement/discouragement is superfluous and he is expected to give count. His ◇2 indicates an odd number. A singleton, leaving South with seven, is clearly out of the question. A trebleton, leaving South with five, is also out. With six hearts and five diamonds, South would have rebid 2◇

rather than insist on a heart suit missing all four tops. Thus partner has five or seven, leaving South with three or one respectively.

Clubs: Three missing – we know little at the moment, but South is unlikely to have all three. This would imply that partner has two voids and surely he would have bid, even without a point in his hand.

Points: We have 11 and the board 13, leaving 16 unaccounted for and South has already shown the three top spades and the ♢A. The club honor position is not yet clear.

Tricks: The early play has made the position an open book. South would only play on spades *before pulling trumps* if he was desperate to discard the board's diamond loser before losing the lead to our ♡A. This means that not only has South a diamond loser in his hand but also that he is unable to discard it on the board's clubs. There is only one layout consistent with this: South must have a trebleton diamond, leaving him with a singleton club. That singleton cannot be the ♣Q. If it were, he could discard his two losing diamonds on the board's ♣A and ♣K, gaining an entry to the board by ruffing the ♠Q. Thus partner will have to have the ♣Q and the full deal will need to look something like this:

```
              ♠ J 6
              ♡ K J 7 4 2
              ♢ J 7
              ♣ A K 5 4
♠ 8 5                        ♠ 10 9 7 4 3 2
♡ A Q         ┌─────────┐    ♡ –
♢ K Q 10      │    N    │    ♢ 9 6 4 3 2
♣ 10 8 7 6 3 2│ W     E │    ♣ Q 9
              │    S    │
              └─────────┘
              ♠ A K Q
              ♡ 10 9 8 6 5 3
              ♢ A 8 5
              ♣ J
```

We have three options. If we refuse to ruff the ♠Q at all, the losing ◇J will be discarded. After that, a low trump from the South hand will ensure only one trick lost. Similarly, if we ruff with the ♡A, the ◇J will still be discarded and we will take no further trick. We must therefore observe the guide of ruffing with a *losing* trump, the ♡Q. Now South is obliged to overruff or lose two trump tricks.

After that, the diamond loser cannot be avoided. South can discard one diamond from his hand on a top club but that does not help. If you found this defence, you can reflect on whether you should have doubled after all!

Problem 6

Spades: Six missing – partner has led an obvious fourth-high, leaving South with two.

Hearts: Seven missing – we know little at the moment but South is unlikely to have more than four, leaving partner with at least three.

Diamonds: Seven missing – South preferred to rebid his own suit rather than support partner, so he is unlikely to have more than three, leaving partner with at least four.

Clubs: Six missing – South, having repeated his suit, will have at least five. Remembering that, after our intervention, he was no longer forced to speak, he could well have all six.

Points: We have 11 and the board 16, leaving 13 unaccounted for; South opened the bidding and partner gave us a raise. It is clear, therefore, that there is a great deal of distribution around and the picture is now becoming clearer. Partner does not have enough to raise us without a void of clubs, leaving six for South.

Tricks: South will have plenty of tricks in clubs, diamonds and hearts as well as a spade ruff and it is a question of whether we can take a second trick. There is clearly no hope in the red suits and the only realistic candidate is the ♣Q. Once South plays a club to the board's ♣A and partner shows out, the position will be clear and all South needs to do is to take two finesses through our ♣Q. To prevent this, we must remove one of the board's trumps by forcing a spade ruff. We thus return a spade at trick two.

The deal:

```
              ♠ 6
              ♡ Q J 5 4
              ◇ A K Q 10 9
              ♣ A 10 6
♠ J 9 7 2                      ♠ A K Q 8 5 3
♡ 10 9 8 2      N              ♡ 7 3
◇ 7 6 5 4 3   W   E            ◇ 8
♣ –             S              ♣ Q 7 4 2
              ♠ 10 4
              ♡ A K 6
              ◇ J 2
              ♣ K J 9 8 5 3
```

Problem 7

Spades: Open book – they have all gone.

Hearts: Open book – South promised at least six for his call and partner's ability to follow three times confirms that South started with exactly six.

Diamonds: Seven missing – we already know ten of South's cards (three spades, six hearts and one club) so he cannot have more than three. So he has none, one, two or three, leaving partner with seven, six, five or four respectively.

Clubs: Four missing – South has already shown one. He could have up to all four, leaving partner with three, two, one or none respectively.

Points: We have 8 and the board 12, leaving 20 unaccounted for. For his jump to game with a six-card suit, South ought to have a minimum of about 11, leaving partner with 9 at most and he has already shown up with ♠A and ♠K leaving, at best, only 2 outstanding. South has the three outstanding heart honors and has shown the ♠Q and ♠J. That leaves only the ◇Q unaccounted for.

Tricks: South has one spade and six hearts to total seven so far. The ◇A brings it up to eight and therefore, if he makes two club tricks, he has ten. On our side, there are the two top spades and the ♣A, but we shall be too late to set up a diamond.

Going up with the ♣A at this point is therefore ruled out. We have to hold up, allowing the board to win, and if it turns out that this costs us our trick, we will get *two* diamond tricks in return provided partner has the ◇Q in this type of layout:

```
                    ♠ 6 5 3
                    ♡ Q 9
                    ◇ A J 5
                    ♣ K Q 6 5 3
     ♠ 10 9 8 4                      ♠ A K 2
     ♡ 7 4          ┌─────────┐      ♡ 6 3 2
     ◇ K 10 9       │   N     │      ◇ Q 8 3 2
     ♣ A J 9 4      │ W   E   │      ♣ 10 7 2
                    │   S     │
                    └─────────┘
                    ♠ Q J 7
                    ♡ A K J 10 8 5
                    ◇ 7 6 4
                    ♣ 8
```

This was a position we discussed at some length in the beginners' book. What we had to consider was whether to rise with the ♣A, winning one trick and losing two, or to play low, winning no trick and losing one. Within the context of the club suit itself, there appears to be no difference, but once we consider the whole hand, notably the diamond position, we see that holding up is a winning play, while rising is a loser.

Problem 8

Spades: Six missing – South has promised at least four and could well have more, leaving partner with two or fewer.

Hearts: Six missing – we know very little at the moment.

Diamonds: Nine missing – again we know little.

Clubs: Five missing – again we know little.

Points: We have 8 and the board 17, which leaves 15 unaccounted for. Partner has already shown the ♡K and, unless that is a singleton, will almost certainly have the ♡Q as well (although a doubleton king is not out of the question).

Tricks: With the ◇Q and any black-suit honors in partner's hand badly placed under the board, South will have at least four in each black suit and at least two in diamonds, to total ten. It is thus a question of whether we can take four tricks first. We can see two top hearts (assuming South has at least a doubleton) and the ◇A. The fourth can only come from a diamond ruff.

It is going to be impossible to tell partner to shift to diamonds immediately – remember that he does not know the diamond position. It is therefore better to take charge of the defence ourselves by overtaking partner's ♡K with our ♡A, cashing the ◇A and then returning a low heart to partner's assumed ♡Q. All he needs do is ask himself why we have adopted this defence. He will conclude that the deal is something like this:

```
                 ♠ A Q J 9
                 ♡ 7 2
                 ◇ K J 10
                 ♣ A Q 10 5
   ♠ 6                            ♠ 8 5 3
   ♡ K Q J 10      N              ♡ A 9 8 5 4
   ◇ 8 7 6 3 2   W     E          ◇ A
   ♣ J 6 3          S             ♣ 8 7 4 2
                 ♠ K 10 7 4 2
                 ♡ 6 3
                 ◇ Q 9 5 4
                 ♣ K 9
```

A diamond return now sets the contract.

SECTION 5:
Bidding

In *The Expert Beginner*, we studied the basics of bidding and introduced one or two 'conventional' calls, i.e. calls which do not mean exactly what they say. We learnt that calls tend to fall into three categories:

1 Forcing – the call is unlimited and partner is expected to bid.
2 Invitational – the call is limited and partner has the choice of whether to bid on or pass.
3 Sign off – the call is limited to the degree that partner, who will always have limited his own hand by this stage, is expected to pass.

We then studied a fair cross-section of sequences which crop up regularly. Nowadays, the tournament bridge world is packed full of conventional calls and the higher the standard of play one reaches, the further one progresses from Dutch to Double Dutch and the more there is to learn. This is not, however, our concern in this book and indeed, we shall only be learning one or two new conventions. It is far more important to understand what you are doing when bidding naturally on straightforward hands than to worry about a minority where a clever conventional call could be useful.

In this section, therefore, we shall first of all consolidate what we learnt in the beginners' book, laying heavy emphasis not only on finding the best call in a given situation (bearing in mind that, on many occasions, there is scope for a difference of opinion and experts have frequent disagreements) but also on understanding the reasons behind it and the likely aftermath.

We shall therefore begin with a test on the basics and in each case I shall want you to demonstrate a full understanding of each position by answering the following:

1 How much do you know about the hand so far? Of course, with the opening call, you will have to say 'nothing'.
2 Was partner's last call forcing, invitational or sign-off?
3 Has the auction so far improved, worsened or made little difference to the value (i.e. trick-taking potential) of your hand?
4 What do you intend to bid now?
5 Will your choice be forcing, invitational or sign-off?
6 How do you expect the auction to develop from here?
7 What final contract(s) do you have in mind?

In other words, you should be able to demonstrate that, not only can you find the best call in a given situation, but also that you know what you are doing.

This might appear to be stating the obvious but, as I indicated in the beginners' book, the standard of bidding throughout the bridge world is, to put it kindly, modest. At the top, it is scarcely better. The gravity of the situation was summed up only recently at the world championships when two 'world class'(?) pairs bid a grand slam with the ace of trumps missing! Any pair of absolute beginners could have improved on that. This and countless similar, if not quite so spectacular, mishaps regularly prove that you only have to bid sensibly (missing out on the brilliancies but avoiding the lunacies) to reach a reasonable standard, and yet this seems to be beyond the vast majority of the world's players.

Let us start with the opening call – in each case, I shall expect a full discussion as set out above. Assume you deal as South at love all and that you are playing strong twos in the non-club suits. Start your stop-watch and see if you can complete the test in ten minutes.

(1) ♠ K 8 6	(2) ♠ Q J 8 5	(3) ♠ K Q 7 5
♡ K 7 5 3	♡ 6 3	♡ Q 8 6 4
◇ K Q 4	◇ A K 5	◇ A J 6
♣ A 4 2	♣ K J 6 3	♣ J 4

(4) ♠ K J 8 6 4   (5) ♠ K Q 4   (6) ♠ K Q 7 5
    ♡ K 7 5 3   ♡ Q 6 5 2   ♡ K Q 6 4
    ◇ K 6   ◇ A 7 4   ◇ 6
    ♣ A 4   ♣ Q 10 3   ♣ A Q 4 3

(7) ♠ A K Q 6   (8) ♠ 5   (9) ♠ K Q 4 2
    ♡ K Q 5 3   ♡ K Q J 5 3 2   ♡ K
    ◇ K 6 4 2   ◇ A K J 2   ◇ A 6 4 2
    ♣ 2   ♣ A 3   ♣ 7 5 4 2

(10) ♠ Q 7 5   (11) ♠ 8   (12) ♠ K Q 4 2
     ♡ K Q 6 4   ♡ A 3   ♡ A K
     ◇ A J 6   ◇ A Q 7 5   ◇ A 6 4
     ♣ A K 6   ♣ A K J 6 3 2   ♣ K Q 7 5

(13) ♠ A K Q J 8 5 (14) ♠ K Q J 8 6 5 4 (15) ♠ A K 8 6
     ♡ A Q 3   ♡ 5 3   ♡ A K 5
     ◇ K 7 5   ◇ 6 4   ◇ A K J
     ♣ 3   ♣ 4 2   ♣ Q 4 2

For the last five examples, assume you have agreed to play weak
twos in the non-club suits.

(16) ♠ 4 2   (17) ♠ Q J 10 8 5 2   (18) ♠ J 4 2
     ♡ 6 5   ♡ K J 3 2   ♡ 6 5
     ◇ 10 9 8 7 6 4 2 ◇ K 5   ◇ K J 10 7 4 3
     ♣ A K   ♣ 9   ♣ K 7

(19) ♠ K Q J 7 5 2 (20) ♠ K 8
     ♡ 4   ♡ Q 8 7 5 3 2
     ◇ 7 5   ◇ Q 6
     ♣ J 10 9 4   ♣ 7 4 2

Let us work through the answers. To save repeating it each
time:

One-level suit calls are wide-ranging and therefore invitational.
Two-level suit openers other than clubs are as agreed and the
strong ones are only limited in that the opener did not open 2♣.
All no-trump openers are limited but also invitational.
2♣ is unlimited and therefore forcing and game will be reached
in all but one situation.
Three-level or higher preemptive calls are strictly limited and
partner will either need a fit to push the preempt higher still or a
strong hand (of at least opening strength) to reply.

(1) A balanced hand in the 15–17 range – 1NT. Goal contracts: 3NT, 4♡.

(2) With only 14 points and no five-card major, we open our longer minor (should they be of equal length, then it is clubs with 3–3 and diamonds with 4–4 or longer suits.) We shall rebid the spade suit over a red-suit reply with a view to 4♡, 3NT or possibly 5♣.

(3) With 13 points and no five-card major, we have to open our longer minor – here 1◇. Goal contracts: 4♠, 4♡ or 3NT.

(4) Here we call in the normal manner with our longest suit, 1♠, intending to rebid 2♡ next round. Goal contracts: 4♠, 4♡, possibly 3NT.

(5) Here, lacking a five-card major, we open with 1♣ when we have two three-card minors. Goal contracts: 3NT, 4♡.

(6) Lacking a five-card major, we open 1♣, though remember that does not guarantee more than three cards. However, we are not entitled to rebid the suit without five cards. Goal contracts: 4♡, 4♠, 5♣.

(7) Here, lacking a five-card major, we open 1◇. Goal contracts: 4♡, 4♠, 5◇.

(8) With 18 points and two very good suits, this hand qualifies for a strong two-opener, forcing for one round. We are primarily looking for 4♡ but 5◇ or a slam in either red suit could well be on.

(9) Only 12 points, including a stiff king, combined with a 4441 shape which tends to play notoriously badly, justifies passing on this hand.

(10) Here we open 1♣, intending to rebid 3NT over any reply other than hearts. Goal contracts: 3NT, 4♡.

(11) This hand is easily strong enough to reverse and we should open our longest suit, 1♣, intending to reverse into 2◇ and then, if necessary, repeat the clubs to show this shape. This could well lead to 3NT but at the moment our goal contracts are 5♣ and 5◇.

(12) A balanced hand in the 20–22 range makes an ideal 2NT opener. Goal contracts are 3NT, 4♠.

(13) This is just under 2♣ opening strength but has every prospect of eight tricks with spades as trump and therefore

is ideal for opening 2♠. Goal contract: 4♠ or hopefully a slam.

(14) This hand has little, if any, defence and with all the points concentrated into one long suit, it is ideal for a preemptive 3♠. Goal contracts: 3♠, 4♠.

(15) A balanced hand in the 23–24 range qualifies for a 2♣ opener, intending to rebid 2NT over a negative 2◇. That is the only sequence which is passable after what is otherwise a game-forcing opening. Goal contracts: 3NT, 4♠.

(16) Here we have another seven-card suit but it is very weak and we have two likely defensive tricks outside. This is not a hand on which to pre-empt. We pass and await developments.

(17) This time the suit is good enough and the hand is in the correct 6–11 point range for a weak two. However, in first seat, we should pass, as we have a good four-card suit in the other major and are liable to miss 4♡ if we give partner the impression of a one-suited hand. In third seat, however, a weak 2♠ would be fully justified as there is now no danger of missing game. We just want to play in the part-score.

(18) This hand is suitable for a weak 2◇ – a good suit in the correct point range and a one-suited hand.

(19) This time we should take advantage of the pre-emptive value of the spade suit with a weak 2♠. The four-card side suit is a weak minor and there is little danger of a disaster in the form of missing 5♣. If game is on, it is almost certainly going to be in 4♠.

(20) This is best passed as the heart suit is not really good enough. In third seat, non-vulnerable against vulnerable opponents, there is more of a case for breaking the rules and opening a weak 2♡.

There remains the question of what to bid with the strong two hands had weak twos been agreed. Let us look at the two examples again:

(8) ♠ 5
♡ K Q J 5 3 2
◇ A K J 2
♣ A 3

(13) ♠ A K Q J 8 5
♡ A Q 3
◇ K 7 5
♣ 3

On (8), we open 1♡ and jump in diamonds to force to game. Then rebid the hearts. On (13), with the solid suit, we open 1♠ and then jump to 4♠. With a less solid suit, we have to 'manufacture' a three-card minor at the three-level before repeating the spades and hope that partner realizes that he should not give preference back to the minor unless his preference is very strong – say at least a three-card difference. With strong hands where the long suit is clubs, we often have to improvise in this way.

We are now going to turn to the responder's first call and the same considerations will apply except that he knows more about the hand than the opener and is better placed to direct the conversation towards the final contract. Let us go through another thirty questions. Each time, when you give your response, you should be prepared for the next round of bidding, i.e. state what you intend to do over partner's possible rebids and the likely final contract(s) in each case.

Start your stop-watch and see if you can complete the test in ten minutes. In each example, assume that you are sitting South, North deals at love all and the opposition are silent.

(1) Partner opens 1♡. What do you reply with:

(a) ♠ Q 7 6 5
♡ 6 5 3
♢ J 7 5 3
♣ 10 9

(b) ♠ J 7 6 4
♡ K 5
♢ A 7 5 3
♣ 6 4 3

(c) ♠ J 7 5
♡ 7 5
♢ A 6 4 2
♣ Q 7 5 3

(d) ♠ 7 5
♡ Q 7 5
♢ Q 8 5 3
♣ K 8 5 2

(e) ♠ K 7 6 4
♡ 9 5
♢ Q 3
♣ A K 6 4 3

(2) Partner opens 1NT. What do you reply with:

(a) ♠ 9 7 6 4
♡ 5
♢ A 9 7 5 3
♣ 6 4 3

(b) ♠ 8 7 5
♡ 7 5
♢ 6 4 2
♣ Q 10 7 5 3

(c) ♠ 9 8 7 6 3
♡ Q 7 5 2
♢ 5 3
♣ 5 2

(d) ♠ Q 10 5
♡ A Q 5
♢ A Q 9
♣ K 8 5 2

(e) ♠ A 9 8
♡ A K 6
♢ Q J 8
♣ A K 8 2

(3) Partner opens 2♣. What do you reply with:

(a) ♠ A 7 6 5
♡ 6 5 3
♢ J 8 5 3
♣ 9 4

(b) ♠ K Q J 7 6 4
♡ 8 5
♢ 7 5 3
♣ 4 3

(c) ♠ J 7 5
♡ 8 6 4
♢ K Q 5 3
♣ K 8 5

(d) ♠ 9 7 5
♡ Q 7 5
♢ 5 3
♣ A K J 5 2

(e) ♠ K 9 3
♡ 8 6 4
♢ K Q 5 3
♣ K 8 5

(4) Partner opens 2♡ (strong). What do you reply with:

(a) ♠ –
♡ 6 5 3
♢ J 8 5 3 2
♣ J 9 8 7 4

(b) ♠ A Q 4
♡ 8 5
♢ K 7 5 3
♣ Q 4 3 2

(c) ♠ J 7 5
♡ Q 7 5 2
♢ K 6 4 2
♣ K 7

(d) ♠ 9 7 5 4 2
♡ Q 7 5
♢ K 5 3
♣ A 5

(e) ♠ 9 8 7 3
♡ 8 6 4
♢ A K Q 5 3
♣ 5

(5) Partner opens 3♢. What do you reply with:

(a) ♠ A K 6 5
♡ A 5 3
♢ –
♣ K Q 9 8 6 2

(b) ♠ A K Q J 7 6 4
♡ 5
♢ 3
♣ A J 3 2

(c) ♠ 7 5
♡ 7 5
♢ A 6 4 2
♣ 7 6 5 3 2

(d) ♠ J 7 5 2
♡ K 5
♢ K Q 3
♣ A K 7 2

(e) ♠ A K 9 3
♡ A K 4 3
♢ K Q 3
♣ K 5

(6) Partner opens 2♠ (weak). What do you reply with:

(a) ♠ –
♡ A K 8 5
♢ A 5 4 3 2
♣ A 7 6 2

(b) ♠ K Q J 7 3
♡ 5 3
♢ 9 8 4 2
♣ 9 2

(c) ♠ A 7
♡ A K Q 5
♢ 9 8 5 3
♣ J 10 2

(d) ♠ A 7 2
♡ 5
♢ Q J 10 7 5 3
♣ 9 5 2

(e) ♠ 4
♡ J 5 2
♢ A K Q J 10 7
♣ A Q 6

Let us work through the answers:

(1) (a) We need at least 6 points to reply to a suit-opener unless we have exceptional distribution. Here we have no right to disturb 1♡ and should pass.

(b) With 8 points, we have enough to reply and have no reason to suppress the spade suit. Many players would call 1NT because they have been taught that 1NT shows 6–10 points balanced and therefore this hand qualifies. What they miss is that, if we bid 1♠, we can still play in 1NT but, if we bid 1NT, a possible spade fit may be lost. Thus 1♠ is better and not only for that reason. Partner will need about 17+ points for game to be on and, in that case, 3NT may well be the goal contract. We shall want this contract to be played from his side of the table rather than have the lead coming round to those three low clubs. 1♠ is forcing for one round and the goal contracts are 3NT and 4♠.

(c) Here we do bid 1NT with the goal contract of 3NT. This is limited and therefore non-forcing.

(d) With five-cards in hearts guaranteed by partner, this hand is a simple, non-forcing raise to 2♡, hoping for 4♡.

(e) Here we do have enough to go to the two-level and can therefore show the two suits in natural order. We bid 2♣, forcing for one round and guaranteeing another call. The goal contracts are 3NT, 4♠, 5♣.

(2) (a) Here we have a weak hand and it is probable that those diamonds will not produce tricks unless they are trumps. It is therefore preferable to play in diamonds, even if it means raising the level of bidding. 2◊ is a sign-off, showing 0–7 points and at least five diamonds.

(b) Similar considerations apply here and it would be desirable to take out into 2♣ with a view to playing there. Unfortunately, as we learnt in the beginners' book, 2♣ has been assigned a different meaning and we should therefore pass 1NT. Should the contract be doubled, we can *then* remove to 2♣, which now resumes its meaning as a natural sign-off.

(c) Again, we do not want to play in 1NT and a straightforward removal to 2♠ is a possibility. However, partner may have four hearts and, as we can always play in 2♠, it costs nothing to find out. We bid a Stayman 2♣ (forcing one round), intending to convert 2◇ (denying a major) to 2♠ (which will then be a sign-off). Should partner bid 2♡ or 2♠, we are happy to pass. Our goal contracts are thus 2♡ and 2♠.

(d) With 17 points, we shall want to be in a slam if partner is maximum, but not otherwise. We invite with 4NT, a non-forcing limit-call, and partner is expected to reply according to his point-count. He also has the option to show a suit at the five-level with a view to a suit slam. Goal contracts: 4NT, 6♣, 6NT. We may have to stop in a *hippopotamus* 5NT.

(e) With 21 points, it is a question of a small or grand slam and we invite with 5NT. This is forcing at least to 6NT but, as with the previous example, partner has the option to look for a 4–4 fit by showing a suit at the six-level. Goal contracts: 6NT, 7♣, 7NT.

(3) (a) We need an ace and a king or about 8 points including at least two kings for a positive response, so here we make the negative response of 2◇. This is forcing as partner has guaranteed another call. Partner, with the bulk of the strength, will hopefully be taking the decision on the final contract but we are primarily looking for 3NT, 4♠, 5◇ or a slam in any one of those denominations.

(b) Again this hand does not qualify for a positive response and a forcing 2◇ must be the choice. We shall be showing our spades strongly on subsequent rounds, hoping for a game or slam in that suit.

(c) This hand does qualify for a positive response and, as it is balanced, 2NT is the best choice. It means that a no-trump contract will be played by the weak hand but, with a minimum of about 30 points combined, this is unlikely to matter. Note that, with a slam likely, conservation of bidding space is of first importance. Therefore, the sequence 2♣ 3NT does not exist. The partnership will be going to game anyway and a jump like that merely makes it very difficult for partner to describe what may be a very distributional hand.

(d) Again this qualifies for a positive response and we show our excellent club suit with 3♣, hoping for 6♣, 6NT or more.

(e) Here a slam is virtually guaranteed but again there is no need for rush as partner could be very distributional. For the moment, we bid a quiet 2NT but will go at least to 6NT, hoping for 7NT.

(4) (a) This hand is nowhere near a positive response and, in the beginners' book, we learnt to play the Herbert negative, i.e. bid the next suit up, here 2♠. The call has nothing to do with spades and is forcing as partner has guaranteed another call. We hope to finish in 4♡ but must warn partner that we have no greater ambition.

(b) Here a slam is likely but again a positive response is forcing to game so there is no need to rush. Just a quiet 2NT, hoping to finish in a slam in any denomination other than spades, is all that is needed for the moment.

(c) This hand is worth game opposite a strong two-opener and with no ace, we jump directly to 4♡, hoping to play there or in 6♡.

(d) Same applies but, with one ace, we raise to 3♡, giving partner more room for cue-bidding about which we will learn later on.

(e) This is a positive response. We shall obviously be playing in at least 4♡ but partner is best able to judge whether to try for more if he knows about our excellent diamond suit. So we bid 3♢ first. Note that we did not show the five poor spades in (d) because we want partner to revalue rather than devalue a singleton or void in that suit.

(5) (a) This hand is a disastrous misfit and it is most unlikely that we can find a better contract than 3◊, bearing in mind that partner's hand will be of little or no value unless those diamonds are trumps. It is therefore best to pass.

(b) Here it will take very little from partner to make 4♠ and a direct game call over a pre-empt is a sign-off.

(c) This time we have a fit and little, if any, defence. With partner in a similar position, it is likely that opponents will be cold for anything up to a grand slam in one of the majors. West must have an enormous hand and it is important to make life as difficult as possible for him by bouncing the pre-empt as far as we can afford. A case can be made for 5◊ or, as I prefer, 6◊. An increase in a pre-empt like that is always a sign-off and it is a general principle that, once a player has pre-empted, he should not bid again unless forced to do so, the exception arising if he has an unexpected defensive value (typically a void in a side-suit with his partner on lead). Now a double is certainly in order and indeed necessary as it increases the partnership's chance of setting the contract.

(d) Here, with an excellent fit, the diamond suit will surely fulfil its full potential and with stops in the other three suits, there are excellent chances for 3NT. The defenders may have a chance to take the first five tricks but the contract will be a near certainty on anything but a spade lead and even then, we might still make it if the ♡A is well placed with East.

(e) This time, we shall be unlucky to lose more than the ♣A but it is important that the hand be played from our side so that the ♣K will be protected. We therefore sign off in 6NT. This will be certain on a club lead and, at the worst, will need a queen in partner's hand on any other lead. Note that partner must pass even if he has a very unbalanced hand. If we had wanted more information about it, we could have proceeded more slowly. Partnership respect is crucial in this type of situation and it is usually a very expensive error for the weak hand to dictate to the strong – a classic example of the tail wagging the dog. This point is emphasized because it happens continually at all levels of bridge!

(6) (a) This hand is a hopeless misfit and it is most unlikely that game is on even if partner turns up with a maximum eleven points. It is best to pass, hoping to make 2♠.

(b) Here, particularly if partner is weak in the 6–11 range, the opponents may well have anything up to a slam on and it is wise to bounce the bidding as far as possible. Vulnerability is crucial here and I would recommend 4♠ except when vulnerable against not, when 3♠ is probably enough.

(c) Here game could be on and we should call an enquiring 2NT to find out more about partner's hand. The responses were explained in the beginner's book but briefly, he will repeat his suit when minimum. With a maximum, he shows a side-suit feature or calls 3NT with solid trumps.

(d) Again we have plenty of support and little defence and should try to extend the pre-empt. I recommend 3♠, except when non-vulnerable against vulnerable, when 4♠ is justified.

(e) In this type of situation, you want partner to show a heart feature, crucial for no-trump, irrespective of his strength. Therefore, rather than the 2NT enquiry, we prefer 3◇ (forcing) and partner will call 3♡, repeat his spades or support diamonds according to his hand. With diamond support, he is even entitled to show a club feature, which costs nothing as partnership is then committed to at least 4◇ anyway.

We are now going to consider the next stage, opener's rebid. There are so many possibilities that we can do little more than look at a cross-section. Two aspects will be emphasized: first, the situations where players continually go wrong; second, major-

and minor-suit trials, which were very briefly mentioned in the beginners' book

We shall start with another test, which I should like you to do against the stop-watch. You ought to be speeding up by now, particularly in this position, because you should have had your rebid planned before opening the bidding and should, therefore, be able to produce answers almost without thinking. However, I shall still expect you to state the effect partner's response has had on the value of your hand, how you expect the auction to continue and, above all, the goal contracts.

Start your stop-watch and see if you can finish in under fifteen minutes. On each of the following hands, you deal as South at love all.

(1) You open 1♣ and partner responds 1♠. What do you rebid on:

(a)	♠ K 4	(b)	♠ Q 7 6	(c)	♠ K Q 4
	♡ 7 5		♡ Q 10		♡ 8 6
	◇ A 7 6 4		◇ A 8 6		◇ 8 5 3
	♣ A K 7 5 3		♣ A J 8 7 2		♣ A K J 10 8

(2) You open 1♡ and partner responds 2◇. What do you rebid on:

(a)	♠ 7 6	(b)	♠ K Q J 6	(c)	♠ 6 2
	♡ A K Q 10 8		♡ K Q J 10 6		♡ A K Q J 10
	◇ 7 5		◇ 6 4		◇ 7 5 4 3
	♣ A K 8 2		♣ 5 4		♣ Q 8

(3) You open 1◇ and partner responds 2♡. What do you rebid on:

(a)	♠ K 4 2	(b)	♠ 4	(c)	♠ Q 7 6 4
	♡ 7 5		♡ K 10 2		♡ K Q 7
	◇ A Q J 9 7		◇ A K Q J 8		◇ A J 6 4 2
	♣ K 8 3		♣ 8 5 3 2		♣ 5

(4) On each of the following hands, you open 1NT. What do you rebid if partner responds: (a) 2♣, (b) 2♡, (c) 2NT, (d) 3◇, (e) 3NT, (f) 4NT, (g) 5NT?

(i)	♠ K 5 4	(ii)	♠ K Q 7 4	(iii)	♠ Q 7 5
	♡ A 10 8 5		♡ K 6		♡ A K 5
	◇ A 8 4		◇ A J 7 3		◇ K 7
	♣ K J 6		♣ A 7 2		♣ A 10 9 8 5

(5) On each of the following hands, you open 2 ◊ (strong) and partner gives the positive response of 2♠. What do you rebid on:

(a) ♠ K 8
     ♡ Q 7 4
     ◊ A K Q J 7 5
     ♣ A 6

(b) ♠ K 7
     ♡ 7
     ◊ A K Q J 8 6 4
     ♣ A 7 4

(6) On each of the following hands, you open 2♡ (weak) and partner makes the forcing enquiry of 2NT. What is your rebid on:

(a) ♠ 9 8
     ♡ A Q J 7 4 2
     ◊ 9 7 5
     ♣ 8 6

(b) ♠ 9 7
     ♡ A K Q 7 6 4
     ◊ 8 6 4
     ♣ J 4

(c) ♠ 9 6
     ♡ K Q J 9 7 5
     ◊ Q J 10
     ♣ 10 7

(d) ♠ K J 7
     ♡ Q J 8 7 6 4
     ◊ 5 3
     ♣ 9 6

(7) On each of the following hands, you open 3 ◊. What do you rebid if partner responds: (a) 3NT, (b) 4 ◊, (c) 5 ◊, (d) 3♡, (e) 4♡?

(i) ♠ K J 7
     ♡ –
     ◊ K Q J 8 6 5 3
     ♣ 6 3 2

(ii) ♠ 2
     ♡ 9 6
     ◊ A K J 7 5 4 3
     ♣ 8 6 4

Let us work through the answers:

(1) (a) We would like to show our second suit, diamonds, but we are not strong enough to do so. A reverse after a one-over-one call promises about 17 points, although we might allow it on less if we have sensational distribution and/or considerable support for spades. Neither applies here and, in any case, partner's 1♠ call indicates that he is unlikely to have a four-card diamond suit. If he has, he will have a five-card spade suit (otherwise he would have shown the diamonds first) and now he can still bid diamonds over our correct rebid of 2♣. Goal contracts: 3NT, 5♣, 5 ◊ ; 4♠ might be considered later if partner repeats the suit.

(b) With 13 points, we are in the 1NT rebid range and, as we shall want the lead in a no-trump contract to come round to that heart holding, have every reason to bid it with goal contracts of 3NT and 4♠. 5♣ is still an outside chance if partner turns out to have a four-card suit and has weak or very short hearts.

(c) Here again, we are in the 1NT rebid range but it would be a most ill-advised call. If partner has five spades or more, we shall want to be in 4♠. If he has only four, 3NT is the most likely goal contract and we shall want it played by partner rather than have the inevitable red-suit lead come round to our poor holdings. It is therefore preferable to bid 2♠, far more encouraging than 2♣. Goal contracts: 4♠, 3NT (by partner), 5♣.

(2) (a) 16 points are enough to go to the three-level after a two-over-one response and if we finish in 3NT, we shall want partner to be declarer to protect his diamond and spade holdings. We therefore reverse with 3♣, goal contracts being 4♡, 3NT (by partner), and 5♣. Contrast this with ♠ K x ♡ A Q 10 8 x ◇ x x ♣ A K x x, where we would like to be declarer in 3NT and are advised to bid 2NT now. Partner, having guaranteed another call, can always show a club suit, so a possible fit will not be lost.

(b) This is similar in shape to (2a) and a reverse at the two-level is allowed with no extra values as partner has guaranteed at least 11 points and therefore enough to go at least as far as 2NT. We therefore may bid 2♠, hoping to finish in four of a major or 3NT, played from partner's side with his club holding protected.

(c) We have four-card diamond support and no reason to refuse to support partner's suit. However, the number of people who would rebid the hearts (with 150 honors, partner, and my diamonds are so poor) is alarming. There are several arguments against the 2♡ call:

(i) The five-card heart suit has been promised anyway and therefore 3 ◇ gives more information to partner at no cost. Even though 2♡ is forcing, to call the suit twice and then support the diamonds will give the impression of six hearts and three diamonds.

(ii) The solid hearts will take tricks whether they are trumps or not. The poor diamonds will be of little value unless they are trumps.

(iii) Should our left-hand opponent have a black two-suiter, he may feel strong enough to compete with a take-out double at the two-level but not at the three-level.

(iv) With four-card trump support and most of our points in a long suit, we should aim to encourage, rather than discourage partner.

Our goal contracts are 4♡ and 5◊.

(3) The basic principle to follow when answering a game-forcing jump in a new suit is to call exactly as we would have done had partner called the same suit without jumping. However, a large number of exceptions arise: firstly, because partner has announced a categorically one-suited hand; and secondly, because we are in a game-forcing situation and therefore there is no need to rush.

(a) Here there is no reason to depart from the basic principle. We rebid 2NT, showing 12–14 points with goal contract of 3NT or a red-suit slam.

(b) This time, there is no point in showing those very poor clubs; we want partner to revalue rather than devalue a singleton or void. We could raise the hearts to 3♡ immediately to agree the trump suit but it is better to repeat the diamonds first and then support the hearts. Partner will then realize that we repeated the diamonds with good reason and will thus have a far more accurate picture of our hand. He will thus be better placed to decide whether to investigate a slam. Goal contracts: 4♡ or a slam in hearts.

(c) Here we should support the hearts immediately as it is worse than useless to show those poor spades for the reason explained under (3b). Goal contracts: $4\heartsuit$ or a slam in hearts.

(4) (a) These are straightforward responses to a Stayman enquiry: (i) $2\heartsuit$, (ii) $2\spadesuit$, (iii) $2\diamondsuit$, denying a major. We have little idea of goal contracts at the moment but have no need to worry as partner is in charge of the auction.

   (b) Partner has made a weak take-out and has stated that he wishes to play in $2\heartsuit$. We must accept his decision and pass on all three hands.

   (c) Here partner has made an invitational call and is asking about our strength. On (i), we are minimum and pass. On (ii), we are maximum and can accept with 3NT but it costs nothing, notably with a useless doubleton, to try Stayman ourselves ($3\clubsuit$) in case partner has four spades in a 4333 hand. He would not use Stayman himself with such a hand. Expert opinion varies on the wisdom of this. I would recommend it on this type of hand with a predominance of quick tricks. With a pile of queens and jacks, it is probably better to settle for 3NT direct. On (iii), with 16 points and a five-card suit, with good intermediates it is reasonable to bid 3NT.

   (d) Here partner has made a game-forcing call. Over 1NT, this is not so categorically a one-suited hand as over a suit call. However, on (i), there is little point in bidding those poor hearts. With a minimum and no ruffing values if diamonds were trump, we should quietly bid 3NT and await further developments. At the moment, our goal contract is 3NT, but partner can take things further if he so wishes. On (ii), we have a maximum, excellent trump support and ruffing values and should move towards a slam. We can agree the suit with $4\diamondsuit$, but a better call is $4\clubsuit$, which, as we shall learn later, agrees diamonds and shows first-round control (obviously the ace rather than a void in a no-trump hand!) in clubs. Goal contracts: $6\diamondsuit$ or $7\diamondsuit$. On (iii), we have little reason to be excited and should bid 3NT, intending to play there unless partner makes a further move.

(e) Partner has signed off and we have no reason to bid on any of the three hands. We therefore pass and play 3NT.

(f) Partner has made a non-forcing invitation. On (i) we are minimum and pass, intending to play in 4NT. On (ii), we are maximum and can accept direct with 6NT. It is debatable whether we might try 5◇, giving the possibility of finding 6◇ or 6♠. Remember that the 5◇ call forces at least to 5NT. On (iii), we are in the middle of the range and there are a number of possible actions. We can bid 5♣, inviting a club fit but prepared to stop in 5NT; we could simply bid 5NT to say that we have 16 points exactly; we could shut our eyes and bid 6NT, hoping that the five-card club suit will be worth something extra. My choice would be 6♣, offering that contract or 6NT. With the good intermediates in the club suit, I would take the view that, at the worst, a slam will need a bit of luck.

(g) This time, partner has made a forcing invitation. On (i) we are minimum and sign off in 6NT. On (ii) we are maximum and sign off in 7NT. It is probably better to stick to no-trump; the advantage of a possible ruff is likely to be outweighed by the risk of a bad trump split when 7NT could still be on. On (iii), for similar reasons to those discussed in (4f), I would recommend 7♣, with a view to playing there or in 7NT.

(5) (a) Apart from the six-card diamond suit we have already announced, the hand is balanced with stops in the other suits and is best described by 2NT. Remember again that, once partner has responded positively to a strong two-opener, the partnership is committed to game and therefore any sort of jump achieves nothing except the loss of bidding space and therefore should not be made unless it carries a very specific meaning. Goal contracts: 3NT or a slam in diamonds, spades or no-trump according to partner's subsequent bidding.

(b) This is an exceptional case in point. The spade call has improved our hand considerably and we are entitled to investigate a slam. A direct call of 4 ◊ shows a solid suit and sets it as trump. Now Blackwood or (preferably) cue-bidding to show controls can follow. Goal contracts: 5 ◊, 6 ◊, 7 ◊.

(6) When we have opened a weak two and partner makes a forcing enquiry, we are expected to repeat our suit if we are minimum in the 6–11 range (i.e. 6–8), bid 3NT if we are maximum (9–11) with a solid suit (i.e. A K Q x x x or better), and show a side-suit feature, typically a stop, for no-trump. Therefore:

(a) Minimum – simply rebid 3 ♡.
(b) Maximum – solid hearts, rebid 3NT.
(c) Maximum – diamond feature to be shown with 3 ◊.
(d) Minimum – not strong enough to show spade feature, rebid 3 ♡.

(7) In (a), (b), (c) and (e), partner's call is a sign-off and we must accept it and pass. If opponents compete, any further move is in his hands although, with hand (a), we should double a club or spade contract, if partner is going to be on lead, to indicate the heart void.

(d) Here partner has made a forcing call and is asking for more information. On (a), the heart call has weakened our hand but there is no harm in showing our good spade holding with 3 ♠. This is forcing and shows a feature rather than a suit. We do not normally pre-empt in a minor when we have a four-card major outside (except in third seat opposite a passed partner). If partner has the ◊ A, 3NT could well be on and the spade stop may be what partner needs. At the worst, we shall play in 4 ◊. Goal contracts: 3NT, 5 ◊. On (b), your two trumps and outside singleton are certainly some help for partner and there is a good case for bidding 4 ♡ rather than merely repeating the pre-emptive suit with 4 ◊.

We are now going to look at trial calls in some detail. They fall into two categories:

1 After a major suit has been opened at the one-level and raised to the two-level and the partnership is discussing whether to play in a part-score, game (primarily in four of the major, but possibly 3NT) or slam.

2 After a minor suit has been opened at the one-level and raised to the two- or three-level and the partnership is discussing whether to play in a part-score, game (primarily in 3NT, but possibly five of the minor) or slam.

The major-suit trial calls

A raise from, say, 1♠ to 2♠ promises a point-count in the 6–10 area but covers quite a wide range of hands in that the spade length can be three or more and the rest of the hand may be relatively balanced or could contain a singleton or void. Also the few honor cards could be spread over the four suits or concentrated in one or two. The opener now has a number of options:

1 To accept that there is no hope of game and pass.

2 To bid game direct, confident that there is no slam.

3 To make a trial call, prepared to stop in three of the major or bid game, dependent on the response to it.

4 To make a trial call, intending to bid a game at least but with the possibility of investigating a slam.

5 Simply to bid three of the major as a pre-emptive sign-off (this is not an invitational trial) as opponents can usually compete with little risk of a disaster if the bidding dies at the two-level with a fit announced.

Let us, first of all, show some hands illustrating these five options after you have opened 1♡ and partner has raised you to 2♡.

(a) ♠ K 8 6   This is a minimum opener and there is no
     ♡ A 9 8 7 5   reason to bid on.
     ◇ K 7
     ♣ Q J 4

(b) ♠ K 8   Here we have 22–25 points with a good fit, so
     ♡ A K 7 5 3 2 there should be a play for game but we have
     ◇ A 8 5   no aspirations for a slam. We sign off in 4♡.
     ♣ Q 5

(c) ♠ 8
    ♡ A K 6 5 3
    ◊ Q 7 5 4 2
    ♣ A J

Here much depends on how much partner can help with those diamond losers. If he has honors in the suit or a doubleton, singleton or void with plenty of trumps, there will be a good chance for game. If not, for example if he has three small diamonds and values in spades, we could well be disappointed in 3♡, never mind game. A trial call is needed.

(d) ♠ –
    ♡ A K 8 7 5 4
    ◊ 9 8 6 4
    ♣ A K 7

Here we shall certainly be going to game but if partner has a singleton or void diamond, or plenty of honors in the suit, anything up to a grand slam could be on. Again, a trial call is useful.

(e) ♠ Q 6
    ♡ A K Q 6 4 3
    ◊ 7 5 3
    ♣ 6 3

With nearly all the points in hearts and therefore little, if any, defence, the principal worry is that opponents will compete if the bidding dies in 2♡. 3♡ is unlikely to be doubled as opponents have little in trumps and even if it is, the penalty should be minimal compared to the value of the game that is probably available to opponents.

In the two cases where trial calls were recommended, we make the trial in the suit in which we have losers, i.e. where we want 'help', either in the form of honors or in that of shortage with plenty of trumps. In the above examples, the trial call would obviously be 3◊.

We now have to consider how to answer a trial call. Some authorities recommend the following:

If you are maximum for the raise, bid the game outright.
If you are minimum for the raise, sign off in three of the major.
If you are mid-range, then look at your holding in the trial suit:

    If you have honors, or shortage with four or more trumps, bid game;

    If you have a weak holding, sign off in three of the major.

This certainly has the advantage of being easy to remember, but shows a poor understanding of the position. If the opener makes a trial, he is showing a two-suited hand, in which case an extra couple of points in the form of a queen or jack in one of the other suits will be of no value, and yet they could make the difference between being minimum or maximum.

My recommendation is to look at the overall picture of the whole hand, taking the following into account:

1 Length and quality of trumps.
2 Contents of trial suit –particularly higher honors.
3 If there is a doubleton or, better, singleton, or, better still, void, look again at the trumps. Now, if there are four or more, value up. If there are only three, then much depends on whether they are honors or low cards. If they are honors (e.g. K Q x), they will be used for ruffing and thus are not pulling the full weight with which they were credited.
4 The honor cards in the other two suits (this is very important and yet neglected by the majority of players). When the opener makes a trial, he will probably have at least nine cards between trumps and the trial suit. That implies that he will probably have doubletons or even less in the two remaining suits. Thus, while aces will certainly score, kings are of dubious value and queens and jacks are virtually worthless.

Let us illustrate with some examples. In each case, we raise 1♠ to 2♠ and partner bids 3◊.

With ♠ K 8 6 5   we are minimum with no help in diamonds
       ♡ K 7 6 4   and must reject outright with 3♠.
       ◊ 7 5 3
       ♣ 6 4

With ♠ K 8 6 4   we are maximum with an excellent dia-
       ♡ 7 5 3 2   mond holding and accept with 4♠.
       ◊ A J
       ♣ 7 5 3

With ♠ 7 5 3 2   we have a doubleton and four low trumps
       ♡ Q J 5   which favor acceptance, but we are mini-
       ◊ 10 5   mum in point-count and the points we
       ♣ Q 6 3 2   have are likely to be worthless; reject with
                      3♠.

With   ♠ 7 6 4 2   the club and heart honors are worth count-
      ♡ A 7 4   ing and the extra trump makes it worth-
      ◇ 5 3   while accepting; we bid 4♠.
      ♣ A 7 4 3

With   ♠ K Q J   it is more debatable but we will be ruffing
      ♡ 8 7 6 5 3   with trump honors which we counted
      ◇ 7   towards the raise. A trump lead is likely to
      ♣ 7 5 3 2   set 4♠. I recommend rejecting with 3♠.

With   ♠ K Q J 6   the extra trump and singleton diamond
      ♡ 8 7 6 5   make it well worthwhile accepting with
      ◇ 7   4♠.
      ♣ 7 5 3 2

With   ♠ 9 8 6 5   we are maximum but all the points are in
      ♡ K Q   the wrong place and the diamond holding
      ◇ 8 6 4 3   is hopeless; we reject with 3♠.
      ♣ Q J 6

This should give you the idea and we can extend it in that, if
there is room to bid between the trial call and three of the major,
we can show a feature in an intermediate suit in situations where
we are not sure whether to accept.

With   ♠ K 8 6   the situation is debatable, but there is no
      ♡ K Q 6   need to commit ourselves. It costs nothing
      ◇ 7 5   to bid 3♡. Now, if opener is 5341, those
      ♣ 7 5 4 3 2   heart honors will be useful and he will
                  probably bid 4♠. However, if he is 5143,
                  those heart honors will be facing a single-
                  ton and therefore be of little use, and now
                  he will probably sign off in 3♠.

Also in cases where we have sensational support, we can make
an intermediate call between three and four of the agreed major.
Let us look again at the second hand:

    ♠ K 8 6 4
    ♡ 7 5 3 2
    ◇ A J
    ♣ 7 5 3

With a maximum hand, a fourth trump and an excellent diamond holding, we had no hesitation in accepting game. But it may well be that partner was making a trial call with a view to a slam, and it costs nothing to bid 4♢, showing the ace and a sensational hand in the light of the bidding so far. Similarly, with

♠ J 8 6 4
♡ 7 6 5 4
♢ –
♣ A 7 5 4 3

it costs nothing to bid 4♣. Partner will then have extra information on which to decide whether to look for a slam. Partner need have no more than

♠ A K 9 5 3 2
♡ –
♢ J 8 6 4
♣ K Q 6

thirteen points and the grand slam is a good bet.

I am very keen on these detailed exchanges of information as they enable a partnership to find the correct contract with far greater frequency. I have to mention, however, that there is a school of thought which believes that these bidding sequences give away a great deal of information to opponents (no argument about that) and their standard of opening leads and defence will improve accordingly. They recommend that it is better to 'shut your eyes and bid it' and leave the defenders in the dark. The result of this is that, while you will occasionally look silly, you will also, on many occasions, get away with daylight robbery. However, there is much to be said for the argument and plenty of examples to prove it. In the end, it comes down to frequency, i.e. overall long-term gain or loss. I can only speak from my own long experience and say that, while I will have to accept the occasional hiccup, I will back the pair who bid accurately to beat the pair who shut their eyes, particularly in the long term.

The minor-suit trial calls

So, assuming that your eyes are still open, we shall now turn to sequences in which a minor has been bid and supported and 3NT is, at least to begin with, favorite as goal contract. Let us look at a couple of examples:

(a) ♠ K J 5   (b) ♠ K Q 6
    ♡ A J 5   ♡ K Q 6
    ◇ K 8   ◇ K 7
    ♣ A Q 6 4 2   ♣ A Q 7 3 2

On each hand, we open 1♣ and partner raises to 2♣. On (a) in the 18–19 range and with stops in the other three suits, we bid 2NT and on (b) with 19 and a five-card suit, we bid 3NT – no problem. But how about these next two?

(c) ♠ 6 2   (d) ♠ A Q 7
    ♡ K Q 6   ♡ A Q
    ◇ A K 4   ◇ 9 7 2
    ♣ A Q 6 4 2   ♣ A K 6 4 2

We have a sufficient point-count for 2NT on (c) and 3NT on (d) but we are wide open in spades on (c) and in diamonds on (d), which means that a no-trump contract could fail, while anything up to game or more in clubs could be on. Clearly, therefore, another trial call is required, but the form is slightly different. Whereas, when discussing a major-suit game, we bid the suit where we have losers and want help, here we bid the suits we *can* stop in ascending order, and partner bids his as cheaply as possible. Where we miss out a suit, i.e. inform partner that we cannot stop that suit, partner may bid no-trump if he can stop that suit.

Let us illustrate with the two examples above. On (c) we bid 2◇, which is forcing (we will never play there as clubs are the agreed trump suit) and we shall play in 3♣ if no-trump is ruled out. Now partner will bid:

  (i) 2♠ if he can stop the spades,
 (ii) 2NT if he can stop both majors,
(iii) 3♣ if he can stop neither major.

On (d) we bid 2♡ (note that, despite the strength to go to 3NT, there is no need to jump at the moment). Now partner knows that we can stop hearts, we cannot stop diamonds, and we may or may not be able to stop spades. He now bids:

  (i) 2♠ if he can stop both spades and diamonds,
 (ii) 2NT if he can stop diamonds but not spades,
(iii) 3♣ if he cannot stop diamonds (in that case his ability to stop spades is irrelevant as no-trump is now ruled out).

All this has so far assumed that responder is minimum for the 2♣ call. If he is maximum, then he is entitled to raise the level where his call would otherwise be non-forcing. Let us go through those six answers again.

(c) (i) 2♠ as before. If opener bids 2NT, he can raise to 3NT. If opener signs off in 3♣, then responder knows that there are losers in hearts and will aim for 5♣ if he is singleton or void in that suit (in the latter case, there could well be a slam on).

   (ii) 3NT which is a sign-off.

   (iii) Now again there will be losers in at least one major and he will need a singleton in a major to think about looking for 5♣. The best way to show this is to bid the singleton at the three-level (3♡ or 3♠). Now the opener can settle for 4♣ or 5♣.

(d) (i) 2♠ as before. If opener bids 2NT, he can raise to 3NT.

   (ii) 3NT which is a sign-off.

   (iii) Now it depends on his length in diamonds. With a singleton or void, he can bid 4♣ (actually there are cleverer calls, but it will pay to keep it simple for the moment).

This should give you the idea. The same principle applies to bidding after 1♣ 3♣ but there is obviously less room for conversation. However, this is game-forcing, so there need be no discussion about minimum or maximum.

If diamonds is the agreed suit, we bid as follows:

The sequence 1♢   2♢
           2♡   promises a stop in hearts and

possibly one black suit. Responder bids:

  (i) 2♠ with a spade stop but no club stop.
 (ii) 3♣ with a club stop but no spade stop.
(iii) 2NT with both black suits stopped (minimum).
(iv) 3NT with both black suits stopped (maximum).

In (i) and (ii), the strength has not yet been shown but there is no problem with the 2♠ call. If opener limits his hand with 2NT, responder can raise to 3NT. The problem arises with 3♣, when opener does not know his partner's strength and, if the stoppers are right, will have to risk 3NT, which may be an overbid.

After 1◇ 3◇, there is limited room for discussion and it is recommended that emphasis be placed on the majors, most likely to be led against no-trump.

Thus 1◇   3◇
    3♡   promises a heart stop but denies a spade
stop and 1◇   3◇
    3♠   promises a spade stop but denies a heart
stop. Responder bids 3NT if he can stop the other major, but he has the option to bid 3♠ over 3♡ in the first case to show a half-stop (Q x or J x x), which may be enough to go with a half-stop in opener's hand.

After trial calls of this kind, responder always has the option to return to the original trump suit if his original raise was based on distribution rather than points and it is clear that 3NT is unlikely to be on. Thus with ♠ 4
            ♡ 7 5 4 2
            ◇ Q J 6 5 3
            ♣ Q 7 5
after 1◇   2◇ it is probably better to suppress the club stop and
     2♡   sign off in 3◇.

Let us try another test against the stop-watch. You should be able to give a full explanation of the bidding so far, state your choice of call with reasons and, of course, the likely final contract(s).

Once again, assume that you are sitting South at love all, that the dealer is the first player to make a call and that the opponents are silent throughout the auction.

(1) You open 1♠ and partner responds 2♠. What do you rebid on:

(a) ♠ A Q 6 5 3
  ♡ K 8 6
  ◇ K 5 2
  ♣ Q 2

(b) ♠ K Q J 8 6 4
  ♡ K 6
  ◇ Q J 7 4
  ♣ J

(c) ♠ K Q J 8 5 3
  ♡ A 6
  ◇ A 4
  ♣ Q 4 2

(d) ♠ A K 8 6 4
  ♡ K 6 5 2
  ◇ A Q
  ♣ J 4

(2) Partner opens 1♠, you respond 2♠ and partner bids 3♣. What do you rebid on:

(a) ♠ Q 6 5 3
  ♡ 8 6
  ◇ K J 5 2
  ♣ 5 3 2

(b) ♠ J 9 6 4
  ♡ K 6
  ◇ K J 7 4
  ♣ J 7 5

(c) ♠ Q J 5 4
  ♡ 7 6 4 3
  ◇ 5 4 3 2
  ♣ A

(d) ♠ 8 6 4
  ♡ Q J 6 4
  ◇ Q J 7 4 3
  ♣ 7

(3) You open 1♣ and partner responds 2♣. What do you rebid on:

(a) ♠ K Q 4
  ♡ K 6 5
  ◇ A J 4
  ♣ A J 10 7

(b) ♠ 10 5 3
  ♡ 8 6
  ◇ A 4
  ♣ A Q J 5 4 2

(c) ♠ 6 4
  ♡ K J 6
  ◇ K J 2
  ♣ A K Q J 2

(d) ♠ K 4
  ♡ 8 6
  ◇ K Q J 4
  ♣ A K J 10 7

(4) Partner opens 1♣, you reply 2♣ and he now bids 2◇. What do you rebid on:

(a) ♠ 7 5 3
  ♡ 8 6
  ◇ A 5 2
  ♣ Q J 7 6 2

(b) ♠ 8 6 4
  ♡ K 6 5
  ◇ 7 4
  ♣ K J 7 5 4

c)   ♠ Q 5 3
    ♡ 8 6 5
    ♢ 4 3 2
    ♣ K Q 4 2

(d)   ♠ Q J 5
    ♡ K 8 6
    ♢ 5 2
    ♣ J 8 7 4 2

(5) Partner opens 1♢, you reply 2♢ and partner rebids 2♡. What do you rebid on:

(a)   ♠ Q J 3
    ♡ 8 6
    ♢ K Q 5 2
    ♣ 8 7 6 2

(b)   ♠ Q J 6
    ♡ 8 6
    ♢ Q 9 7 4
    ♣ Q 9 7 6

(c)   ♠ 8 5 3
    ♡ 7 6
    ♢ K Q 4 2
    ♣ Q J 4 2

(d)   ♠ J 4
    ♡ 8 4
    ♢ Q J 5 3 2
    ♣ J 9 8 4

(6) You open 1♣ and partner responds 3♣. What do you rebid on:

(a)   ♠ Q 6 5
    ♡ 6 5
    ♢ K 5 2
    ♣ A Q J 5 2

(b)   ♠ 6 4
    ♡ A Q
    ♢ Q J 7 4
    ♣ A Q J 7 6

(c)   ♠ Q J 8
    ♡ 6
    ♢ A 5 4
    ♣ A K 9 6 4 2

(d)   ♠ A K
    ♡ A J
    ♢ 8 5 4
    ♣ A J 10 5 4 3

(7) You open 1♢ and partner responds 3♢. What do you rebid on:

(a)   ♠ Q 5 3
    ♡ K 8 6
    ♢ A K 5 2
    ♣ A Q 2

(b)   ♠ K 8 4
    ♡ A J 6
    ♢ A Q J 7 4
    ♣ J 8

(c)   ♠ 5 3 2
    ♡ A 6
    ♢ A Q 8 4 2
    ♣ A Q 2

(d)   ♠ J 5 4
    ♡ A K 7
    ♢ A J 9 8 5
    ♣ K Q

(8) Partner opens 1♢, you respond 3♢ and partner now bids 3♡. What do you rebid on:

(a) ♠ Q J 3
     ♡ 8 6
     ♢ A K 6 5 2
     ♣ K 4 3

(b) ♠ 8 4
     ♡ K Q 6
     ♢ Q J 7 5 4
     ♣ A J 8

(c) ♠ J 3 2
     ♡ A K 6
     ♢ A Q 5 4 2
     ♣ 10 2

(d) ♠ 4
     ♡ K 8 6
     ♢ A K Q 8 5
     ♣ J 9 4 2

(9) You open 1♢, partner responds 3♢, you bid 3♡ and partner bids 3♠. What do you rebid on:

(a) ♠ Q 3
     ♡ K 8 6
     ♢ A 9 8 5 2
     ♣ A 10 2

(b) ♠ 8 6 4
     ♡ A K 6
     ♢ A 9 5 4 2
     ♣ Q 8

(c) ♠ 9 5 3 2
     ♡ A K
     ♢ Q 10 9 4 2
     ♣ A 2

(d) ♠ K
     ♡ K 9 6
     ♢ K 10 8 6 5
     ♣ K Q 6 5

Let us work through the answers:

(1) (a) With only 14 points, scattered values and a balanced distribution, there is no reason to bid any more and we pass, happy to play in 2♠.

(b) This is a far more distributional hand. There is little prospect of game but, especially if partner has the ♠A and an opponent has a singleton or void, our defensive prospects against a club or heart contract could be very poor. It is important, therefore, to pre-empt with 3♠, a sign-off, to make it as difficult as possible for opponents to compete.

(c) Here we have enough strength for game but have no interest in a slam so we sign off in 4♠.

(d) Here, we have a number of potential losers in hearts and we should ask partner for help with a trial call of 3♡. He will sign off in 3♠ or 4♠ (or make a four-level call in a non-spade suit if his hand becomes sensational). In the case where both majors have been called, some pairs allow a 4♡ call to be passed because it may well be that we shall be playing in a 4–4 fit in that suit, preferable to a 5–3 or 5–4 fit in spades because discards may be possible on the unbalanced side-suit. This is something that has to be agreed between the partners and although clearly advantageous at slam-level, is debatable at lower levels because opponents can usually take their minor-suit tricks early. Now spades may make the better trump suit if there is a bad split in hearts.

(2) (a) Here we are minimum with a disastrous club holding, so we sign off in 3♠.

    (b) This time, we are maximum but again the club holding is hopeless and the red-suit holdings not much better. Some players might try 3NT, but I recommend signing off in 3♠.

    (c) Here the club holding is sensational and we know there is no loser in the suit. We shall certainly want to be in 4♠ but it costs nothing to bid 4♣, to show our first-round control, and now, if partner has a hand which warranted making a trial with slam intentions, he may be able to go up to 6♠ or more!

    (d) Here we certainly have help in clubs but the trumps are very poor and none of our six red-suit points are likely to be worth anything. I therefore recommend signing off in 3♠.

(3) (a) This hand is strong enough for 2NT, angling for 3NT and, with all the side-suits stopped, we have no reason to bid anything else.

    (b) There will be no game on this hand but with most of our honors in the long club suit, our defensive prospects are very poor. This is a time to pre-empt the bidding with 3♣. Even then, the opponents may compete but at least it will be difficult for them to call accurately.

    (c) This hand is strong enough for at least 2NT but the lack of a spade stop makes a direct call inadvisable. We make the trial call of 2 ◇, giving partner a chance to show his major-suit stops. We are aiming for 3NT but may finish in a club part-score or game.

(d) Here the same applies – again we bid 2 ◇. Remember that this shows a diamond feature, not necessarily a suit. As far as trumps are concerned, clubs have been agreed.

(4) (a) We have been invited to show major-suit stops but this hand has none. We therefore sign off in 3 ♣.

(b) Here we have a heart stop but no spade stop – we show it with 2 ♡.

(c) Here, the spade stop and the absence of a heart stop is shown by 2 ♠.

(d) Here we have both major suits stopped and a minimum raise so we bid 2NT, hoping to finish in 3NT.

In all these last three cases, the prime goal contract is 3NT but partner could have a very distributional hand and be debating between part-score, game or slam in clubs and this is a good way to find out where our values are. We do not really have to worry about final contract in this type of situation because partner is in charge of the auction and he will take the decision. Nevertheless, I have mentioned it because it should never be far away from your mind!

(5) (a) We have been invited to show black-suit stops and we have spades but not clubs; thus we bid 2 ♠.

(b) Here we have both black suits stopped and a minimum raise, so we bid 2NT.

(c) Here we have the clubs stopped but no spade stop so we bid 3 ♣.

(d) The same applies but the hand is so poor that it is best to discourage partner by trying to sign off in 3 ◇.

(6) The sequence is game-forcing and we are, in the first place, expected to show stops, in ascending order, in the other three suits:

(a) 3 ◇. If partner bids 3 ♡, we shall be able to bid the goal

contract of 3NT. If the spade holding is ♠ J x x, we bid
3♠ to show the half-stop.

(b) 3◇, this time hoping that partner bids 3♠ or 3NT.

(c) 3◇. If partner bids 3♡, we shall bid the goal contract of
3NT; if he is weak in hearts, 5♣ or 6♣ could be on.

(d) This time, we need a diamond stop from partner and
bid 3♡, promising a heart stop but denying a diamond
stop. Partner replies:

   (i)   3♠ with both spades and diamonds stopped.

   (ii) 3NT with diamonds only stopped.

   (iii) 4♣ with no diamond stop.

(7) (a) This is strong enough for 3NT and, with the other suits
stopped, there is no reason to bid anything else. This is
a sign-off in principle and partner should not call again
unless he is very distributional.

(b) Again, the best call is 3NT despite the weak clubs. In the
absence of major-suit bidding, partner is likely to have
some clubs in his hand and a major-suit lead is most
likely on this auction.

(c) Here we can find out if partner has no stop, half a stop
or a full stop in spades by bidding 3♡. Partner replies
3♠ with a half-stop (which will not be enough), 3NT
with a full stop and 4◇ with no stop.

(d) The same applies as in (c). This time, however, the half-
stop will be enough and we shall be able to bid 3NT
over 3♠.

(8) (a) Here we have a full spade stop and bid 3NT, hoping to
play there.

(b) Here we have no stop and must revert to 4◇. When we
get to a more advanced stage, we will learn that we can
call 4♣ to show our club feature, which may help
partner to decide whether to play in 4◇ or 5◇.

(c) With a half-stop, we can bid 3♠, which partner may be
able to convert to 3NT. Otherwise, we shall play in a
part-score or game in diamonds according to partner's
strength and distribution.

(d) Here we have no spade stop but, as partner has

advertised spade losers, our singleton justifies calling
5◇ rather than 4◇. (Yes, you are technically in a game-
forcing situation but a partnership should have the
right to stop in four of the minor on a minimum point-
count with one suit wide open.) In more advanced
studies, we shall learn more accurate extensions of
these sequences.

Just to give you a foretaste, change the hand to

♠ 4
♡ A 8 6
◇ A Q J 8 5
♣ 9 7 4 2

and we can show our ♡A on the way to game with 4♡ and
if you really want to be sophisticated, change the hand to

♠ –
♡ K 8 6
◇ A Q J 8 5
♣ J 9 7 4 2

and we can show what must surely be a crucial void with
4♠! This is all getting a bit advanced but these calls very
often pave the way to 6◇ or 7◇.

(9) Here we have been asked for a half-stop in spades.
 (a) We accept and sign-off in 3NT.
 (b) We reject and bid 4◇.
 (c) More debatable, but with plenty of top controls and the
     probability that the defenders will only be able to take
     four spade tricks, 3NT is worth trying.
 (d) A stiff king can be a half-stop but with a large number
     (at least nine) guaranteed against us and a lamentable
     lack of aces, 3NT is going to be dubious at best and
     could be heavily set. It is best to settle for a sign-off in
     4◇.

The bidding of short suits to show features or stops rather than as
suggestions for trump is an excellent lead-in to the study of cue-
bidding.

Cue-bidding

Cue-bids fall into two main categories:

1 Control-showing – carrying a definite message.
2 Unassuming – asking partner to describe his hand.

The unassuming cue-bid will be discussed later when we allow our opponents to enter the auction, but for the time being, we shall assume that they are maintaining their polite silence.

The control-showing cue-bid is used as an alternative to Blackwood and is far more efficient. The use of Blackwood implies that the enquirer has to take a decision on a slam based on one solitary piece of information, partner's *number* of aces. It works reasonably well when there are plenty of second-round controls (kings and singletons) around but, as soon as voids, doubletons and longer suits arrive on the scene, the convention fails miserably. A couple of simple examples will illustrate:

(a) ♠ A K 7 6 3   (b) ♠ Q J 10 5 4
    ♡ A Q 8 5   ♡ –
    ◊ 8 6   ◊ A K Q
    ♣ K 9   ♣ J 5 4 3 2

Look at hand (a) considered in isolation. You open 1♠ and partner answers 3♠. You try Blackwood and partner's 5◊ shows one ace. What now? The truth of it is that you have little idea of what to do. If that ace is the ◊A, the slam will probably be on. If it is the ♣A, the slam will probably be on. If it is the ♣A, partner will need the ◊K to have any chance at all and even then, in the absence of the ◊Q, a lead through it (and it will be on the board) could be fatal.

Now consider hand (b), which could be the responding hand, but again, let us look at it in isolation. Partner opens 1♠ and you reply 3♠. Partner now gives a Blackwood 4NT. How do you answer? You could ignore the void and simply call 5◊, answering the question literally, or you could employ one of two commonly used modifications which were explained in the beginners' book. These are certainly improvements, but the whereabouts of the void may not be shown until the partnership is too high!

The cue-bid enables the partnership to hold a much more detailed discussion, starting at a lower level. Once a suit has been agreed, i.e.

(a)   both partners have bid it or
(b)   one has announced a solid suit, for example after the sequence 2♣ 2◇
               3♠

spades is deemed the agreed trump suit; and

(c)   in the case of a minor, the bidding has, at least, reached the four-level (otherwise 3NT is still under discussion and we are cue-bidding stops rather than aces as we have just seen); or
(d)   in the case of a major, the bidding has reached at least the three-level (otherwise we make trial calls to decide whether to play in a part-score or game),

any call of a side suit shows first-round control (ace or void) in that suit or, if the first-round control has already been categorically promised by either partner or categorically denied by the player about to call, it shows second-round control (king or singleton). A call of the agreed trump suit indicates that the player feels he can do no more. Also, once cue-bidding has started, 4NT is no longer Blackwood but is used by many pairs to cue-bid the ace of trumps. When cue-bidding, always work in ascending order, making the cheapest cue-bid available.

Let us illustrate with a few examples:

South	North
1♠	3♠
4♣	4◇
4♠	Pass

Here South promised first-round control of clubs. North promised first-round control of diamonds and South denied first-round control of hearts and felt that he could not go beyond game.

South	North
1♠	3♠
4◇	4♡
4NT	5♣
5◇	5♠
Pass	

Here South promised first-round control of diamonds but denied first-round control of clubs. He then showed the ♠A and second-round control of diamonds. North showed first-round control of hearts and then first-round control of clubs.

South	North
1♠	3♠
4◇	4NT
5♣	5◇
5♡	5♠
6♠	Pass

Here South promised first-round control of diamonds but denied first-round control of clubs. He then showed second-round control of clubs, having categorically denied first-round control on the previous round and then first-round control of hearts (which he had not denied on the previous round). North denied first-round control of hearts but felt he was strong enough to go past game and cue-bid the ♠A. He then showed second-round control of diamonds, but felt he could do no more over 5♡ but sign off in 5♠. After that sequence, South decided that the slam was worth bidding.

Note very carefully that any other call – 5NT or six of a non-spade suit – would commit the partnership to at least 6♠ and is therefore an investigation for a possible grand slam. Again the final contract consideration is paramount.

Notice in particular how much information was exchanged between the two partners below 5♠, as compared with Black-wood, so that the partnership was in a far better position to take a decision on the final contract. Once again, it can be argued that a sequence like 1♠   3♠

        6♠   leaves the defenders wondering what to lead and how to defend, while detailed sequences like the above virtually guarantee impeccable defence. I can only refer you to what I said earlier.

Let us try some examples against the stop-watch. Each one should take no more than ten seconds as there is little to think about.

(1)   You open 1♠ and partner responds 3♠. As this is game-forcing, you are expected to cue-bid below game unless you have a very weak opening call. So, assuming you decide that a slam is worth investigating, how do you cue-bid on the following?

(a) ♠ A K Q J 7
    ♡ 8 6 5
    ◇ 4
    ♣ A K Q 6

(b) ♠ A K Q 7 5
    ♡ A Q 6
    ◇ A J 6
    ♣ 4 2

(c) ♠ K Q J 7 5
    ♡ A K Q 8
    ◇ K 9
    ♣ 8 6

(d) ♠ A K J 6 4
    ♡ A K Q 7
    ◇ 8 5 4 3
    ♣ –

(e) ♠ K Q J 7 5 3
    ♡ A 8 5
    ◇ –
    ♣ K Q J 6

(f) ♠ A K Q 9 7 5
    ♡ –
    ◇ K Q 7 5
    ♣ K 6 5

(g) ♠ A Q J 7 5
    ♡ A K Q 8
    ◇ K 9 7 4
    ♣ –

(h) ♠ A K J 9 8 4
    ♡ A Q 7
    ◇ –
    ♣ K J 6 5

(2)   Partner opens 1♠ and you reply 3♠. Partner now cue-bids 4♣. What do you bid now on:

(a) ♠ K Q J 6 5
    ♡ J 6 5 2
    ◇ Q
    ♣ A 7 6

(b) ♠ K Q J 7 5
    ♡ 9 6 2
    ◇ A K 2
    ♣ 7 2

(c) ♠ K Q J 7 5
    ♡ A 8 4
    ◇ K 9 2
    ♣ 8 2

(d) ♠ A K J 6 4
    ♡ 10 7 6
    ◇ 8
    ♣ K Q 6 5

(3)   You open 1♠ and partner replies 3♠. You cue-bid 4♣ and partner bids 4♡. What do you bid now on:

(a) ♠ A K Q J 7
    ♡ 8 6 5
    ◇ 4
    ♣ A Q 6 5

(b) ♠ A Q 7 5 3
    ♡ A J 7 6
    ◇ 8 6
    ♣ A 2

(c) ♠ K Q J 7 5   (d) ♠ A J 7 6 4
    ♡ A Q 7   ♡ K Q J 7
    ◇ 10 9 4   ◇ –
    ♣ A 6   ♣ A 9 8 6

(4) The bidding goes:

South	North
	1♠
3♠	4◇
4♡	4NT

What do you bid now on:

(a) ♠ K Q J 6 5   (b) ♠ K Q J 5 3
    ♡ A 6 5 2   ♡ A 6 2
    ◇ 6   ◇ 2
    ♣ A 7 6   ♣ Q J 10 6

(c) ♠ K Q J 7 5   (d) ♠ K Q J 6 4
    ♡ –   ♡ A 7 6
    ◇ Q J 10 2   ◇ Q 7
    ♣ Q J 10 2   ♣ J 8 5

(5) The bidding goes:

South	North
1♠	3♠
4◇	4♡
5♣	5◇

What do you bid now on:

(a) ♠ Q J 8 7 6   (b) ♠ Q J 9 8 4
    ♡ K 6 5   ♡ 6 5 3
    ◇ A   ◇ A
    ♣ K Q 6 2   ♣ K Q J 2

(c) ♠ Q J 8 5 2   (d) ♠ J 10 8 6 4
    ♡ K Q 8   ♡ K Q J 7
    ◇ A Q 9 4   ◇ –
    ♣ 6   ♣ K Q J 5

Let us work through the answers:

(1) In each case, we cue-bid the cheapest first-round control (ace or void) possible: (a) 4♣; (b) 4◇; (c) 4♡; (d) 4♣; (e) 4◇; (f) 4♡; (g) 4♣; (h) 4◇. Note that, in all cases, the bidding is still below game and that partner has maximum

space (often still below game) to show his controls. This must be an improvement on Blackwood, which commits the partnership to at least 5♠ and on occasions (it happens all too often) even that contract fails. The result is the loss of a game when there was nothing to be gained.

(2) The same principle applies and should certainly be followed below game as that costs nothing.

    (a) Partner clearly has a void of clubs and that is bad news because our ace is likely to be of little or no value. As we have no red-suit first-round control, it is advisable to discourage with 4♠, hoping to play there. If partner now bids 4NT, it will be more helpful to him to cue-bid our second-round control in diamonds in preference to 5♣. If we do bid 5♣, though technically not wrong, we may never be able to show the diamond singleton below 5♠.

    (b) 4♦.

    (c) 4♡.

    (d) This is more debatable. We are entitled to cue-bid 4NT to show the ♠A but that involves going past game. In this case, with the singleton diamond, we are likely to be able to underwrite 5♠, so it is probably worth risking. Without the singleton diamond, 4♠ is probably enough.

(3) (a) The heart control is just what we wanted. There is no need for a decision yet so we just carry on cue-bidding with 4NT to show the ♠A and see what second-round controls partner has.

    (b) Partner's heart void is both good and bad news. On the one hand, our three low hearts are looked after; on the other, the ♡A is of little, if any, worth. With good controls and only two diamonds, however, it is unlikely that 5♠ will go down, so it is worth cue-bidding the ♠A with 4NT. Hopefully, partner will bid 5♦, after which 6♠ will be a fair bet.

    (c) Partner's heart void and lack of diamond control is bad news. He could, of course, have strong diamond

honors and the ♠A, but even then there is no guarantee
that we can avoid a club loser so it is probably best to
stop in 4♠. Partner may turn up with the ♠A and
strong clubs, in which case three top diamonds would
defeat 5♠.

(d) Here we have control of all four suits and there is every
reason to bid on – we cue-bid the ♠A with 4NT and
await more news.

(4) Here partner has gone past game and it is up to us to make
the cheapest cue-bid available:

(a) 5♣.

(b) 5♦ (the first-round control has already been shown);
this denies first-round control of clubs.

(c) 5♡ (a void is both first- *and* second-round control); this
denies first-round control of clubs and second-round
control of diamonds.

(d) 5♠ – nothing more to show.

(5) In all cases, we are unable to take a decision – that must rest
with partner, who knows that we are missing the two black
aces. All we can do is to bid 5♡ on (a), (c) and (d) to show
the second-round control of hearts, and 5♠ on (b) to deny
it.

Competitive bidding

We are now going to allow the opponents to enter the auction.
This has a number of effects:

1 It gives them a chance of buying the contract.
2 They may be able to indicate an opening lead or line of defence
if they nevertheless have to defend.
3 They may rob us of valuable bidding space, notably if they can
pre-empt at the three- or higher level.

On the other hand:

4 It may give us valuable information regarding the whereabouts of enemy cards.

5 It gives us the opportunity to bid their suit at a low level as a forcing bid – this is the unassuming cue-bid (UCB).

6 It gives us the opportunity to bid their suit at the three-level to investigate stoppers for no-trump – this is the directional asking bid (DAB).

There is a certain amount of confusion between the two latter calls and the distinction can indeed be somewhat blurred. At this stage, I shall try to set out an easy-to-remember rule:

The direct cue-bid This is unassuming and forces to game or suit agreement, i.e. to a position where both partners have bid the same suit. It arises when an opponent has opened at the one-level and the bidding goes either:

W	N	E	S	or	W	N	E	S
1♡	2♡				1♡	Pass	Pass	2♡

Assume West has dealt and has opened 1♡. The cue-bid shows a strong hand (worth about eight tricks at least playing on its own) but one not suitable for a take-out double. That usually means a desperate shortage (singleton or void) in one of the side suits. The commonest are big one- or two-suiters:

♠ A K Q J 8 7	♠ –
♡ 9 7	♡ K 7
◇ A K 7 5 3	◇ A K Q J 8 6 5 3
♣ –	♣ K Q 7

would both be typical. On the first hand, if we made a take-out double, partner, with long clubs, might think Christmas had arrived early and, particularly if the opponents preempt in hearts (they often do in this type of situation) could propel us into an embarrassing club contract when we ought to be playing in spades or diamonds. On the second hand, we shall definitely want to play in diamonds or 3NT, but doubling one major is primarily orientated towards finding a fit in the other – the last thing we want here. Once a cue-bid of this kind has been made, the discussion can proceed *quietly* as all calls are forcing until game or suit agreement has been reached. In fact, no jump call should be made unless it carries a very definite message.

The UCB opposite partner's call This normally arises when partner has overcalled. The bidding might go:

W	N	E	S
1♣	1♡	Pass	2♣

What South is saying here is that he has a good hand but does not know what to bid. Again it forces to game or suit agreement. Assuming West passes, North is expected to describe his hand further, either by bidding another suit, if he has one, repeating his own suit if he hasn't, or bidding no-trump if he is strong in clubs (usually means a minimum of about a stop and a half, typically A J x). The conversation continues until game or suit agreement is reached, when either partner is entitled to pass if he has no extra strength.

The directional asking bid This occurs where an opponent makes an opening call or overcall and 3NT is being discussed. Now the call of opponent's suit promises at least a half-stop and asks for help in the form of another half-stop. Dependent on the number of top controls held by the partnership and their ability to run a long suit quickly, it may take from one to two stops in the opponents' suit to make 3NT viable.

Thus, while the unassuming cue-bid asks for a considerable holding in opponent's suit for no-trump, the DAB only requests a half stop and therein lies the potential for confusion. My suggestion is that a direct cue-bid over opponent's bid is always unassuming. A cue-bid made opposite partner's bid is unassuming at the two-level, but directional asking at the three-level. Let us illustrate with examples:

W	N	E	S	
1♢	1♡	Pass	2♢	is UCB

W	N	E	S	
1♢	1♡	Pass	1♠	
Pass	2♡	Pass	3♢	is DAB

but remember that

W	N	E	S
1◇	1♡	Pass	1♠
Pass	2♠	Pass	3◇

is still a trial-call in diamonds with spades the agreed suit.

W	N	E	S	
1◇	1♡	2◇	3◇	is UCB

W	N	E	S	
1◇	1♠	Pass	2♣	
Pass	3♣	Pass	3◇	is DAB

As always, as if it needed repeating, the goal contract should be uppermost in the mind of both partners and these calls give the widest scope for options. Indeed, they have a far wider application than we are going to learn at this stage, but for the time being, let us confine ourselves to understanding the basic principles and do another test against the stop-watch. In each case, I want you state whether the cue-bid made is a UCB or DAB; what you propose to bid; whether your call will be a sign-off, invitational or forcing; and, above all, the goal contract(s). Assume you are always sitting South at love all.

Start your stop-watch and see if you can answer each example in under fifteen seconds.

(1)   East deals and opens 1♡. What would you bid on:

(a) ♠ A K J 8 6 4
      ♡ –
      ◇ K Q 10 8 7 4
      ♣ A

(b) ♠ A K Q 8
      ♡ K 8 6
      ◇ A K Q J 5 3
      ♣ –

(c) ♠ –
      ♡ K J 8 7
      ◇ A K
      ♣ A K Q J 8 5 3

(d) ♠ K Q J 8
      ♡ –
      ◇ A K 7 5 3
      ♣ A K 7 5

(2)   West deals and opens 1♡. Partner bids 2♡ and East passes.
What do you bid on:

(a) ♠ 8 7 6 4   (b) ♠ A K Q 5
     ♡ 9 6 5   ♡ 8 6
     ◇ 8 7 4   ◇ J 5 3
     ♣ 9 6 5   ♣ 8 6 5 3

(c) ♠ 5 3   (d) ♠ 8 7 5
     ♡ 7 6   ♡ A Q 4
     ◇ 8 6   ◇ 5 3 2
     ♣ A K Q J 10 5 3   ♣ 6 5 4 2

(3)   West deals and opens 1♡; North bids 1♠ and East passes.
What do you bid now on:

(a) ♠ 8 6   (b) ♠ Q 7
     ♡ A   ♡ K 8
     ◇ K J 10 8 7 4   ◇ A K J 8 5 3
     ♣ A Q 5 4   ♣ 7 5 2

(c) ♠ 9 7   (d) ♠ 9
     ♡ J 8 7   ♡ 8 6
     ◇ A K Q 8   ◇ A K 7 4 3
     ♣ K Q J 8   ♣ A K Q 4 2

(4)   East deals and the bidding goes:

W	N	E	S
		1◇	2♣
Pass	3♣	Pass	?

What do you bid now on:

(a) ♠ Q 8   (b) ♠ Q 8
     ♡ K 8   ♡ K 6
     ◇ J 7 4   ◇ A 3 2
     ♣ A Q J 8 7 6   ♣ K Q J 8 6 5

(c) ♠ A   (d) ♠ J 8 7
     ♡ A 9 8 7   ♡ A 8 7
     ◇ 8 6   ◇ Q 3
     ♣ K Q J 9 5 3   ♣ K Q 10 7 5

(5)   West deals and the bidding goes:

W	N	E	S
1♡	2◇	Pass	3◇
Pass	3♡	Pass	?

What do you bid now on:

(a) ♠ Q 6 4   (b) ♠ A K 8 4
     ♡ Q 6   ♡ 8 6
     ◇ J 10 7 4   ◇ Q J 5 3 2
     ♣ A Q 10 7   ♣ 7 5

Let us work through the answers:

(1) (a) With this very strong two-suited hand, we are near to
          making a slam single-handed, and it is purely a ques-
          tion of locating the ◇ A and establishing whether to
          play in diamonds or spades. For the moment, all we
          need do is establish a forcing situation with a UCB of
          2♡, after which we can have a lengthy discussion with
          a view to a slam in diamonds or spades.

     (b) This is a similar position. Again there is no rush – we
          just bid 2♡ as a UCB and await further developments.
          Game or slam is possible in diamonds or spades but we
          might even finish in no trump.

     (c) Again, we have an enormous hand, unsuitable for a
          take-out double because of our lack of the other major.
          Again, we establish a forcing situation with 2♡. If
          partner bids 2♠, we can settle for 3NT, otherwise we
          may be looking for a game or slam in clubs.

     (d) This hand is ideal for a take-out double and there is no
          reason to bid anything else. The call is forcing and,
          contrary to the belief of many players, there is virtually
          no such thing as being too strong. Partner will only
          leave it if he has long and solid hearts, in which case the
          penalty will be huge. Only in the case where we are
          near to a slam in our own hand and genuinely fear that
          the penalty will be inadequate compensation, should
          we prefer the cue-bid on a three-suited hand. Vulnera-
          bility will, obviously, be an important consideration.
          Goal contracts: 4♠, 5♣, 5◇ or a slam in one of those
          suits.

(2) (a) We have been forced to bid and all we can do is bid our
          longest suit, 2♠. It is a sobering thought that this is
          forcing, but partner is responsible and will decide the

final contract. We have little idea of the goal contract at present but that hardly matters as partner is in charge.

(b) Here we have a much stronger hand, but as a forcing situation has been established, there is no need for rush. Again we just bid 2♠ and await further developments – we will certainly reach game, probably slam.

(c) This is the one exception where we have a very definite message to send to partner and it is worth sacrificing a round of bidding to express it in one breath. Our call of 4♣ shows a solid suit which we are willing to have as trump, even opposite a void. This sets the trump suit and any bid that follows from partner is a cue-bid. Goal contracts: 5♣ or a club slam.

(d) Here, with a good double heart stop, we can describe our hand with 2NT with a view to 3NT. We can, however, give some support to any suit partner chooses and will not mind playing in a suit game.

(3) (a) We have game-going ambitions here but any non-heart denomination could be right. This is ideal for a UCB of 2♡ and we will bid diamonds afterwards (still forcing) to describe this hand. Goal contracts: 3NT, 4♠, 5♣ 5♢.

(b) Here again we have game-going ambitions, but there is no need to ask partner to describe his hand when it is more convenient to describe ours. A jump in a new suit opposite an overcall is forcing for one round and gives the opportunity for 3NT (if partner bids it or makes a DAB of 3♡) 4♠ or 5♢. We thus bid 3♢.

(c) Here we must insist on game but any non-heart denomination is possible and this is ideal for a UCB of 2♡. We may be able to follow up with a DAB of 3♡ to give the opportunity of 3NT. Other goal contracts are 4♠, 5♣ and 5♢.

(d) Again, we are almost certain that game will be on despite the misfit but again we do not know where. We make the UCB of 2♡ and then start bidding our minors (forcing until a suit is agreed). We avoid the DAB this time. If 3NT is to be played, partner will have to bid it on his own as we cannot assist with even a half-stop in hearts.

(4) (a) There is every chance that 3NT will be on if partner can help stop the diamonds. We therefore make the DAB of 3 ◊, hoping to play 3NT, but we may have to settle for 4♣ or 5♣.

(b) Here, with one definite stop, we could take a stab at 3NT ourselves, but with such a lack of aces, the chances are that we shall need a second stop in diamonds. The DAB of 3 ◊ is therefore arguably preferable. If partner turns up with a singleton diamond, 5♣ may be makeable while 3NT fails. We may, of course, have to be content with 4♣.

(c) Here we certainly want to make a forward move but, if we are to play 3NT, partner will have to produce a stop on his own. The DAB of 3 ◊ is thus ruled out and our best bid is 3♡ (forcing) so that we end in 3NT, 4♣ or 5♣. It will be interesting to see how we decide which. If partner bids 3NT, we pass. If he cannot stop the diamonds, he has the option to bid 3♠, showing values in that suit. That is just what we do not want and we will probably sign off in 4♣. If he fails to bid 3♠, then it is reasonable to assume that he does not hold values in spades, and as he clearly has little in diamonds, then he must have something in hearts, and now 5♣ is a good bet. There is also the chance that partner has a four-card heart suit and we can then play in 4♡.

(d) Here we have little more than our two-over-one overcall and there is little reason to move over 3♣.

(5) Here we have been asked for a half-stop in hearts with a DAB (at the three-level opposite our bid) and we are happy to accept with hand (a), bidding the goal contract of 3NT. Giving partner ♡ K x x or ♡ A x x gives us a second stop in the suit when our hand is declarer. One of the disadvantages of the DAB arises when the hand sitting *under* the original opener has Q x in the suit. If the layout is

                              A x x

            K J 10 x x   x x x

                              Q x

then North-South have one stop if North is declarer but two if
South is declarer. For that reason, many players tend to bid no-
trump themselves holding Q x under the call, risking looking
silly if partner turns up with nothing and the opponents reel
off five or more tricks, but very often gaining in the above
situation or if the leader, with a holding of something like
AK x x x, leads fourth-high at trick one.

It is, however, quite in order to make a DAB with Q x when
sitting *over* the original bidder. Now he will be on lead if
partner is declarer and nothing is lost. Thus this sequence
would be appropriate:

W	N	E	S
		1♡	2♢
Pass	3♢	Pass	3♡
Pass	?		

Now, if North bids 3NT, East has to lead away from his
holding.

On hand (b) we have no semblance of a heart stop and
must return to 4♢. However, it costs nothing to bid 3♠ on
the way. Partner should realize that this promises no more
than four spades. With five or more, we should bid 2♠ over
2♢ as 4♠ is a serious candidate for goal contract. Here,
showing our good spade suit may help partner decide to
play 4♢ or 5♢. Had our ace and king been in clubs, we
could call 4♣. Both bids are below 4♢ and therefore cost
nothing. We shall presumably finish in 4♢ or 5♢ but 4♠,
possibly on a 4–3 fit, is not out of the question. Notice in all
these sequences, how the partnership keeps as many
options open for goal contract as possible.

Bidding after an overcall

We are now going to consider the position arising when partner
opens the bidding and the next hand overcalls. These overcalls
fall into a number of categories.

1 A simple overcall of (a) one of a suit, (b) two of a suit.

2 1NT, promising about 15–17 points including at least a stop in partner's suit.

3 A jump overcall, promising a good six-card suit but a weak hand of about 6–10 points.

4 An unassuming cue-bid as discussed in the last section.

We shall consider each in turn.

A one-over-one simple overcall

A typical example would be 1◇ from partner and 1♡ from the next hand. The first point to realize is that partner will now have another chance to bid and therefore there is no need for our hand to stretch to compete on minimal values. However, in principle, we bid as we would have done in the absence of the overcall.

1♠:   6 points up as usual, forcing; there is no need to alter this.

1NT: 6–10 points as usual, but you must have a stop in the overcalled suit. In the absence of a stop, you should pass (especially if you are at the minimum end of the range) unless you can support partner; he will have another chance to bid.

2♣:   Normal: 11+ points and forcing.

2◇:   Normal raise: 6–10 points and at least four trumps.

2♡:   UCB as discussed before.

2♠, 3♣: Game-forcing, one-suited hand a usual.

2NT: 13–15 as usual, forcing with at least one-and-a-half stops in hearts. With less than that, it is better to change suit and make a DAB later.

3◇:   Normal jump raise – about 13–16 points, forcing.

Here, however, there are two schools of thought, especially regarding raises in major suits. Normally, we play 1♡ 3♡ as 13–16 supporting points, forcing. Where opponents come in, particularly with jump overcalls, bidding space has been lost and, especially as we are guaranteed a five-card suit, we may wish to compete at the three-level despite being understrength and indeed it would be a pity not to be able to do so. It is therefore recommended that the forcing raise to three-level be abandoned if the opponents enter the auction, and therefore that 1♡ (2♣) 3♡ be a limit raise, showing 11–12 points, non forcing. With a strong hand, you can always cue-bid the opponent's suit first and then support hearts to show game-going values, or call 4♡ direct with a primarily heart-orientated hand. This is what I recommend but be sure to agree it with your partner.

Double: Penalties – indicates shortage in hearts, doubleton at the most but preferably singleton or void, at least a good four-card heart suit and a minimum of about 10 points. The message to partner is that we wish to defend and therefore he should not repeat his diamonds unless they are so long and strong that he is happy to have them as trump, even opposite a singleton or void.

Two-over-one simple overcall

A typical example would be 1♡ by partner, 2◇ by the next hand. The position now changes appreciably as considerable bidding space has been lost.

2♡: Simple raise as usual.

2♠: This is forcing and therefore commits the partnership to 2NT or the three-level and must therefore have at least 11 points as usual and ideally a minimum of five spades. You might do it on less with a longer suit.

2NT: 13–15 points (forcing) with a good diamond stop as usual.

But again, a similar problem arises as with 1♡ 3♡ and it is recommended that with the 13–15 point range, you bid 3NT direct, intending to play, with 2NT as 11–12, limited and non-forcing. Again you must be sure to agree it with your partner.

3♣: Again much depends on our attitude to hearts, but we should be near to opening strength; this is forcing for one round.

3◇: UCB – promises a minimum of opening strength and forces at least to suit agreement; in practice, the partnership will rarely stop short of game.

3♡:   A forcing jump raise as usual or limit non-forcing raise (recommended), as explained above.

3♠:   One-suited game-force – opening strength or better; again attitude to hearts is important unless the spades are so good that we are happy to play in 4♠ even with a complete misfit.

Double: Penalties – this can be a little lighter than at the one-level but care must be taken with calls higher than two diamonds, when we are doubling opponents into game.

The 1NT overcall

Let us say that partner has opened 1♡ and the next hand overcalls 1NT. This changes the picture considerably because 15–17 points have been advertised on our right, including at least one heart honor. The chances of game are now reduced dramatically and indeed, in practice, game is rare against that kind of strength. In any case, it would imply that the combined strength on our side would be enough to extract a huge penalty in 1NT doubled. For that reason, our bidding is orientated towards contesting the part-score.

2♣, 2♢, These all show one-suited hands, five-card at least but
2♠:   usually six. The calls themselves are the goal contracts, although partner can look for game with a big supporting hand. They are unlikely to contain more than 9 points. With 10 or more, we shall want to double 1NT for penalties.

2♡:   Raise as usual – note that a trump stack is now more likely and three small cards is a dubious holding.

3♣, 3♢, These are similar to the two-level calls but show six-card
3♠:   or longer suits. Like the two-level calls, these are non-forcing but invitational to game in those suits.

3♡:   Jump raise as usual.

Double: Penalties – about 10 points or more.

The weak jump overcall

Here a great deal of bidding space may be lost, but the damage

can vary considerably, ranging from 1♣ 2♢ to the most harmful
1♠ 3♡. A change of suit forces for one round, promising a
minimum point-count according to level: 9+ at two-level; 11+ at
three-level; 13+ at four-level.

When competing, how strict we have to be depends on the
length and quality of our suit, our attitude to partner's suit, and
our holding in the opponents' suit. The shorter we are in that suit,
the less likely we are to run into trouble (in the form of an
opponents' misfit) if we stretch the bidding, and vice versa.

With so many factors to be taken into account, it is difficult to
make hard and fast rules and in these competitive situations
judgement, which only comes with experience, plays a considerable role. We only have to look at the regular bidding competi-
tions in magazines to see that even top players can differ widely
in their views.

Raises of partner's suit are as usual, but it is permissible to
stretch one level to be able to compete. A no-trump call is as
usual, but a double stop is desirable as there will be a long and
possibly strong suit against us. A double is for penalties. Pre-
emptive jumps are treated in a similar manner.

The unassuming cue-bid

Here the opponents are in a forcing situation and if we pass now,
we are guaranteed another call. For that reason, there is little
point in bidding if the hand is a misfit, as we are likely to want to
defend. Any call should therefore be orientated towards competing and/or taking bidding space away from opponents.

A double of the cue-bid replaces a simple raise in partner's
suit, i.e. we were going to make the call ourselves.

Raises to higher levels in partner's suit are as usual, but often a
little under strength as the fit implies little defence against a game
likely to be on for the other side. We are thus prepared to
'sacrifice' to make life as difficult for opponents as possible. How
high we should go depends on the amount of our potential
defence and the vulnerability. With plenty of honors in side-suits,
there is little to worry about as opponents are unlikely to be able
to make anything spectacular. With all our points in partner's
suit, we have no defence and now anything up to a slam could be

on. A penalty of 500 or even more could then be well worth conceding.

A new suit shows a strong suit of our own and at least tolerance (say three to an honor or any four or more cards) for partner's suit. This situation often arises when the cue-bidder has a massive two-suiter in the other suits. With a more detailed knowledge of our hand, partner will be better informed when it comes to taking a decision as to whether to defend or sacrifice. Mistakes at a high level in this situation can be very expensive and it is worthwhile developing good judgement in this area.

Let us try another test against the stop-watch. You should be able to answer each problem in well under fifteen seconds. Give your choice of call, stating whether it is forcing, invitational or sign-off and the probable goal contracts. As usual, assume you are sitting South at love all.

(1)   Partner deals and opens 1♡; East overcalls 1♠. What do you bid on:

(a) ♠ 7 6 5
     ♡ Q 7 5
     ◇ Q 5 4 3
     ♣ 8 5 4

(b) ♠ K J 5
     ♡ 8 5 4
     ◇ A J 6 5
     ♣ 8 6 2

(c) ♠ A Q J 7
     ♡ 8
     ◇ K 8 6 5
     ♣ J 7 5 4

(d) ♠ 8 6 5 4
     ♡ Q
     ◇ A 5 4 3
     ♣ J 6 5 2

(e) ♠ K Q 7
     ♡ 8 5
     ◇ A J 6 2
     ♣ K 5 4 3

(f) ♠ 7
     ♡ Q 8 6
     ◇ K Q 8 6 5
     ♣ J 7 5 4

(g) ♠ K 5
     ♡ Q 5
     ◇ A Q J 7 5 3
     ♣ K 5 4

(h) ♠ 7
     ♡ K 8 6 4
     ◇ K 8 6 5
     ♣ K 7 5 4

(2) Partner deals and opens 1♡; East overcalls 1NT. What do you bid on:

(a) ♠ 5
     ♡ Q 7 5
     ◇ K 5 4 3
     ♣ J 8 5 4 3

(b) ♠ A J 7
     ♡ 8 6
     ◇ 8 6 5
     ♣ 9 8 7 5 3

(c) ♠ J 5 3
     ♡ 8 4
     ◇ J
     ♣ A K Q J 8 5 4

(d) ♠ A Q J 8 6 4
     ♡ 8
     ◇ 10 6
     ♣ 5 4 3 2

(e) ♠ –
     ♡ Q 10 8 6
     ◇ Q 5 4 3
     ♣ K Q 6 5 2

(f) ♠ 7
     ♡ 6
     ◇ Q 8 6 5
     ♣ K Q J 8 7 5 3

(g) ♠ Q 7
     ♡ 8 5
     ◇ Q 10 9 8 7 6 2
     ♣ Q 5

(h) ♠ A 7
     ♡ Q 8 6
     ◇ K 8 6 5
     ♣ Q 5 4 2

(3) Partner deals and opens 1♡; East overcalls 2♣. What do you bid on:

(a) ♠ J 8
     ♡ Q 7 5
     ◇ K 5 4 3
     ♣ 8 5 4 3

(b) ♠ J 5
     ♡ 8 6 2
     ◇ 10 8 6 5
     ♣ K Q 5 3

(c) ♠ K J 5 3
     ♡ 8
     ◇ K J 9 3
     ♣ Q J 8 5

(d) ♠ K J 4
     ♡ 8 4
     ◇ K Q J 10 6
     ♣ 5 4 3

(e) ♠ K J 8 6
     ♡ 8 6
     ◇ Q 5 4 3
     ♣ 6 5 2

(f) ♠ K 8 7
     ♡ K 6
     ◇ A 8 6 5
     ♣ Q J 5 3

(g) ♠ A J 7 6
     ♡ 8 5
     ◇ Q 6 5 2
     ♣ K J 9

(h) ♠ A K Q 7 3
     ♡ J 6
     ◇ 8 6 5
     ♣ 5 4 2

(4)   Partner deals and opens 1♡; East overcalls 2♠. What do you bid on:

(a)   ♠ 5
      ♡ Q 7 4 2
      ◇ K 5 4 3
      ♣ J 8 5 3

(b)   ♠ A J 10 7
      ♡ 8
      ◇ K 8 6 5
      ♣ J 7 5 3

(c)   ♠ K 3
      ♡ 8 4
      ◇ J 4 2
      ♣ A K Q J 5 4

(d)   ♠ A Q 7
      ♡ 8 4
      ◇ K 10 6 5
      ♣ Q 10 3 2

(e)   ♠ 5
      ♡ 8 6
      ◇ A Q J 5 4 3
      ♣ K 6 5 2

(f)   ♠ 7 4
      ♡ 6
      ◇ Q 8 6 5
      ♣ K Q J 7 5 3

(g)   ♠ 7
      ♡ Q 10 8 5
      ◇ 7 6 2
      ♣ A K Q 5 2

(h)   ♠ A J 7
      ♡ Q 8 6
      ◇ K J 5
      ♣ Q 5 4 2

(5)   Partner deals and opens 1♡; East cue-bids 2♡. What do you bid on:

(a)   ♠ 5 2
      ♡ K Q 5
      ◇ 5 4 3
      ♣ J 8 5 4 3

(b)   ♠ A J 7
      ♡ 8
      ◇ K Q 6 5
      ♣ Q 8 7 5 3

(c)   ♠ J 10 5 3 2
      ♡ K 10 8 4 2
      ◇ J
      ♣ 5 4

(d)   ♠ A Q J 8 6 4
      ♡ Q 8 3
      ◇ 10
      ♣ 5 4 2

(e)   ♠ –
      ♡ Q 10 8 6
      ◇ 7 5 4 2
      ♣ K 6 5 4 2

(f)   ♠ 7
      ♡ 10 9 8 7 6 5
      ◇ Q 8 6 5 4 2
      ♣ –

(g)   ♠ Q 7
      ♡ Q 8 5
      ◇ K 8
      ♣ 10 8 7 6 5 3

(h)   ♠ J 7
      ♡ Q J
      ◇ J 8 6 5 3
      ♣ A 5 4 2

(6) Partner opens 1♡ and East overcalls 3♣. What do you bid on:

(a) ♠ 5
♡ Q J 7 5
◇ K 5 4 3
♣ J 8 4 3

(b) ♠ A J 7
♡ Q 8 6
◇ 8 6 5
♣ 8 7 5 3

(c) ♠ 10 5 2
♡ 4 2
◇ A K Q J 8 4
♣ A 9

(d) ♠ A K Q J 6 4
♡ 8 4
◇ 6 5
♣ 4 3 2

Let us work through the answers:

(1) (a) Although we have modest support for partner's suit, we have neither the strength nor shape to compete. We therefore pass and hope that partner can reopen. We may then have the opportunity to show the heart support.

(b) With 9 points and a double spade stop we are happy to compete with 1NT, the goal contract being 3NT.

(c) Here, with a very unpleasant spade stack against East and – just as important – a shortage in partner's suit, we are keen to defend and therefore double 1♠, intending to defend that contract. Partner should not move it unless his hand is totally unsuitable for defence. There are two circumstances in which this might apply:

(i) He has very long and solid hearts and precious little outside so that, despite our singleton, he has plenty of playing strength and little or no defence;

(ii) He has very poor hearts and a long solid minor outside. Now he knows that there will be a big crossruff available to us in a minor-suit contract and again, he will have little to offer in defence.

In both cases, he will have a singleton or void spades. Examples would be:

♠ 3
♡ A K Q J 10 2
◇ Q 7 5 4
♣ 8 5

♠ –
♡ J 8 7 6 5 4
◇ J 6
♣ A K Q J 6

In both cases, 1♠ doubled will hardly be successful, while we can make at least a part-score, if not a game, in hearts (on the left hand) or in clubs (on the right).

(d) This is a similar shape to (c) but the quality of the spades and general strength of the hand do not warrant a penalty double. We certainly do not want to compete with such a misfit and, as a general rule, low cards sitting over an overcalled suit are a bad sign. We therefore pass and hope that, if partner reopens, it will be with a take-out double (which we shall answer by bidding our minor suits in ascending order, i.e. 2♣) or with a minor suit of his own. If he does repeat his hearts, we shall pass – at least the ♡Q will be a useful card.

(e) Here we would have bid 2NT (13–15 points, forcing) without the intervention and, if you have agreed to stick to it, then this is your call. However, as explained above, it is easier to play 2NT as 11–12, a limited invitational non-forcing call and thus here, with 13 points and a double stop in spades, we should bid 3NT direct, hoping to play there.

(f) This is a straightforward raise to 2♡ and we have no reason to bid anything else. We hope to finish in 4♡ and the singleton in opponent's suit is likely to be an important asset.

(g) Here, we have a game-forcing hand and, being one-suited, should describe the hand directly with 3♢, primarily looking for 3NT (which we shall be happy to bid if partner makes the DAB of 3♠), 5♢ or even a slam.

(h) This is worth a limit-raise to 3♡. Without the overcall, we would have had to bid a minor on the two-level before making the limit-raise. Here we can either do the same, or, according to agreement as discussed above, bid 3♡ direct, non-forcing.

(2) (a) Here we would have raised to 2♡ without the inter-vention and there is little reason to do anything else

now. Note that both red-suit honors are well-placed behind East's announced strength, but the spade singleton is of limited value with only three trumps. East will know that we are likely to have bid on distribution rather than high-card strength and this auction calls for a trump lead, even if it has to be from an embarrassing holding.

(b) Here the spade holding is likely to be well-placed over the bid, but 5 points, especially with such poor hearts, is nowhere near good enough to warrant competing. We therefore pass.

(c) With seven top tricks in our own hand and an opening bid opposite, a huge penalty is likely if they play 1NT and we have no hesitation in doubling. It is likely that West will remove to spades or diamonds, and after that we can bid our clubs, possibly with a view to playing in 3NT.

(d) Here we have a strong suit of our own and despite the misfit, this is probably more suited to play rather than defence. 1NT doubled could be sensational if we get the spades going and the ♠K is almost certain to be well-placed for us in partner's or East's hand. However, we have little defence against a diamond contract and if we double 1NT now and then bid spades, we are showing a stronger hand. An immediate 2♠ is therefore advisable.

(e) This is well worth a raise to 3♡ (a case could be made even for 4♡ direct) and it is best to bid it now rather than double 1NT, after which opponents are almost certain to get together in spades. 3♡ is invitational to our goal contract, 4♡.

(f) Here we have quite a strong hand but success in 1NT doubled (which is most unlikely to be played anyway) would depend on bringing in the club suit and we are short of side-suit entries. Despite the dislike of hearts, this hand is best suited to playing in clubs rather than defending but it is certainly worth 3♣, bid with a view to 5♣ or perhaps 3NT, if partner is strong with a club holding and a good spade stop. Remember that we have limited our hand by failing to double 1NT and therefore that 3♣ is non-forcing.

(g) This is a poorish hand and partner has bid the suit we least wanted to hear. Nonetheless, it will be worth a lot of tricks if those diamonds are trumps and it is worth competing with 2◇ (with a view to playing there) rather than trying to defend 1NT.

(h) Here we have a strong hand with a fit for partner and the ♡Q will be well placed behind East's heart stop. There should be no hesitation in doubling 1NT for penalties.

(3) (a) Here we have enough strength to compete with 2♡. Note, however, the four small clubs are a poor feature, but against that our three honors are outside clubs and are therefore likely to be useful. Goal contract: 4♡.

(b) This time, most of our points are in clubs and are probably facing a shortage in partner's hand. Worse still, if partner has three or more clubs, West will be left with a singleton or void and will be able to ruff our honors. With only three poor trumps, it is best not to compete and it is advisable to pass, intending, at least for the moment, to defend 2♣.

(c) This time, we have a strong hand, a misfit and a very unpleasant trump stack against East. We therefore have no hesitation in doubling for penalties, with the added bonus that we can treat the two other suits with similar contempt.

(d) Here the club and heart holdings are most discouraging but the point-count, solid diamond suit and respectable spade holding make it worthwhile competing with 2◇. Goal contracts: 5◇, 3NT (more likely if partner can stop the clubs).

(e) Here we would have been strong enough to bid 1♠ over 1♡ without the interference but with only 6 points and unattractive holdings in both clubs and hearts, it is best to pass, remembering that partner has another chance. If he reopens with a take-out double, he will be promising a spade suit and we can then bid ours, confident of a fit.

(f) With this stronger hand, we have to judge whether to double and defend 2♣ or call a game in 3NT. In this kind of situation, the heart position is critical. K x is a positive holding rather than a dislike and I therefore prefer 3NT (or 2NT if you have agreed to play this as forcing). Give partner a six-card broken heart suit and a singleton or void in clubs and it may well be that 3NT or 4♡ will be made while 2♣ is going for a very small penalty. If partner has length in clubs, 3NT will be comfortable as the defenders will have poor communications with their 5–1 or 6–0 club misfit.

(g) This is a hand where we can bid an invitational, non-forcing 2NT. If you still play this as forcing, then you must bid 2◇ now, intending to bid 2NT over a rebid of 2♡.

(h) With the solid spade suit and 10 points, it is worth competing with 2♠ (forcing one round) despite the poor club and heart holdings. We are primarily aiming for 4♠.

(4) (a) We have been pushed up to the three-level but it is well worth competing with a hand which, although low in point-count, has improved considerably on the bidding. We bid 3♡, hoping for 4♡, but partner will have to take into account the fact that we have been pushed and therefore that our call is wider-ranging than it would have been without the interference.

(b) Here we have a misfit and a very unpleasant trump stack against East. Even if partner has a minimum opening call, we have at least half the points in the pack and 2♠ doubled is most unlikely to be made. We are also able to double any 'escape' to 3♣ or 3◇.

(c) With a well-placed ♠K and six quick tricks in clubs, 3NT must be a near certainty and it is reasonable to bid it direct. Alternatively, we can bid 3♣ (forcing) intending to rebid 3NT next time. This does give the option of playing in 5♣ (or 4♡ should partner have a long suit) which will be preferable if it turns out that partner is very short and/or weak in diamonds. For that reason, I prefer 3♣ but 3NT (or 2NT if it is played as forcing) can hardly be criticized in that it has the advantage that we do not pinpoint the diamond weakness.

(d) Without the interference, we would have called a minor intending to follow up with 2NT (11–12 invitational but non-forcing). This option has now been removed and the ideal call now is a direct 2NT, still invitational and non-forcing. If you are still playing it as 13–15, forcing, you have little alternative but to call a minor on the three-level, hoping to follow with 3NT. A case could be made for doubling but we do not have enough trumps and the hearts are too long (note that a doubleton is hardly a 'shortage'). Goal contract: 3NT.

(e) We have a good diamond suit, and the singleton spade improves this hand slightly. We therefore compete with 3♢ (forcing for one round), looking for 5♢ but 4♡ and 3NT are possibilities.

(f) This time, the bidding has weakened this hand with the singleton heart and doubleton spade being undesirable holdings from the declaring point of view. It is therefore not worth competing with only 8 points, particularly as it would be with a minor, requiring eleven tricks for game. We therefore pass.

(g) Here we are easily worth a raise to game but, particularly with a singleton spade, a slam could well be on. It therefore costs nothing to bid 3♣ first and 4♡ on the next round and partner will realize that we have slam ambitions.

(h) This hand is a balanced opening call with a double stop in spades and we have little reason to consider anything other than 3NT. We bid it direct and let partner pass or choose an alternative contract. If you are still playing 2NT as 13–15, forcing, you can bid that instead, leaving room for discussion if partner has slam ambitions.

(5) (a) We have strong values in hearts and would have bid
2♡ without the interference. We can cheaply suggest a
sacrifice (or, at any rate, a safe lead for partner) by
doubling the cue-bid. We have no idea of final contract
at the moment, but that will be for partner to decide
with the information we have given him. He will elect
to sacrifice or defend accordingly. Thus we do not have
to worry unnecessarily over that consideration.

(b) Here we have a strong hand which will be excellent for
defence with the heart misfit and plenty of honors in
enemy suits. We are therefore happy to pass and force
West to bid. He is likely to have a desperately weak
hand with long hearts – but that is his problem.
Opponents are forced at least to suit agreement and we
are advised to wait until they get as high as possible
before doubling.

(c) Here, it is almost certain that East has a big minor two-
suiter and our length in hearts suggests that he may
well be void in the suit. In any case, we have little or no
defence and, with the big heart fit, this is the time to
preempt or *bounce* the bidding. Opponents will almost
certainly have a game on and could well make anything
up to a grand slam if partner has bid on a good heart
suit and little else. Thus we should bid at least 4♡ and a
case could be made for bidding 5♡. After that, we
should not bid again but leave any further action to
partner, who will be better placed to decide the final
contract.

(d) Again, it appears that East has a big minor two-suiter
and whether we should play or defend will largely
depend on partner's attitude to spades. As we are
happy to play in 3♡, we should give partner the extra
information by bidding 2♠. Again the goal contract is
not our worry.

(e) How far we should bounce here is more debatable.
Opponents clearly have a spade fit but the ♣K is a
possible defensive trick. The club suit is not good
enough to warrant bidding 3♣ and I would be content

to bid 3♡, although 4♡ can certainly be justified. Either way, any subsequent action should be left to partner.

(f) This is a very extreme case of a bouncing hand with not a defensive trick in sight and the possibility of anything up to a grand slam on for either side. My recommendation would be 5♡, but 6♡ is certainly justifiable. Again, after that, partner calls the tune. This point is being repeated because the number of people who bid their hand twice (or more often!) in this type of situation, even in the higher echelons, is alarming. The excuse that partner may not have heard them the first time does not really stand up at any level!

(g) Here the heart support is modest and the honors in the short suits are likely to be valuable in defence. This is not the time to even suggest a sacrifice to partner and it is best to pass and defend whatever opponents choose.

(h) Similar arguments apply and again we should pass. Note that we should not even contemplate doubling the cue-bid, even if it were only for lead purposes. We would not want partner to lead hearts from a holding like A 10 x x x.

(6) (a) This would have been a comfortable raise to 2♡ without the interference and we are justified in pushing up a level although the club holding is unattractive. We hope that partner will be very short, otherwise West will be void and we could lose a lot of tricks. Nevertheless, it would be a pity to be talked out of what may be an excellent 4♡ contract and this is the sort of situation where we have to take the rough with the smooth.

(b) Here we are very flat, the club holding is disastrous behind the overcall and we have no justification in competing at the three level. We must pass and await further developments, if any.

(c) This is similar to (4c); arguments for 3◇ or 3NT apply similarly.

(d) Despite the poor club and heart holdings, it would be a

pity to be talked out of a good game in 4♠ with six near-certain tricks in our own hand. We bid 3♠ (forcing) and are prepared to play 3NT or 4♠.

We complete this section by discussing the modifications that apply if the partner of the opening hand has already passed. He is thus limited to 11 points or less and therefore the guides change as follows:

1 A simple change of suit (previously forcing) is now non-forcing.
2 A jump in a new suit (previously forcing to game) is now forcing for one round and expresses willingness to play at least at the three-level in partner's bid suit.
3 The cue-bid forces to suit agreement and guarantees at least three-card support for opener's suit (there is no reason to get excited otherwise).

   A call of 2NT (and this applies even without interference) shows about 11 points, with at least a good stop in opponent's suit where applicable.

Try these examples in which you hold: ♠ Q 8 7
                                        ♡ A K 7 6 4
                                        ◇ K J
                                        ♣ 8 6 4

North deals at love all and the bidding goes:

W	N	E	S
	Pass	Pass	1♡
2♣	*	Pass	?

What do you bid now if North's call (*) is: (a) Double, (b) 2◇, (c) 2♡, (d) 2♠, (e) 2NT, (f) 3♣, (g) 3◇, (h) 3♡?

Let us work through the answers:

(a) The double is for penalties and with the top hearts, three trumps and 6 more points in short suits, we are delighted to stand it and pass.

(b) The call is non-forcing, but with only a doubleton diamond it is probably advisable to return to 2♡. Partner is likely to have at least a doubleton heart (with less, he might well have passed or doubled 2♣). We hope to play in 2♡. Note that, if partner now bids 2♠, the responder's reverse (previously forcing for one round) is now non-forcing. However, on this hand, we shall be expected to give false preference to 3♢.

(c) Here partner has given a simple raise and with a minimal opener, we have little reason to bid on. We thus pass, expecting to play in 2♡.

(d) This is non-forcing and, with game being unlikely, we are justified in passing 2♠.

(e) This promises about 11 points, balanced. With only 23 points combined and partner likely to have a doubleton heart (with three, he might have made a more positive call), it is best to pass and let him play 2NT.

(f) This is still a UCB, forcing to suit agreement. The only explanation for partner's rush of blood is an exciting heart fit and the cue-bid in this position is often used by many players to show a club control (singleton or void). For the time being, we have no new suit to show so we must just quietly bid 3♡ and await further developments. If the UCB guarantees club shortage, 4♡ is justified, with all our points working.

(g) This shows a raise to 3♡ with a good diamond suit on the side. Our diamond holding is therefore ideal and despite the minimum opener, I would recommend accepting the try with 4♡.

(h) This is a straightforward jump raise and with a minimum opening, I suggest passing, content to play there.

The double and redouble

In *The Expert Beginner* we discussed the take-out double at some length, and I explained that my method of handling it is rather different from those commonly taught and played. I say 'those' because there are at least two others. We also discussed situations in which a penalty double is appropriate. We are now going to deal with bidding after a take-out or penalty double has been made.

The first essential is to realize what is happening. A double is for take-out if partner has not already bid and one or two suits have been bid by the opposition. A double is for penalties if an opponent has opened 1NT or if partner has already bid. Let us start with a short test to make sure we can distinguish the two. Here are ten sequences. State the type of double in each case and give general comments on what type of hands the doublers are showing:

(1)	W	N	E	S
				1♡
	Dbl			

(2)	W	N	E	S
				Pass
	Pass	1NT	Dbl	

(3)	W	N	E	S
				1♡
	2◇	Dbl		

(4)	W	N	E	S
				1♡
	Pass	1NT	Dbl	

(5)	W	N	E	S
				1◇
	1♠	2♡	Dbl	

(6)	W	N	E	S
				1♠
	Pass	2♣	Pass	2♠
	Dbl			

(7)	W	N	E	S
				2◇
	Dbl			

(8)	W	N	E	S
				1♡
	1NT	2♣	Dbl	

(9)	W	N	E	S
				1♡
	1♠	Pass	Pass	Dbl

(10)	W	N	E	S
				1♡
	Pass	Pass	1NT	Dbl

Let us work through the answers:

(1)   Partner has not yet bid, therefore this is take-out, suggesting shortage in hearts and inviting another suit.

(2)   No suit has been bid, therefore this is for penalties, showing at least a point above the top of the non-trump range (i.e. 18 or more) and preferably a good suit from which to lead.

(3)   Partner has bid a suit, therefore we do not ask for his best suit and this is for penalties, suggesting a trump stack and –

more important – an intense dislike of hearts (doubleton at most, preferably less).

(4) Here a suit has been bid and therefore the double is for take-out. East should be fairly strong for this; both opponents have bid and the no-trump bid suggests that they may have a misfit. The risk in entering the bidding is considerable, particularly as we are likely to be contesting no more than a part-score.

(5) Again partner has bid, so this is for penalties. Note here that partner has only overcalled and may have little in defence. Thus an intense dislike of spades (singleton or void) is essential and East ought to be able to double a rescue back into diamonds. If he cannot, he is merely helping the opposition when they are in a forcing situation. Doubles in this position are very rare.

(6) Partner has not bid and this is take-out, clearly asking for the red suits. West did not double the first time because he is very short of clubs.

(7) Again partner has not spoken and this is take-out. With a strong hand advertised, this is likely to be sacrifice-orientated and should be very distributional.

(8) Partner has made a call so this is for penalties and East should be intending to double a heart rescue as well.

(9) This is a take-out as partner has not bid. In addition to his heart suit, South will have at least three cards in each of the two minors, 0544 being the ideal hand.

(10) East has shown about a 12–14 1NT in the protective position and, as no suit has been mentioned by the opposition, the double is for penalties. South will probably have about 18–19 (remember his partner has promised 0–5) and is also likely to have a good solid lead. With his partner unlikely to be able to help, leads away from tenaces are going to be costly.

Handling a take-out double was discussed in detail in the beginners' book and there is no need to repeat it here. We must, however, discuss bidding after a penalty double has been made and we shall distinguish between no-trump and suit calls.

Bidding after 1NT has been doubled

Let us first consider the general position after partner has opened 1NT and the next hand has doubled. Partner has limited his hand to 15–17 points, balanced, and the doubler has announced 18 points minimum (unless he has a long solid suit to lead) and could theoretically have up to 25 points. Most of the time, therefore, we are in some trouble and the aim should be to escape as cheaply as possible.

In the absence of a five-card suit, it is usually advisable to pass. Trying to find what would, at best, be a 4–4 fit would involve going on to the two-level, which means that we must make an extra trick to break even and two or more extra tricks to show a profit. This is likely to be advisable if the doubler has a long running suit, but we have to weigh up that consideration against the extra penalty likely to be sustained through being a level higher with no guarantee that we shall find more than a 4–3 fit.

With a five-card or longer suit and less than about 9 points, it is advisable to take-out into the suit, irrespective of quality. A long suit in a weak hand is unlikely to be brought in for tricks in no-trump but will usually be worth two or more extra tricks as trump; it is therefore worth paying the price of playing one level higher.

With 7 points or more in a balanced hand, we can be confident of a comfortable balance of the points and can redouble. 1NT redoubled is game, and we hope to play there. We are also expressing the intention to double if opponents choose to bid at the two-level. The partner of the doubler is almost certain to be very weak and he must now consider what to do. He is best advised to bid as though his partner has promised a strong no-trump (say 15–17 points). Again, with a balanced hand, he is advised to pass. The doubler may have the contract beaten in his own hand, for example with a long running suit, and he has, in any case, another chance to bid. It is always advisable in these situations for the stronger hand of a partnership to take a critical decision as he knows so much more.

With 9 points or more and an unbalanced hand, the position is more debatable. The probability that the doubler has a long running suit is now increased and it is a question of whether to redouble and hope to scrape home or to rescue into a long suit, where anything up to game could be on, especially if we have a singleton or void in the long running suit. It is usually advisable to bid rather than redouble or pass. A redouble is unlikely to be profitable. Even if the doubler's partner stands it, the doubler still has the option to run to his long suit or let the redouble stand according to his hand. If he does run to his long suit, we shall still have to take a decision about whether to compete or defend. A simple removal to the two-level is a sign-off. A jump to the three-level is invitational but non-forcing. The only forcing call in this situation is 2NT, which obviously cannot be natural, and is treated as a UCB, usually on a two-suiter. The 1NT opener describes his hand by bidding his four-card suits in ascending order until a fit is found.

Suit bids doubled for penalties

This can occur in a number of circumstances. If a take-out double is left in, as in:

W	N	E	S	or	W	N	E	S
			1♡					1♡
Dbl	Pass	Pass	?		Pass	Pass	Dbl	Pass
					Pass	?		

then the partner of the take-out doubler will have a very unpleasant trump stack, particularly in the first case where East is sitting under the call. The take-out doubler himself will probably be rich in at least two, if not all three of the other suits, and we are in desperate trouble.

Another situation arises when an overcall has been doubled (either directly for penalties or after a reopening take-out double has been left in):

W	N	E	S	or	W	N	E	S
1♡	2♣	Dbl	?		1♡	2♣	Pass	Pass
					Dbl	Pass	Pass	?

When a low-level *suit-contract* has been doubled for penalties, it is generally accepted that it is most unlikely that we shall want to redouble for 'business', i.e. hoping for a bigger profit on success. The redouble is used as 'SOS'. It is universally known as Kock-Werner, after the two Swedish players who first publicized it. A typical hand for an SOS redouble would include at least five cards in the unbid suits and a singleton or void in the doubled suit, as here: ♠ Q 10 8 6 5

      ♡ 8 7 4

      ◇ K J 6 4 3

      ♣ –

Partner should always remove the redouble; his partner could have up to all thirteen cards in the rescue suits and a doubled contract in one of them is almost certainly going to be cheaper than a redoubled contract in his own suit.

Alternatively, the partner of the overcaller may have a long suit of his own (it could even be that of the original opener) and will be considering whether to rescue to it. The wisdom of this is very much a matter of judgement, but the relevant considerations are:

1 Length in partner's suit: with a trebleton or more, we should be happy to accept partner's trump suit. The case for rescuing strengthens progressively as we shorten to a doubleton, singleton or void.
2 Length and quality of our suit: it is usually unwise to rescue to less than a six-card suit. A very strong five-card suit may well be worth tricks without being trump.
3 Will a rescue involve a higher-level contract? Rescuing 2♣ into 2◇ only means that we have to make one extra trick to show a profit. On the other hand, rescuing from 2◇ into 3♣ implies that we need the extra trick to break even and must take *two* extra tricks to show a profit. So we must be sufficiently confident that the rescue is worthwhile.

We will conclude with a test against the stop-watch. In each case, you will be on the run from opponents and will be expected to judge how best to keep the penalty (if any) to a minimum. You should state what the bidding has told you to date, what action you think is appropriate and above all, our old friend, the goal contract. See if you can do each example in under ten seconds. In all cases, you are South at love all, and the dealer is the first player under whose letter a call or pass is mentioned.

(1)

W	N	E	S
	1NT	Dbl	?

What do you bid with:

(a) ♠ 8 7 5 4
♡ 8 4 2
◇ 7 5 3
♣ 5 4 2

(b) ♠ 7 6
♡ J 7 4
◇ 7 5 3
♣ 10 9 6 5 3

(c) ♠ A J 8
♡ Q 5 3
◇ 10 8 5
♣ 7 5 3 2

(d) ♠ K Q J 7 6 4
♡ 9 7 6
◇ –
♣ 8 6 4 3

(2)

W	N	E	S
1♡	2♣	Dbl	?

What do you bid with:

(a) ♠ J 5 4 2
♡ 8 5 4 2
◇ 7 5 3 2
♣ 5

(b) ♠ Q J 8 7 6
♡ J 7
◇ K Q 7 5 3
♣ 3

(c) ♠ A J 8 4
♡ 7 6 5
◇ A K 8 5
♣ 7 5

(d) ♠ Q J 10 8 7 6 4
♡ 8 7 6
◇ 9 8
♣ 3

(3)

W	N	E	S
1NT	Dbl	Rdbl	?

What do you bid with:

(a) ♠ 5 4 2
♡ 8 5 4 2
◇ 7 5 3 2
♣ Q 5

(b) ♠ K J 8 7 6
♡ J
◇ Q J 10 5 3
♣ 8 3

(c) ♠ J 10 8 7 4
♡ 7 6 5
◇ 8
♣ 7 6 5 2

(d) ♠ 6 4
♡ 8 7 6 5 4
◇ A K
♣ 8 7 6 3

(4)	W	N	E	S	
			1♡	2♣	What do you bid with:
	Dbl	2♠	Dbl	?	

(a) ♠ 4
♡ 8 4 2
◇ 7 5 3
♣ A K Q 5 4 2

(b) ♠ 7
♡ J 7 4
◇ A K 3
♣ K J 9 6 5 3

(c) ♠ 8
♡ A Q 3
◇ K 7 5
♣ K Q 7 5 3 2

(d) ♠ –
♡ K Q 7 6
◇ K J 6
♣ K Q 10 6 4 3

(5)	W	N	E	S	
			1♡	2♣	What do you bid with:
	Dbl	Rdbl	Pass	?	

(a) ♠ 4
♡ 8 4 2
◇ 7 5 3
♣ A K Q 5 4 2

(b) ♠ 7
♡ J 7 4
◇ A K 3
♣ K J 9 6 5 3

(c) ♠ K Q 8 7
♡ Q 3
◇ 5
♣ K Q 7 5 3 2

(d) ♠ 9 7
♡ K Q 6
◇ 9 7
♣ K Q 10 6 4 3

(6)	W	N	E	S	
				1♡	What do you bid with:
	Dbl	Pass	Pass	?	

(a) ♠ 4
♡ A K 8 4 2
◇ 7 5 3
♣ K Q 4 2

(b) ♠ K Q 7
♡ K 10 9 3 2
◇ A 6 3 2
♣ 3

(c) ♠ A K Q 6
♡ 9 8 7 5 3
◇ K 7
♣ K 2

(d) ♠ 9 8
♡ 9 7 6 4 3
◇ A K 7
♣ A K Q

(7)	W	N	E	S	
		1♡	Pass	Pass	What do you bid with:
	Dbl	Pass	Pass	?	

(a) ♠ 6 4 3
    ♡ 8 4 2
    ◇ 7 5 3
    ♣ J 6 4 2

(b) ♠ Q 9 8 7 3
    ♡ 4
    ◇ 9 7 6 3 2
    ♣ 3 2

(c) ♠ 6 2
    ♡ 9
    ◇ 9 7 6 5 2
    ♣ K 8 7 6 4

(d) ♠ 9 8 5
    ♡ K 7
    ◇ 7 5 4 2
    ♣ 8 6 4 2

(8)	W	N	E	S	
				1NT	What do you bid with:
	Dbl	2♣	Dbl	?	

(a) ♠ K 4
    ♡ A Q 4 2
    ◇ K 5 3
    ♣ K J 4 2

(b) ♠ K Q 7 3
    ♡ K J 4
    ◇ A 6 3 2
    ♣ Q 3

(c) ♠ Q 6 5
    ♡ Q 7 3
    ◇ A K J 8 7
    ♣ Q 2

(d) ♠ J 9 8 6
    ♡ Q 4 3
    ◇ A K 7
    ♣ K Q 10

(9)	W	N	E	S	
				1NT	What do you bid with:
	Dbl	2♣	2♡	?	

(a) ♠ K 7 4
    ♡ A K J 2
    ◇ K 5 3 2
    ♣ Q 2

(b) ♠ Q 3
    ♡ K J 4
    ◇ A 6 3 2
    ♣ K Q 8 3

(c) ♠ K Q 5
    ♡ Q 7 3
    ◇ A J 8 7
    ♣ A 6 2

(d) ♠ Q J 6
    ♡ 6 4 3
    ◇ A 9 7
    ♣ A K Q 10

Let us work through the answers:

(1)   (a) This is an obvious disaster but we are unlikely to achieve anything by attempting to find another contract

which would be on the two-level anyway and more likely to lead to a heavier penalty. It is best to pass.

(b) Here, with a five-card suit, we have a potential gain by playing in 2♣. Remember that, after the double, 2♣ reverts to being a natural weak take-out.

(c) With 7 points, we have a clear balance in our favor and can redouble, hoping to double any contract to which the opponents may run. We should be able to beat anything they play at the two-level by sheer weight of high cards, bearing in mind that partner will contribute at least a doubleton in any suit.

(d) Here we have 6 points and again the balance is in our favor, but it is possible that the double is based on a long diamond suit so we should prefer to play in spades. If partner has some fit for the suit, game could well be on so we should invite with a non-forcing but encouraging 3♠.

(2) (a) This is a nightmare but trying for another contract is likely to make matters worse. We pass and take our medicine.

(b) This time, we have two good five-card suits to offer and give partner the choice with an SOS redouble, intending to finish in 2◊ or 2♠.

(c) Here we have, in the circumstances, a tremendous hand and it appears that South has little outside a good heart suit. There is, however, no better contract than 2♣ doubled and we should pass and hope for the best. South may well refuse to stand it.

(d) If those spades are trumps, our hand is worth five tricks more than it would be in clubs. It must therefore be advisable to rescue to 2♠ with the intention of playing there.

(3) (a) This looks grim but partner has another chance to bid and we have no right to bid in front of him with a relatively balanced hand. He is much better placed to take a decision and he knows that we are weak on points. Actually, another point missed by many play-

ers, this is quite a good hand – two points stronger than it might have been!

(b) Here we have 8 points and it will pay to have a look round. Give the opener 15 and the redoubler 7, leaving 10 for partner – and he has doubled 1NT. It is clear, therefore, that he has doubled on a long running suit in clubs or hearts and what reason have we to disturb it? Rescuing in this situation is likely to convert a big penalty in our favor into a possibly similar penalty against us. Electing to play in a misfit in preference to defending is a common and expensive error.

(c) Here we have a five-card suit and a desperately weak hand and should rescue to 2♠, intending to play there. Partner should realize that this is the situation and, if he decides on another contract, we shall respect his decision.

(d) Here we have a five-card suit, but with 7 points we have no reason to run from the present contract. Again, partner is likely to have a long running suit and we have two top tricks to add icing on the cake!

(4) Here we have described our hand and should respect partner's decision to remove into what must be a very long suit which will be useless unless it is trump. We should pass on all four hands. We should not be tempted to bid 2NT on (d) as we would have to play it on our own and will be lucky to escape for down four.

(5) Here partner has made an SOS redouble and must have a big diamond and spade two-suiter. Thus we sign off in 2♦ on (a) and (b), 2♠ on (c) and on (d) it is usual to make the cheapest bid, here 2♦, when we have nothing to choose between the two suits.

(6) (a) Here our hearts are quite good and should yield at least three tricks. We have therefore little reason to remove the double.

(b) This is more debatable, but again we have three trump tricks and partner is likely to have long clubs. The hand is therefore a disaster and trying to find another contract is likely to make it worse. We therefore pass.

(c) Here the heart suit is very weak and partner is likely to be short. We will, therefore, save a large number of tricks by getting out of that trump suit and, for the moment, we should bid 1 ♠. Partner should realize that we have this sort of hand and even two of a minor should be better than 1 ♡ doubled.

(d) Again we should rescue, this time to 1NT. Partner should realize that, this time, we have no interest in spades and he should choose the final contract, crediting us with this sort of hand. Again, we are hoping to finish in two of a minor.

(7) (a) Partner is obviously in for a hammering but we have nowhere to go so we pass and put down three more trumps than we might have done!

(b) Here a rescue is certainly advisable. There are two approaches. We could make an SOS redouble. Then, if partner bids 2♣ and is doubled, we make another SOS redouble (it can be used more than once) asking him to choose between diamonds and spades. The alternative, which I prefer, is simply to bid 1♠, keeping the level low. This might involve missing a diamond fit but that would, in any case, mean playing a level higher.

(c) Here it is best to remove to 1NT, by-passing the spade suit and making it clear to partner that we want him to choose a minor. There is never any point in removing 1♡ doubled to 1NT, intending to play there. It simply makes matters worse.

(d) There may be a 4–4 fit in a minor here but, as that would involve playing at a higher level, the risk of a bigger disaster precludes anything but a pass.

(8) Partner has rescued us into his long suit and we have neither right nor reason to argue with him on any of these hands.

(9) This time, East has elected to play rather than defend. Partner will have another chance to bid and could have

absolutely nothing. Admittedly, East is likely to be weak, but West is unlimited. Again, we have no right to bid on any of these hands.

I think you have worked hard enough. Allow me to conclude by stressing the importance of understanding what you are doing as well as getting the right answers. You will then be well placed to go on to more advanced studies.

Index